YANKEE
REPORTER

WILFRED FUNK ᴵⁿᶜ· NEW YORK

YANKEE REPORTER

* * * * * *

S. BURTON HEATH

TO MY DAD

Contents

Contents

Chapter One

HORSE & BUGGY YOUTH

★ 1 ★

Horse & Buggy Youth

I WAS raised in Vermont.

Some pleasant day in the future, I hope to turn over to a new owner the key to my New York house, which squats in the shadow of six-story-and-elevator suburban apartment houses, and drift leisurely back to a verdure-clad hillside that overlooks lovely Lake Champlain.

There, from a velvet lawn as expansive as the apartment houses that surround me now, I hope to watch an unobscured sun sink behind the Adirondacks across the lake, covering mountains and rippling water with a glorious cavalcade of color that no artist would dare reproduce, lest he be condemned for gross exaggeration. And there, and then, I hope to recapture some of that gracious peace and that homely friendliness of which, by the exigencies of earning a living, I have been deprived too long.

3

I admire New York. I am grateful to the big city for standing tolerantly by while I pulled myself up by my own bootstraps into a degree of material comfort which, negligible as it may be by the standards of Wall Street and Park Avenue, is greater than any predecessor members of my family have achieved.

New York is a great city, a wonderful city, a tolerant city, a sensitive city. There is nothing like it. Its buildings rise higher, its utilities are submerged lower, its intellectual opportunities are more lavish and its moral obliquities more dedecorous than those of any other community. It combines the best features of the South, the West, New England and the Middle West, along with their worst features, because its significant population is so richly fertilized with carpet-baggers from every cross-road and whistle-stop between the oceans.

In New York I can see better theatre better presented, hear better music and know better art. I can ride fifty miles or more for a nickel. I can stand firmly planted inside a building quarter of a mile above the ground, and look down upon scurrying ant-like creatures that really are full-size men and women. Twenty minutes from my front door is Times Square, cross-roads of the nation, and equidistant in another direction is the largest, most active airport in America.

In New York are men who are making America— bankers through whose tills pass millions of dollars a day, industrialists who control world supplies of basic commodities, actors and playwrights and musicians and artists and merchants who rightly acknowledge no peers. In my daily work I know many of these people, some casually and a few rather intimately.

To a youngster who grew up on a farm quarter of a mile from his nearest neighbor, to whom a village trustee seemed to have attained the pinnacle of worldly success, it is like living on the set of a lifelong moving picture production. I wouldn't have missed it for the world. I couldn't have had it in Vermont. I'm glad I have lived in New York.

But I confess with neither pride nor shame that I remain one of the great unassimilated. I admire New York, but I love Vermont. I am grateful to New York, but I want to go back to Vermont. I shall stay in New York long enough, if fortune is kind, to acquire the competence wherewith to spend my declining years in a state where no elevated trains rattle and bump over my head, where it doesn't matter if I lose ninety seconds by missing a subway train, where my rest is disturbed by frogs or crickets rather than by late-departing callers at the house next door.

I want to go back where I can not walk down the street without meeting friends who matter; where I can reach fields and woods in a few minutes' walk, and loll there without fear of being warned off a private estate; where I can nap under a tree without being trampled by picnickers;

where wants are as simple as needs; where there are no
Joneses with whom to keep up; where I can be Burt Heath,
and not "a reporter from the World-Telegram."

In every sense of the word, I am a Yankee. My blood
stream is impregnated with whatever of good or of bad
there may be in Connecticut and New Hampshire, Massachusetts and Vermont. I have a long head and a sharp
face. I have a nasal twang. I overplay terminal r's, because I have a born tendency to overlook them entirely.

My actual birth occurred in West Lynn, Massachusetts.
That was an accident, due indirectly to the temporary
aberration which led other states to elect the Democrat,
Grover Cleveland, as president. Vermont had no part in
that error of judgment. From the day that Vermont first
consented to give up its status as an independent nation
and join the United States, my state has never sent to either
house of Congress, or elected as governor, or cast its presidential votes for anybody who was not a candidate of the
Republican party in one of its successive incarnations.
Right or wrong we are consistent, persistent, and occasionally obstinate.

When my father was ready to take a wife and set up
his own home, he left his father's hill farm in the back part
of Lebanon, New Hampshire, and moved to the village of
Etna, where he invested his little savings in a grain mill
and a shingle mill.

Benjamin Harrison had been elected president, though he had not yet taken office. The country had tried the Democrat, Cleveland, for one term, and had repudiated him and his party. It didn't seem likely that the voters would revert to radicalism for a while, which made the prospects good for business success under sound Republican policies.

Dad did well for a time. He was unable to save because his wife had become a confirmed invalid, and doctors' bills and nurse hire ate up what came in. But he managed in spite of this handicap to keep on an even financial keel.

Then, with a perversity which has never ceased to mystify Republicans of Dad's generation, the people turned face and elected Grover Cleveland again. What happened? Exactly what Dad could have foretold, and probably did. The country went bust. Cleveland had been in office no more than three months when there was a financial panic. Dad's customers couldn't pay him, and he couldn't pay his creditors. His friends rallied around with offers of help, but he could not see his way clear to borrow what he had no idea how he might be able to repay. Soon he was in Lynn, working for the General Electric Company. I was born there.

At times, Dad's explanation of the panic of 1893 has seemed a trifle over-simplified. But I did not have occasion to weigh it, and raise questions, until after I had voted for Harding and Coolidge—and Dad is not yet ready to agree. So far as he is concerned, white is white and black is the Democratic party.

It may appear that I am ridiculing the fixity of my father's political persuasion. Perhaps I am a little. But I am deriding it gently, for the consistency of my father's Republicanism is of the same flavor as the constancy of his moral and ethical convictions, and of his generosity and tolerance in all things that matter. Firm personal convictions, and reluctance to force them upon others, are fundamental ingredients of the Yankee character, and of the Yankee character I am both fond and proud.

In more than four-score years, my father has never questioned that there is right and there is wrong, and everybody must choose one and abide with it. He can understand my own deviations from right, forgive me for them and love me in spite of them. He never volunteers criticism of my current peccadillos, or reproach for those that are past. He realizes that within my limitations, and subject to the loose codes of the twentieth century, I mean well. But I know that he grieves, at times, because to me right and wrong are not the clean-cut issues that they always have been for him.

I was brought up in the fear of God, the belief in His omnipresence, omniscience and omnipotence; in the theory that right eventually makes might and justice always will triumph; in the conviction that if I could do a better job I must keep quiet, let my work speak for itself, and wait for the better employer and the bigger paymaster to find their way to my door. I learned, early, that money is not important of itself, but that if I want things that cost money I have the duty and privilege of getting busy and earning the money with which to pay for them.

The child is father to the man. What I am today, and what I see today and the way I interpret it, inevitably depend upon the fundamental concepts I acquired at the farm fireside, in the fields and gardens and pastures and berry-patches, the barns and the woodshed back in Vermont.

These concepts have been modified by experience. Early lessons have been forgotten or ignored. But neither war nor unemployment, nor the sad failure of the Great Engineer nor the sophomoric experimentations of the New Dealers, have eradicated that reliance upon natural laws which was bred into me by precept and example in the shadow of the Green Mountains.

Fate has dealt more than one blow which seemed unnecessarily cruel, and each time she has hit so far below the belt that she has lifted me another notch above what I asked or had a right to expect. Fate, and a wife who refuses to admit those limitations in me which are apparent to everybody else, have forced me far from scenes where otherwise I should have been content to linger.

Most of the past quarter of a century, beginning when I was a very callow sophomore in a country high school, I have devoted to the commendable task of satisfying human curiosity about what the neighbors are doing. I have known intimately quite a number of the men and women who are keeping the world from bogging down in the morass of its own complacency. I have accumulated some rather definite ideas about these men and women, and what they are doing and the way they do it.

While I was yet a small boy, my father's health became increasingly poor. When I was seven, the doctor suggested that by going back to the country, Dad might survive long enough to provide for my younger sister and me until we were old enough to look after ourselves.

Dad took the advice. The prescription proved good. Last town meeting day, at the age of eighty-two, Dad went into the dirt cellar to get a jar of home-canned vegetables, to round out the noon-day dinner for friends who were in the village for the annual occasion. My mother, failing to notice the open trap door, plunged headlong to the cellar bottom. There, with two hundred pounds of nearly dead weight, she landed full on my father, who was about to come up. Being an oldster, Dad couldn't take it. After my mother had been taken to the hospital, and the excitement had died down, he admitted that he was a bit lame. He refused absolutely to let anybody stay with him that night, but the next day he consented to go to bed for a month while his ribs grew back onto the breast bone whence they had been torn loose. He has not yet stopped apologizing for being so soft and causing so much trouble. His description of what happened epitomizes his attitude toward personal misfortune.

"Ma'am and I have fought together for 45 years," he says, "and that was the first time she ever knocked me down."

We moved to Vermont, when the doctor ordered a change, because it was our kind of country, where Dad's ancestors had lived.   To be near his only sister, we moved onto the eastern foothill of Wright's Mountain, in the town of Newbury.   On this side the hill was slightly more steep than on the Chelsea slope, where Mother declined to ride down, en route to the county fair, because she feared the horse would lose his balance and topple tail over head down the rocky road, buggy and all.

In the night time, owls hooted mournfully in the surrounding woods.   Hawks stole chickens and crows stole corn.   Skunks wandered about the front yard.   Woodchucks grew fat off our gardens, and deer came to our orchards for their dessert.   The family collie occasionally came yelping home with a snout full of hedgehog quills. He never seemed to learn from experience.

Though the town was dry by local option, my uncle always had at least one barrel of potent sap beer in the sugar house.   In the butteries were huge pails of maple sugar, and unlimited supplies of apple and mince and cherry and berry pies, and big stone crocks of cookies.

All were free for the taking by any member of the family or any visiting neighbor, adult or child. The fields were full of delicious caraway seeds. Sweet cherries bore down the trees, if one could beat the birds to them. From midsummer to late fall there was a continual succession of new ripening apple trees.

It was a mile and a quarter to the country store in West Newbury. We lived off the farm in good part, but when we needed something the farm could not produce I went to the store for it, sometimes dragging a little cart downhill empty and uphill loaded. Once a week the butcher from Newbury Street drove his cart into each yard—and if we had the money we could have fresh meat. When we bought beef or pork or veal we could have all the liver we wanted, without charge. Between times, we lived off home-cured salt pork, home-smoked hams, salt codfish, chipped dried beef—and occasionally a gamy roast or steak which the donor would assure us, with a wink, was "mutton." But for the law protecting deer from the huntsman, one might have sworn that it tasted like venison.

I have come to realize, of late years, that we must have been among the underprivileged third of the nation, who have virtually no money, no bath tubs or flush toilets, no electric lights, or gas for their ranges, no telephones, nor any of those things which are essential to the preservation of self-respect and the breeding of character.

At that time we did not realize the inevitable social effects of our sad situation—which made it easier to bear. Not too close relatives from Lynn and Brooklyn came to visit for a week, and stayed for the summer. They called us hicks, and we called them city slickers, and we supposed it was all in fun. Now I realize that they must have been pitying us, and spending the summer to relieve our loneliness and cheer us up. They were most courteous about pretending to like our country fare. One such guest, a lad perhaps fifteen, used to force himself to eat more at our house than Dad, who had been working in the fields, and then would walk quarter of a mile to a neighbor's and, so the neighbor said, would flatter the cook by eating a second meal bigger than any field-hand could assimilate.

Beyond dispute, we found it a bit uncomfortable on some days in winter to visit the little frame cubicle in a corner of the woodshed.

I confess that I prefer my own full-length enameled bath tub, with running hot and cold water, to the galvanized wash tub we used to bring out in front of the kitchen range on Saturday nights in the winter time. The wash tub wasn't big enough to stretch out, or deep enough to immerse properly when hunched up. It was necessary to be sparing of hot water, with four of us to share what could be heated in the stove's attached water tank and in kettles on top. We did make out, however. I even managed to get by during the winter of my senior year in high school when, living with relative strangers, I could not take my tub into the warm kitchen and had to use it in an unheated upstairs bedroom where the bath water would literally freeze if it were left standing in the tub.

We never had much money. I question whether my father ever earned more than $20 a week while we lived in Vermont. He rose to that affluence only for a brief time, as a sort of departmental boss in a wood-turning plant that burned to the ground not long afterward. By that time he was past sixty-five, and was suffering from the after-effects of a neuritic affliction. He found it all he could do to keep a 35-acre farm going during the next fifteen years.

During my early life, the wage scale for Vermont farm workers was one dollar a day, except during haying, when it was $1.25 a day. I remember when the scale rose to $1.25, still with an extra quarter for the haying season. Dad early acquired the reputation of being an able, willing, intelligent worker, who did not mind topping off a ten-hour day in the fields with a couple of hours' help in the barn during rush seasons. Often he was paid twenty-five cents a day above the scale.

My father seldom was at home during daylight hours except on Sundays. When he returned from work each night he found wood to be sawed and split for the fires; a family garden in the summer to be planted, hoed and harvested; pigs and chickens to be fed and cows to be milked—

not all in the same season, but enough at any time to take up the hours until bedtime.

During the greater part of one year the water did not run to our house from the spring in a neighbor's pasture. All the water used by four persons for drinking, cooking, housework, washing clothes and bathing had to be carried some hundred fifty yards uphill from a pasture spring in fourteen-quart pails. In the summer it was merely time-consuming and bothersome. In the winter, when the fields were covered with a couple of feet of snow or, in the alternative, when the snow was covered with a glassy crust strong enough to support a yearling heifer, it was really arduous lugging two full pails of water up to the house.

In such a life, each member of the family must assume some responsibilities. By the time I was eight, it was my task to keep the woodbox behind the kitchen range filled with split wood, and to carry what chunks were needed for occasional use of the parlor stove. Gradually I took over more of the job, first splitting trunk-sized blocks into store-size, and later adding the sawing of four-foot wood into 16-inch stove lengths.

I was able to help with the gardening, shelling beans and peas, husking corn, feeding pigs and hens and cows, and similar tasks. I never did learn to milk to the satisfaction of any cow we had. Cows often are temperamental about giving milk to amateurs.

I was not overworked. I did less than most boys of my

age, in that era and that locality. There was ample time left for schooling and reading, for fishing and swimming, for sliding and skating.

I attended a "little red schoolhouse" that was painted white. There the charming daughter of the village tin-smith, while she waited for her young man to set up his own home, taught about fifteen of us who ranged through the nine grades. In one small, somewhat primitive room, heated with a square sheet iron stove for which older boys brought in the wood, she and other young women like her taught us to sing, to draw, to read and write and spell and figure. They taught us history and geography and civil government, anatomy and physiology and hygiene—not to mention a moiety of elocution and dramatics.

A similar young lady in a not dissimilar schoolhouse, a stone's toss across the road from our farmhouse, is teach-ing a dozen youngsters the same things today, waiting—I hasten to add that I am talking generalities, without inquiry about the particular schoolma'am now dispensing educa-tion on South Hill—waiting for her young man to save the price of furniture, or perhaps for one of the village lads to get up his courage to ask the question.

My teachers carried their discipline in their own com-mon sense, implemented with a wooden ruler, or some-times a short piece of harness strap, or even, when a clump of birch was handy, in switches cut by the culprits themselves under duress.

In my own case, the teacher's discipline was made more effective by my father's assurance that for any chastisement I got at school I would find a more unpleasant one waiting at home. That was no idle threat. What Dad promised he performed—and what he threatened. I received few real whippings from him, nor needed many. After I passed the age of monitory slipperings, administered when I was ready for bed and there was nothing to impede free access to the spot provided by nature, I remember only two. One was after a playmate and I had indulged in accurate target practice with stones at schoolhouse windows. The other was after I had visited the old swimming hole, contrary to express instructions, without asking permission. Each left a lasting impression.

In our school there was no organized play program, nor any scientific play equipment, yet we managed to keep rather busy. Duck-on-a-rock required only an empty salmon can and a round, hard stone. Fox-and-geese required only snow and ingenuity. We played tag, and prisoner's base, and hide-and-seek. In the winter we built snow forts, and fought almost sanguinary battles with wooden swords, lances and shields, with snowballs, and sometimes with stones and fists.

We had sleds, on which we could slide a full three-quarters of a mile straight away—one lying belly-bunt on his sled, steering, while his feet were hooked into the rope of a second sled whose rider sat erect. We built scooters, to slide through the fields and over the crust, with barrel staves for runners, blocks of stovewood for uprights, and pieces of board for seats. Competition among the boys to make the fastest scooter was intense.

In the summer we played baseball. We had never heard of football or, at that time, of basketball. Ordinarily there were five or six boys in the school at a time. Occasionally one was able to acquire a dime with which to buy a store baseball stuffed with cotton and covered with painted canvas. I made my baseballs, using small solid rubber cores that cost a penny each and winding each with a five-cent ball of store twine. For covers, I dried the hides of trapped woodchucks, clipped the fur as closely as possible, reversed the skin, cut it in the standard shape of a baseball cover, and sewed it with shoemaker's waxed ends prepared by Dad, using a stitch copied from the boughten balls. These not only were much the most lively baseballs we had, but they outlasted the others many times.

For bats we used canthook handles. A canthook, or cantdog, is an implement used by lumbermen for handling heavy logs. When good farm muscles snap a cantdog that is hooked into a big tree trunk, the handle often is broken near the lower end. Shortened properly, the remains make an excellent bat capable of poking a home run over the horseshed roof. Most of us had been able to save up the quarter necessary to buy a Reach or Spalding fielder's glove, and one or two had catcher's mitts. I was wearing long pants before I ever saw a baseball uniform, except as pictured in a mail order catalog or the Boston Journal.

From the few boys we had, we formed a baseball team. Sometimes we had an outfielder, but more often the available boypower was sufficient only for a battery and an infield. I alternated with an older lad as pitcher. Only one of our number possessed the phlegmatic nerve required to stand close and pick fouls off the bat, without a mask, breast protector or shin guards. This was particularly true after one foul that he missed struck his lower jaw, while his tongue was out, and nearly amputated the tongue.

We had two three-hour sessions of school each day, with an hour's nooning. One or two days a week, in spring and fall, we used this hour to walk three quarters of a mile to the neighboring village of West Newbury, play four or five innings against the boys of the village school, and walk back in time for afternoon classes. The game was played on the sloping lawn of the Congregational church.

For a time our family lived a good mile by road, and a trifle less through the fields, from the schoolhouse. All of us, boys and girls, from five years old up, walked to school summer and winter. One brother and sister had almost three miles each way to walk. In summer, going through the fields, it was fun. In winter, when the roads were drifted with three or four feet of snow or were covered with ice, and the thermometer ranged downward to as much as twenty-five or thirty degrees below zero, it was a bit trying. The roads never were plowed. They were rolled, and after a rolling one still sank inches into shifty dry snow with each step.

When I finished the sixth grade, for a reason of which I have no remembrance it was decided that I should go to the graded school in Newbury Street, where there was a high school. The next year, in the district school, I took two years' work, and Dad found a boarding place in Newbury for me while I was in the ninth grade.

Newbury was about six miles from our home. Every Sunday night, the school year around, I walked to Newbury, and every Friday night I walked back home. It would seem like a long, lonely, arduous hike now, but it didn't then. I had made a series of weekly trips on foot to Bradford, five miles each way, to have dental work done. Dad and I had walked to Bailey's Eddy, near Newbury Street, at night and back before morning, seeking horned pout. Everywhere we went, we walked. It was natural, fitting and proper.

The manager of the creamery at West Newbury, a carpet-bagger with city slicker ideas, introduced an Overland automobile into our quiet community about that time. He was a friendly, honest, hard-working chap, with a nice wife and an attractive daughter, but he wasn't satisfied to travel like his father and his grandfather and his neighbors, either afoot or behind a fresh-curried horse in a clean-washed top-buggy. He insisted upon dashing about at twelve and fifteen and—it was rumored—even at eighteen miles an hour, kicking up an awful dust, frightening horses, and shaking the daylights out of his womenfolk.

Over in another part of town, a queer character sent out to Sears and Roebuck's for one of their gasoline buggies, which looked like our go-to-meeting horse-drawn vehicles except that it had no shafts for the horse, and instead of a whipsocket on the dash it had a post up through the floor topped with a cross stick, for steering. This man used to ride up onto our hill occasionally. When we heard his engine popping along, we would dash to vantage points to see if he got up the hill without stalling. Later, when I was going to the village school, some of us had a happier idea. Whenever this man approached the school, which he had to pass to get to his farm, we would lay hands onto the machine and stop it in its tracks, holding it until pity or ennui suggested that we go back to playing baseball. It was no use for him to try to avoid us. We could outrun his automobile.

Without motor cars with which to dash thirty or forty miles after supper to the movies—and, for that matter, without movies to dash to—we were thrown back on immediately local resources for our entertainment. I was in high school when the first itinerant exhibitor brought his portable moving picture machine into Bradford and began showing silent pictures in the Opera House, behind the Congregational church. He covered six villages, one each weekday evening. We did not have shows of any kind on the Sabbath. That day was devoted to reading, meditation, quiet walks and church services.

There were no radios, of course. Only a few saw a newspaper regularly, and that was the Bradford weekly, which ignored anything that occurred outside the limits of Vermont. We were always well informed about local happenings, however. We had party telephone lines, and the most conscientious of housewives saw nothing amiss in "listening in," provided, of course, one hand was kept pressed on the transmitter to keep out vagrant sounds. Everybody knew that everybody "listened in," but it was one of the things that nobody cared to talk about.

Our formal social life centered about the Congregational Church supplemented by Adventist prayer meetings. We went to church religiously fifty-two Sundays a year, barring serious illness. After church young and old attended Sunday School. Then we lingered, visiting with folks we had not seen since last Sabbath. Those who did not live too far away came back for Sunday evening prayer meeting, though it was possible to retain community and self-respect without doing this. On Tuesday evenings, many gathered for mid-week prayer meeting.

Thursday evenings, several of us met with the Adventists at their prayer meetings, and even entertained them in our non-Adventist homes.   At Congregational meetings, the minister did most of the work, except for three hymns in which the congregation joined fervently.   But at the Adventist gatherings we all participated with prayer, testimony, and fervent "Hallelujahs" and "Amens" and "Thank Gods."

The only library in the community was in the church. It was devoted to books of religious history and moral inspiration.   My favorite volume, which I borrowed many times and read with avidity, described the tribulations of the early Christians, and their flights to the catacombs seeking to escape being tossed to the lions or subjected to even more painful forms of death.

The men got together most often at the country store, which also housed the postoffice.   There was an occasional barn raising, usually necessitated by lightning.   Husking bees were obsolescent in our neighborhood, though I did go to a few and thought the older boys were very silly to set so much store on finding red ears of corn.   A red ear traditionally entitled the finder to kiss the girl of his choice thoroughly, publicly and properly.   My own lone attempt at kissing a neighbor girl had left me unimpressed, and had produced a hostility which I did not understand until later.   It developed that when, following the suggestion of an older prompter, I murmured "honey bunch," she overlooked the "honey" and applied the "bunch" to her not inconsiderable chubbiness.

The women met, probably monthly, at Ladies' Aid gatherings. The Ladies' Aid was an auxiliary of the church. Its meetings were held in members' homes until a hall was built. The hall afforded us opportunity to put on home talent entertainments, and to enjoy visiting Thespians from Bradford Academy and Newbury High School.

The hall was not an unmixed blessing. It added much to the metropolitan flavor of the village, which theretofore had included only the general store and postoffice, the school, the creamery, the church, and about a dozen houses. But it split our community wide open from top to bottom. One group of ladies felt that another group was assuming too much authority in connection with the building plans. Unable to reconcile their differences, the dissidents withdrew and founded the Church Aid Society. There was no possible neutrality for those who traded and attended church in West Newbury. Every lady was placed, willy nilly, in one camp or other, and with her went her husband, her children, her bosom friends and any visitors from out of town.

The secessionists included some of our socially élite. One, who kept a modest boarding house in which occasionally she entertained summer boarders from Manchester and Boston, was the community litterateur, and wrote a weekly column of local news items for the United Opinion, published in Bradford. A high point of enterprise in the bitter battle, which also marked a distinct departure in rural Vermont journalism, came when this lady included in one week's grist of local gossip an original verse, which was published unexpurgated. I remember it well. It went:

> 'Twixt Hall and Hell
> There's but one letter.
> If the Hall was in Hell
> West Newbury'd be better.

We seldom tried anything as complicated as a play with local talent. Our offerings were more in the way of variety, in its simplest forms. The first such program that I remember was notable for a number of reasons.

I was about eleven years old, and wore my first store suit, which had been ordered sight unseen from the Charles Williams catalog and which, to my intense relief after prolonged worry, did arrive on the very day of the entertainment.

My sister, then about four, intoned a little song about "fishie, fishie in the bwook," with a debonair unconcern which has always distinguished her public appearances from my own stumbling, tongue-tied impotencies.

My contribution was to have been a simple little piano solo. I had been taking piano lessons on our parlor organ,

which gave forth sound whenever I pumped the foot bel-
lows and depressed a key enough to let air into the reeds.
The teacher had neglected to mention that piano keys
must be struck hard enough to force hammers onto the
wires. By the time I discovered this, I had become both
embarrassed and quite furious at the audience's levity. I
started for the wings, and was sent back. What we started,
I was informed, we finished. I compromised on "Home,
Sweet Home," without encore.

To that evening's misery I trace the beginning of a life-
long aversion to getting up in any public place as the center
of attraction. I have done it at times, perforce, because
I lacked the courage to say "no." For a time I played the
organ in church, and Dad and I sang a duet each Sunday.
I am not being unduly modest when I suggest that thirty
years ago New Englanders were willing to go through Hell
for a chance to get to Heaven.

The favorite toast in my youth, always pledged in
good, pure spring water, was to:

"Vermont—the land of brave men, fair women, maple
syrup, and Morgan horses.

> "The first are strong,
> The last are fleet,
> The second and third
> Are remarkably sweet—
> And all are uncommonly hard to beat."

We were and still are very proud of our maple syrup and sugar. Maryland, Texas, Minnesota and perhaps other states stole our turkey trade temporarily, so that while the menus still say "Roast Young Vermont Turkey," for a time much of it was raised elsewhere. But nobody can interfere with the preëminence of Vermont Maple Syrup because nowhere else does the soil put into the maple's sap quite the same delicate flavor as in Vermont. Chemists might dispute me, but I know; I am from Vermont.

The two or three spring weeks when the sun first brings the sap to the surface, with snappily cool nights and pleasantly sunny days, are given over in Vermont to sugaring. There usually is ample snow in the woods for drawing the sap, and Easter vacation leaves school children free to help and hinder.

The prime social events of the spring season were sugaring off parties at the homes of the better sugar-makers. Then the syrup, which had been brewed from sap in the frame sugar house in the woods, would be boiled down on the kitchen range.

There were huge containers of plain, unsweetened doughnuts, and ample supplies of chokingly sharp home-made cucumber pickles. Each guest was given a large sauce dish in which, when the simmering syrup had thickened enough so that drops would "spin a thread" off a spoon, he could stir it vigorously until it hardened into a creamy white, finely-grained confection. When this palled, each was given a big tin pan close-packed with clean white snow from the woods. Syrup poured hot onto the snow forms a waxy thin taffy which, as it hardens, runs into strange shapes. It was, and still is, Vermont's famous "sugar on snow," so incomparable that the Vermont Club in Hartford, Conn., has snow saved each winter, in barrels, in a commercial refrigerating plant, so that each summer its members may have a sugaring-off, and live over again that greatest of youth's gastronomic thrills.

One more event annually rounded out our social life. That was the Fourth of July picnic, always held in one of two pasture sites which offered facilities for a baseball game between married men and single men. The day was given over to visiting, eating, baseball, and a constant succession of feats of skill—eating custard pies with hands tied out of the way, or eating doughnuts hung from trees or apples bobbing in water tubs, under similar handicap; foot-races in which the contestants' feet were encased in grain sacks; three-legged races, in which the adjacent feet of two men were tied together, outer legs free; potato races, in which each contestant had his own row of potatoes, spaced at intervals, to pick up one at a time and carry back to the starting place.

The first big, shiny new dime I ever earned was as an honorarium for making a slight improvement in my use of vowels. I worked harder and longer for that dime than for most larger sums that I have earned.

In common with most Yankees of the rural genus, I used to pronounce "cow" as though it were spelled "caow," and I inserted the same "a" into how, and now, and bow, and row and sow. The head of a Boston department store, summering quietly in our town, offered me ten cents when I could come to him and pronounce any or all of those words without an "a." It was a matter of more than a few days before I was able to claim the award—but eventually I did.

Such free lance employment was too infrequent to provide pocket money for even my modest needs. I required something more dependable, so I undertook to sell Saturday Evening Posts through that section of Bradford known as Goshen. Every week, on foot, I made a grand circle of approximately five miles, stopping at every farmhouse. I built up my clientele to a high of almost twenty a week, which represented something like two-thirds of the homes in my territory. As I remember, I kept two cents a copy as commission. I was then eight years old.

My first regular employment was as a cow-herder. For twenty-five cents a week—which is what I now pay a youngster for brushing a light fall of snow off some thirty feet of sidewalk—I went seven afternoons a week into a pasture, where I walked from half a mile to three times that distance finding the cows, and then drove them a like distance to the neighbor's barn and walked home to supper.

This income was supplemented, during the season, with what I could earn picking raspberries in a pasture clearing. Most folks sold their berries for ten cents a quart, but because my berries were unusually free from stems, leaves, bugs and worms, I had regular customers willing to pay twenty-five cents for two quarts. I was able to pick five or six quarts in a good day at the height of the season.

In haying season I helped a neighbor—raking, cocking, turning, and occasionally loading or pitching on—for which I earned fifty cents for a ten-hour day. This lasted only part of one season. The neighbor, who was generally reputed an ungodly man, so far forgot himself one day as to swear at me, so that he found himself in the hayfield without a helper, with half a load on the rack and a thundershower approaching, while I found myself unemployed.

Up to the time I entered high school, my appearance at any home within a four or five mile radius was the signal for housewives to consider whether they were prepared to buy gold-eyed needles, or Larkin products, or religious tracts, or any of the many products which offered money or prizes to child canvassers.

The sum total of my earnings in those days, from all sources, was probably less than most modern children are given as free allowances, but to me it represented real wealth.

When I was twelve, Dad moved to South Newbury

and ran a grist mill—one of the last in which corn and oats and wheat were ground between huge composition "stones," which had to be sharpened occasionally with a chisel and hammer. He was there less than two years before the mill was closed, and Dad was sent to the company's mill at Bradford.

I found South Newbury a profitable home. During the school term I helped at the mill in spare time, learning to grind corn and oats into mixed feed, and to wangle 140-pound bags of daisy flour into the farmers' wagons, and to keep the simple single-entry books of financial record. For this latter Dad paid me a quarter a week.

No sooner had school closed than the station agent's son and I contracted to pick strawberries, at two cents a quart, at a farm four miles away. Every morning and night we rode to and from work on bicycles. During the height of the season we approached briefly the average of eighty quarts a day. My season's earnings, with some savings, were enough so that I bought a brand new bicycle, with rubber handle-bar grips and a coaster brake, to replace the $5 castoff I had been using.

In South Newbury I served brief apprenticeships in two branches of the building industry. I made a deal with the contractor who was starting to build a new schoolhouse, by which he was to hire me for $1 a day to mix cement with a shovel. If, at the end of the first day, he was not satisfied with my work, he was not obligated to pay me. I found him a good egg. He paid for that first day, though he did not ask me back. The next morning I couldn't have dragged my legs to the spot, or raised a shovel with my arms.

That same summer a neighbor was rebuilding the farmhouse that had been burned down by lightning, and he took me on as a lather, also at $1 a day. I made good on this job, and held up my end until more skilled operations were in process.

I was fourteen the summer we moved to Bradford, a village then credited by the census bureau with 607 inhabitants, but which boasted a hotel, a garage, a high school, an opera house, stores of all descriptions, and most important of all to me, the United Opinion and an electric brougham.

The Opinion was a weekly newspaper, consisting of eight pages of six columns each. For the most part, it was devoted to local news paragraphs recording the day-by-day doings of residents in perhaps a dozen surrounding towns, plus a column or two of brief notes on happenings throughout the state. Unlike most such weekly newspapers, it was not operated by a working printer, but rather by the town's Crœsus, who had inherited a multi-thousand dollar interest in a prosperous lumber company and devoted himself to the Opinion largely because the voters had not yet been able to convince him that they did not need him in politics. It was his daughter who owned the electric brougham, for whose storage battery her father installed a charger in the local garage.

The Opinion was set entirely by hand, as was all of the commercial printing which actually supported the business. I persuaded the publisher to take me on as an apprentice, working from seven to six, with time out for school five days a week. It was my job to set type for the paper, clean up, run a small printing press, operate the folder on publication days and help with addressing and mailing the paper.

No wage was set when I started. I felt that I could trust so wealthy a man to do right by an ambitious youngster. I accepted the better mouse-trap theory trustfully, but I fear that my employer had not heard about it. I worked hard, and in course of time I got so that I could set type as fast as any employee he had except the foreman, who was widely known for his speed as a compositor, and so that I could perform the other simple tasks allotted to me as fast and as well as the others. In addition, for my own pleasure, I began turning in a small column of high school notes each week.

At the end of almost a year, my monthly salary had been increased from around $2 to a few cents more than $4, for a work-month of 110 hours. Still I was not satisfied. I ventured cautiously into the editorial sanctum one day, counted the money in my brown pay envelope, and suggested tentatively that I could use a full four cents an hour, if my employer could not yet see his way clear to make it five cents.

"I'm sorry," he told me with a harried look, suspending his casual watch upon the sidewalk. "I haven't time to talk with you about it. My time is worth $15 an hour, and I can't afford to waste it."

I have always had an aversion to bothering busy men with my personal troubles. There seemed only one thing to do, and I did it. I resigned, in writing so as not to take his time discussing the matter, and rode my bicycle to Wells River, thirteen miles north, where I sold the local printer the idea that his flourishing business required my assistance. It was agreed that he should give me board and room, and pay my tuition and the cost of textbooks, in return for my spare-time work.

My parents tried to squeeze out an allowance of fifty cents a week for spending money. Often they failed, but it mattered little. I was working until ten or eleven o'clock most nights, and there weren't many ways of spending money in what spare time I had. Occasionally I managed to earn eight or ten dollars in one fell swoop by providing advertising programs for the theatrical stock company which came frequently to the Woodsville Opera House, across the river in New Hampshire.

Two men have had the greatest influence on my life. One was my father. His industry, his faithfulness, his calm and kindly tolerance in all personal relationships, his self-reliance, his uncomplaining forbearance under provocation have set me an example which, however much I have deviated, has provided me with a goal toward which to strive.   The other was Roswell Sherwin, the printer in whose home and shop I spent most of my junior year in high school.

Sherwin was the first business man with whom I ever had intimate contact.   He was not and never has become a good business man.   For fifteen years he has had a Model T Ford sitting in his barn, which he has not felt he could afford to fix up and operate.   I doubt if he has been away from his home overnight, on pleasure, during the quarter of a century since I first made his acquaintance.   His only vice, if he still has it, is going to auctions and bringing home decrepit items which, strangely enough, have turned out to be antiques of considerable merit and some value—that, and chewing continuously on two-for-a-nickel cigars which, occasionally, he lights for a few whiffs.

But Roswell Sherwin was a craftsman of the type which it was difficult to find even a quarter of a century ago, and which is yet more rare today.   Self-taught, with inadequate equipment, he has devoted his life to doing the best printing he knows how.   He has never been a typographer of first rank.   Sometimes his taste is questionable.   His product would never win prizes in exhibitions.   But every piece he turned out while I knew him intimately had the merit that, with whatever might be its faults, it was the best of which its creator was capable.   Could Goudy say more?

While I was with him, he became involved in a dispute with the telephone company over a cash discount which had been denied.   With both disputants it became a matter of principle, so that Sherwin's telephone was taken out. Neither having receded, he has had no telephone since that time.

When he had a telephone, he would use it to check upon any question that arose in connection with the copy provided by his customers.   One day after the telephone was gone, he found in the handwritten copy for a program —a job for which the women's club of a back village would pay him perhaps $5—a name whose spelling was undecipherable.   Rather than take any chance, he rode in his car some ten miles to ascertain how the name should be spelled.   Sometimes, when I am inclined to do sloppy work and wonder who will care, I think of my friend Roswell Sherwin, who often sacrificed his comfort and forewent his profit, but never prostituted his integrity.

Our arrangement broke up, to my regret, when the son of the household tried out on me one day some epithets he had acquired from playmates.   I turned him over my knee.   His mother felt that relations were strained, and I relieved them by returning to Bradford for the remainder of the school year.

We moved again—this time back near our original Vermont home, to where an old neighbor was rebuilding his farmhouse and barns which had been burned. Dad threw together a two-room shack in a pine grove, and I rode my bicycle daily, more than five miles each way over steep hill roads, to school. This would be impossible in winter, and we had no idea where we might be living when snow came, so I arranged to work for board and room at the home of an elderly lady near Bradford whose grandson was trying to carry on the farm while attending high school.

Every morning we got up at five, cared for the hens and pigs and cows, milked three cows, had breakfast, changed our clothes, hitched up the horse and drove to the village to school. Every night, after school, we drove home, put up the horse, changed back to working clothes, and did the chores. Saturdays we went into the woods, chopped down trees, cut them up, and got them ready to haul to the house for stove-wood. Sundays we did no work except the chores around the barn.

Along toward spring, I detected a feeling that I was not carrying my weight of the work. Moreover, I was finding it a bit unpleasant bathing in a room in which the temperature had not risen to freezing since winter set in. So when my hostess remarked one breakfast-time, as I dawdled for another slice of brown bread, that I ate more than I was worth, I gave notice and went home, riding my bicycle to school the rest of the year.

After graduation, I took a job in a country store in a little paper mill village near Wells River, where I started at $6 a week and was boarded in my employer's home for $4 a week. His was the only store in the village, and served quite a countryside. We sold food, clothing, yard goods, notions, grain, gasoline home-lighting systems, automobiles, ice cream and soda pop, not to mention Jamaica ginger to those we had no reason to expect would drink it behind the horsesheds.

Every morning I opened the store in time to sell tobacco to men going to work on the seven o'clock shift. I made the fire in the sheet-iron box stove in winter, and in summer I re-packed the ice cream. Five nights a week we closed at six o'clock, and Saturday night soon after nine. One of my tasks was to wait on the postoffice in one corner of the store—selling stamps, writing money orders, sorting incoming mail and preparing and sacking the outgoing. Once a month I prepared the money order report to go to Washington.

Freight cars containing assorted grain were left on a siding beside our door, and the senior clerk and I unloaded them down a gangway with trucks, always trying to set a new record for getting the twenty tons unloaded and stacked up head-high in the storeroom. We never took as much as an hour and a half, unless one of us had to spend too much time in the store waiting on customers.

Once a week four or five of us would go hell-raising to the movies at Woodsville, in an ancient Buick that seldom made the three miles without at least one change of spark plugs. Sundays we dissipated by pitching pennies at the side of a building, or stealing a ride as far as the summit on the freights that were slowed to a crawl by the grade near the store.

After about eight months and two raises, I was getting $8 a week. Besides, I had the privilege of buying anything from the store at cost. I liked the work, the community was friendly and pleasant, and the pay was good. But I had printers' ink in my veins, and when Sherwin tipped me that an editor was being sought for the nearby Groton Times, I gave up my job and set out for Groton.

The Times was owned by one of those enterprising jacks-of-all-trades of whom each small town seems to have one—and usually only one. Scott Welch owned and operated the local meat market. He was the neighborhood auctioneer. He was agent for a moderately popular type of automobile. He was willing to try his hand at anything that would produce a dollar, or to invest in anything that might be turned over for a profit. Knowing nothing about the newspaper business and caring less, he had taken over the Times because he could get it cheap and had an idea he could sell it for more. He needed an editor, a manager, a publisher, a boss printer, an advertising salesman, a circulation manager, and a star reporter.

I got the job at the highly pleasing salary of twelve dollars a week.

That was in May of 1917. The United States, at last catching up with my enthusiasm, had declared war on Germany in April. A New Hampshire recruiting officer had turned me down because I did not have my parents' consent to enlist. The May night I arrived in Groton, the community was giving a proud send-off party to more than a dozen of its best young men, who had enlisted in the National Guard for the duration of the war.

In July, some of those citizen soldiers were home on leave. The First Vermont, they said, was almost full. Only those who rushed could find openings. The next morning I took a train to Montpelier, the state capital, whence the Adjutant-General himself drove me to Fort Ethan Allen and arranged for me to enlist in Company F.

"When you come back," Scott Welch told me, "the job will be waiting for you."

Chapter Two

CITIZEN SOLDIER

★ 2 ★

Citizen Soldier

FOR slightly more than a score of years, at least two million maturing American men have been boasting: "I've learned my lesson. When the next war comes, the whole damned American army can't get me into a uniform."

In common with almost everybody of my acquaintance who helped fight World War I from Yaphank to Belleau Woods, I have said it now and again with more or less conviction.

It appears that I and quite a number of others were mistaken—not perhaps as to the compelling ability of "the whole damned American army," which seems at best to be a decimated corporal's guard, but mistaken as to what would happen inside us when everything in which we believe is being challenged by an Austro-German egomaniac, a self-promoted Georgian bandit and an Italian popinjay.

Most of us who were in the American Expeditionary Forces almost quarter of a century ago, or in the reserves that never got to Europe, aren't volunteering for whatever may be ahead in the immediate future. No longer are we young, ardent and unattached. We have wives and children, parents and other dependents, more than could exist on subdivided portions of $35 a month. We have become accustomed, particularly during the past ten years, to looking ahead and wondering what would happen to our loved ones if our support were withdrawn even temporarily.

Nevertheless I realize, and others are beginning to confess, that if our times should come under a democratic system of conscription, we would be deterred neither by the memories of cooties and trench rats, nor by the dread of death or of maiming, nor even by our still vivid recollection of how true it was, once the emergency had passed, that nothing really was much too good for those who risked their lives in the trenches at one dollar a day.

Emotionalism is abhorrent to me. I am disgusted with persons who have to wipe tears from their eyes whenever they see a regiment marching at attention, with colors flying and bands playing. It is ridiculous for a grown man to have to push his heart back down his throat when a piece of bunting is lowered to the strains of the Star Spangled Banner. All that is hooey, utilized in war time to get men to do what their better judgment says they should

not do. Such emotionalism is unworthy of thinking, rea-
soning adults.

It is, then, with some defiance that I admit being such
an emotionalist, who in his more lucid moments demands
that his country in her relations with other nations shall
ever be right, but at all times is a sucker for the tag line:
"But—my country, right or wrong." It was so when I
was eighteen and first donned khaki. It was so when I
was twenty and first came up the Narrows into New York
harbor, and from a deck of the then proud Leviathan saw
Liberty holding high her torch. It is so today, when I
pretend to be cynical and disillusioned, disingenuous and
alert to propaganda however it may be camouflaged.

I was under no illusion, when I joined the Vermont
national guard "for the duration," that war was a glorious
adventure, with gallant drummer boys and dashing sabre-
waving officers leading the way into battle on prancing
white stallions. At its worst—and it was bad—World War I
never was as unbearable as I had expected it to be.

I enlisted for a very simple reason, sufficient to me then
as it is now. In my opinion, it was the duty of this country
to enter the war against Germany. I urged it. When we
did go in, I could see no possible way to retain my self-
respect without accepting personally the risks and discom-
forts that I had demanded for others.

It is amazing to me now that anybody as little illusioned
about the nature of war as I was in 1917 should have been

the victim of so many illusions about everything else under the sun. Of all the men and boys with whom I served during twenty-two months in the National Army, there was only one more innocent, more ignorant, more naïve and more provincial than myself. He must have been, because he attached himself to me at Fort Ethan Allen as his guide and mentor, and looked up to me as his superior in *savoir faire*. He was a farm boy, from out back of the cross-roads village of East Hardwick. He set out, one crisp September day, to help capture a machine-gun nest. Before he was cut to ribbons he took it single-handed—for a few brief moments the sole survivor of his detachment. He never saw his Distinguished Service Cross.

I was in France for nineteen months. Ten of them, with time out for hospital visits, were spent on the front.

I crawled on protesting belly over open ground between our front lines and the Heinies, hoping desperately that no star shell would disclose my shivering form to some Boche with a machine gun.

I quaked in shamed terror while a mischievous German gunner slowly but inexorably lifted the range of his 88 millimeter gun, a few yards at a time, on a straight line for the observation post where board walls and a slate roof were my only protection from the nerve-wracking "whiz-bangs."

I volunteered from breakfast mess line for stretcher duty. Blood from the head of a comrade dripped over my shoes and leggings, as we carried him up the trench, and for two days I couldn't keep food on my stomach.

A buddy for whom I felt unusual respect and esteem stood with the major, at one moment, and in the next there was only a hole in the ground.

I was halted in trenches by rats that I still believe were as big as full-grown cats. I picked body lice by the score from the seams of underwear that covered flesh on which a mosquito bite itches for days.

Even quarter of a century ago, before Panzer divisions and stukas, war was unpleasant. I came out with fallen arches, and chronic bronchitis, and nerves so taut that a rolling clap of thunder was enough to ruin a night's sleep for months afterward. It reminded me of barrages and strafes, and other things which we who lack physical courage find it hard to forget.

But those are not the things that I remember best when I think now of World War I. Not the filth, the squalor, the cold, the hunger, the danger, the loss of comrades, the enervating fear that was always present. For those I sit and search my memory, and pull them out one by one, and try to recreate some of the horror of war as I would fit together a crossword puzzle. After first shocks those things brought their own welcome anesthesia of numbed acceptance.

What I do remember, first and best, are acres of dainty blue violets, shimmering under the Mediterranean sun, and groves of trees bright with golden oranges, less than a week before Christmas, when in my own home the earth was frozen hard beneath a blanket of white snow, and the air was brittle, and the trees were bare. I remember how the hills were terraced, and covered with vineyards instead of birches and pines and maples.

I remember a beef pie, with crust made from water-soaked hardtack, and filling composed of canned corned beef plus vegetables from a garden left behind by some family that fled advancing Germans near Belleau Woods—the beef pie concocted by a hard-boiled signal sergeant who had soldiered for King George in India, and had short-order cooked in a greasy-spoon lunchroom somewhere in Boston.

I remember the English girl who stood me up at the statue of that eminent theologian and sacred poet Isaac Watts, in Southampton's West Park; and the French girl who used to show me about Toulon and visit me in Hyères, while I learned French and taught her English. I remember the beautiful, sad-eyed wench in a French café who would have none of any of us, and the farm girl who scoffed at us for eating blackberries, which were fit only for turkeys, and the lovely American Red Cross canteen worker—the first of my own kind I had seen in months—to whom I couldn't talk because gas had temporarily sabotaged my vocal cords.

I remember the overpowering vileness of French cigarettes, which drove me to attempt chewing tobacco for relief, and how I lay on my back beside a trench near the Malmaison and watched an aerial dogfight so exciting that I swallowed my first cud and nearly strangled.

The war opened a new world to me. It was new geographically, for since babyhood I had never set foot outside of Vermont and western New Hampshire. I had never been in a city of more than ten thousand inhabitants until I enlisted. I had never been places, seen sights and done things. I have never ceased to believe that for me Vermont is Nature's masterpiece, but I learned that other lands have other virtues not to be despised.

I could get along, though it would be a loss, if I had never had my curiosity aroused by the war, and learned somewhat of the physical endowments possessed by other states and nations than my own. But without the new human world into which the war introduced me, I should have missed most of those things which have made life worth living.

At eighteen, I was an innocent purist by the most charitable nomenclature, and an insufferable prig by the least. I had never touched liquor or seen the swinging doors of a saloon, and there was no question in my mind that he who savored the vile brew was ripe for any indescribable form of turpitude. Only recently I had overcome a suspicion of cigarettes and their smokers so intense

that while I was in high school I made my sister walk to
school because an older boy smoked in the bus.

I was densely and lamentably ignorant about girls. To
me they were divided sharply, accurately and for all time
into two classifications. There was the vast majority of
those who were good, if mysterious, who not only never
committed an indiscretion but, because women were different than men, would never suffer any inner urge to
indiscretion, and who bore the selfish beastliness of men in
marriage only that the race might be propagated.

There was a small minority which not only accepted
but actually seemed to enjoy the approaches of men. One
such, a high school sophomore, had been caught in the hay
mow with the town clerk's son. Another, a town girl,
was reputed to accept the attentions of visiting Dartmouth
students, and once I had seen her sitting on a railroad station bench cuddling on her breast the head of a stranger
who, it must be assumed, was from Hanover. But these
were strictly casual and amateur. I had never so much
as heard of $1 wholesale bargain days under culverts, until
I reached Yale Field, or of the $5 retail carriage trade in
carnality.

It is no exaggeration to say that such things shocked me.
First I learned that mankind and womankind indulge in
activities which had not reached my attention. Then I
learned that at least some of those who now and then

indulged their baser instincts possessed better natures which predominated at most times.

Before the war was old, I tried some liquor myself, and I found that unless I took too much, too often, it didn't seem to convert me into anything very different than I had been. For convenience I laid aside the pipe and smoked cigarettes, and they induced no unusually sordid cravings nor seemed to weaken my powers of resistance. This may have been self-deception, of course, for before the war was over—in a spirit of scientific exploration, to further my education in the mores of that strange race, the French, I visited a couple of Côte d'Azur houses of a sort which I still believe we did not have in Newbury or Bradford.

I mention them because I am trying honestly and frankly to trace the process by which a very narrow-minded youngster, who saw right and wrong as two and incompatible, acquired some measure of tolerance to apply to the seething world of politics and public life into which he later was tossed.

The first, in Hyères, was what I should have expected—a slatternly café, with brazen habitués in wrappers forcing themselves and their questionable merchandise so vigorously that both I and my more experienced companions were ready to force our way out after a single beer.

In the establishment of Miss Louise, the Toulon "flamboyant" who (to quote her business card) conducted a "steam-heathed" maison de premier ordre featuring "a selection of nice girls with absolute security," I discovered that commercial prostitution did not always hide under culverts or in disgusting back-street cafés, nor did it confine itself to frowzy tarts beckoning from windows and inviting from doorways. Here was quiet and superficial dignity. Here were pleasant, if simple surroundings.

Miss Louise's establishment contributed materially to the eye-opening process which had begun largely with my entrance into the army. The town girl who entertained Dartmouth students was a hard, bitter, self-contained person, of whom it was easy to believe the worst. The New Haven street walker who did a mass production business at Yale Field was repulsive of appearance and manner. The entertainers at the Hyères café looked and acted like whores. Miss Louise's girls, on the contrary, were just attractive girls—better looking than the average, to be sure, better-formed, more demure of mien and more considerate of manner, but except for their apparent virtues, quite the sort of charming young ladies one would expect to meet in the most respectable of surroundings.

In other words, in that brothel in a French naval base, catering to all races and every degree of mankind possessing Miss Louise's price and perhaps a pourboire for mademoiselle, I discovered that vice doesn't necessarily wear a scarlet letter, and that every outward evidence of sweetness, and purity, and friendliness and courage and honesty may be only the tinsel wrapper for indiscriminating unchastity in its most obscene forms, for treachery and malice and cowardice and despicably venal corruption.

I did not sit down in Miss Louise's reception room and think these things out, nor did I lie awake that night back in Le Golf Hotel worrying about the deceptiveness of appearances. It has taken a great deal more of experience, in a number of other fields, to build up the iconoclasm I practice. But this was an early lesson.

Vermont small towns, except in the northern portion where there is a heavy infiltration of French-Canadians, and in a few marble- and granite-belt villages where Italian stone-cutters have overflown from Rutland and Barre, are made up almost exclusively of British-descended native-born Americans. In my pre-war youth I had met very few persons who did not trace to England, Scotland or Ireland, and those few, being domiciled with a preponderance of British-ancestried, adapted their customs closely to ours. I had no reason to suppose that there could be any codes of morals or of manners except those in which I was raised.

In Bradford or in Newbury, girls were not supposed to know anything about the procreative processes until, when they were married, perhaps in a vision from on high, they received such enlightenment as was necessary. A farm boy might wonder whether farm girls never, never happened by the barn when a neighbor's cow or mare had been brought for service, but he wondered silently, and our girls would have been shamed to their depths to have been present on such occasions.

When, therefore, walking down the street from my billet in Landaville with some fellows, we passed by an adolescent girl giving assistance to a stallion, I assumed that she would be frightfully embarrassed. On the contrary, she asked if we would help. Her father was at war, her brothers were at war, a mare had been brought and there was something to be done. So far as she was concerned there was no more to it, for all that any of us could determine.

Back in Vermont, when one of us visited the outhouse, he buttoned the door before picking up the mail order catalog, lest one of opposite sex should intrude by inadvertence. In Landaville, while we were using the open trench behind our billet, the scrawny old grandmother and her middle-aged daughter showed no hesitancy about joining us there, in perfect innocence and unconcern.

Amongst us, in my youth, there was a quaint conceit in mixed company that our trousers had no buttons but were solid back and front, and that they were worn for warmth and protection, since nothing that required covering was recognized. It was with amazement, then, that I stood in a sidewalk latrine outside the railroad station at Chaumont and watched a French soldier greet a woman acquaintance with one hand, over the breast high barrier, while with the other he prepared himself to join her outside.

These were isolated but far from unique illustrations to me of the strange idea that other peoples did not all have the same standards that we and our neighbors accepted. But for experimentation in which such groups as soldiers away from home indulge, it might have been supposed that these casual manners demonstrated as casual morals. There proved to be no traceable relationship. These French just had different customs.

Such experiences were not soldierly, and belong here only because they were incidental to my presence in France as a member of the American Expeditionary Forces. Truth to tell, the experiences which most impressed me and which left the heaviest imprints on my personality and character while I wore the army uniform, were not particularly soldierly in the military sense.

I wanted to be a good soldier. I tried hard. I bought a book, and read about the principles of close order drill and of the manual of arms. I tried to hold my belly in and my chest out, to keep head erect and chin in, to get through evolutions without throwing the entire regiment into mad disorder. I achieved the last—seldom more than a platoon was involved when I failed to carry out my assignment on the drill ground.

At the time I enlisted, the first sergeant of Company F was away at officers' school. I didn't know it, for to me one sergeant was quite the same as any other, and I did not miss the diamond beneath the three chevrons on him who acted as company Simon Legree. After I had been there perhaps a month, our top sergeant returned and resumed his duties while he waited for his commission.

I was on guard one day, assigned to Post Number One, in front of regimental headquarters. In that conspicuous and exposed position, where the colonel or even the adjutant-general might have an eye upon my soldierly conduct, I kept well in mind the general orders for guard duty —"to walk my post in a military manner . . . keeping always on the alert . . . observing everything that takes place within sight or hearing . . . to allow no one to commit a nuisance on or near my post . . ." and also the special orders for the post. One of these was to permit nobody to walk between colors which fluttered proudly in front of headquarters.

Well on in the afternoon, then, I came smack up against the major emergency of all my experience on guard duty during the war. As I pivoted smartly at the end of my beat, casting a rovingly alert glance to see that all was well with the headquarters placed under my protection, I saw a sergeant leave the building hastily and start carelessly to walk between the colors. Instantly I rose to the occasion. Snapping my Springfield to a port position, I shouted "Halt." The sergeant looked around inquiringly.

"Go around the colors," I told him, sternly.

He gaped at me for a moment, and started to continue on between them. Slipping the safety catch on my rifle, which was loaded with ball cartridge, I warned him explicitly:

"Halt. If you go through, I'll shoot."

I would have, too, and at that time I had never heard of shooting to frighten, or even of shooting to maim. On the range we had been practicing the kill. I was a better than average marksman. Fortunately for us both he believed me, and went around.

Now, theoretically I was right. A soldier must always obey orders, and I was obeying them explicitly on the one post where failure or neglect would most readily be apparent to my most exalted superiors. But practically, I was wrong. It developed that the sergeant was the executive non-com of my own company. He never mentioned the episode. But when the guard house was cleaned of its denizens, and a few more were needed to complete the complement of fifty ordered to New Haven to fill out the Connecticut regiment of the Yankee Division, I was one that my company felt it could spare.

The Connecticut regiment was the 102d. It was made up of two peace-time guard outfits. Like most national guard regiments, its personnel included all types, from illiterate immigrant mill hands to the sons of Hartford's life insurance aristocracy. The latter, a relatively small group of wealthy, socially acceptable young men and their friends and admirers, had made up the headquarters company of the old First Regiment, and in the merger they became the nucleus of headquarters company in the expanded regiment.

Most of the Vermont delegation was assigned to the Supply Company, because it was assumed that all Vermonters were on social terms with mules. But my playmate at one time was the station agent's son and we had learned the Morse code, so I was put into headquarters company as a signalman.

In late September we started for France, entraining in the dead of night at the Winchester arms plant siding, boarding the Canadian Pacific liner Missanabie in Montreal, steaming down the St. Lawrence, under the Quebec bridge at low water, and into the harbor at Halifax, where for six days we waited for a convoy.

Except for a few steps from train to gangplank on the Montreal docks, it was in Halifax, metropolis of my mother's Nova Scotian girlhood, that I first set foot on foreign soil, when the 102d marched proudly up Citadel Hill and back down again, at our most impressive attention, to let the Canadians know that the Yanks were coming and all would be well.

Eventually we arrived in Liverpool, without adventure or any mishap other than digestive, and were sneaked by train across the countryside to Southampton, where for six days we rested and drilled in barracks that floated in ankle-deep mud, and where I formed my first impression of Johnny Bull at home. In full realization that it is unfair and illogical to reason from a few specific premises to a broad generalization, I confess that I did exactly that, and that I acquired in six days a dislike for Englishmen as individuals that I never have overcome entirely.

In our spare time we wandered around the lovely countryside trying to make friends with the civilian population, who wanted none of us and who repelled our advances with a courteous frigidity that no other race can approach. We had virtually no meat in our slum, though we saw the nearby British soldiers eating liberal portions, and we believed the report that our beef was being diverted by the English, who were supplying us temporarily, to their own troops. Walking down a Southampton street, moneyless and cigaretteless, I saw an Englishman put a nearly full pack back into his pocket, and asked him for a smoke, and was told politely that he had just lighted his last one. His Australian companion pulled out an unopened pack and gave it to me to keep.

Such things might have happened to me in New Haven, or in Peoria or Tacoma, and I would have considered them only as isolated discourtesies. But I was in England, whence virtually all of my ancestry had come; I was in the land I had admired from boyhood as a spiritual fatherland, second only to my own country in my esteem; I was in the homeland of my mother's birth and girlhood allegiance—she was born aboard her father's sailing vessel in an English port.

On insufficient evidence, to be sure, I was let down. The warmth and kindliness of the French, from peasant to aristocrat, when I met them soon afterward, was in striking contrast to the English coldness. Today I admire the British as a nation, but every Englishman has to prove himself to me anew before I will accept him as anything more palatable than an uncooked fish.

Headquarters company trained, with the first battalion, at Landaville, near Neufchateau, in the Vosges, within easy walking distance of the birthplace of Joan of Arc at Domremy.

I was one of about a score who were billeted in the then empty store-room of the village bakery. For a week, perhaps, we slept on the cement floor, with only the thickness of an army blanket to mattress our hip bones and shoulder blades.

Most of my companions in this billet were from the Hartford delegation. The resident sergeant was an ambitious chap who did not belong to the inner circle, but intended to make it. Eventually he sold the company commander on the idea of letting him hand-pick the membership of a one-pounder platoon, which he proposed to make into the Union League Club of the regiment. By sufferance, because I was physically present in the billet and had not made myself obnoxious, I was tapped tentatively for membership. But I muffed my chance. I acquired cooties.

Few will need to be reminded that cooties are body lice, a persistent and most obnoxious form of vermin which no well-bred person will harbor. Our sergeant apparently felt that no socially acceptable person would even acquire them, though very little later he developed and retained an ability to scratch with the best of us.

I learned quite a lot about cooties before the war was over, but when I found the first fat one crawling along a seam in my underwear I felt an intense personal shame. It seemed in some way a reflection upon my character. I had no idea what to do about it. To inquire would have betrayed my ignominy, and before long the whole regiment would have known that Private Heath had cooties. The only thing I could think of I did. Squeezing to death the one I found, and searching vainly for any others, I washed the offending garment carefully in the village laundering pool and hung it back of the billet to dry.

Unfortunately, I did not know about the tiny eggs in the seams, and cold water laundering had not destroyed their fertility. The sergeant found on the line a pair of drawers inhabited by cooties. He inquired its ownership. His indignation, at my effrontery in introducing cooties into the A. E. F., was intense. Soon I was transferred to another billet on the far side of lower Landaville, whose farm-bred occupants would not be so contaminated by association with a private who had cooties.

Not long afterward, I attained briefly my highest military rank of the war. I was a corporal for a matter of hours—not, however, long enough for the promotion to reach the payroll records. When it happened, I was absent without leave, with three friends, in the hospitable little town of Bulgneville, which was out of bounds for Americans. There I was learning about alcohol.

Before we left New Haven for France, most of us were given leaves to see our families and say good-bye. Mine involved a trip to Vermont, so by the time we left Halifax harbor I lacked two dimes to rub together in my pocket. Our next payday was in France, two months later. It was a glorious occasion, the more so for me because it was the day before my nineteenth birthday. Four of us, in our party, were among those who took our pay and walked out of bounds for a celebration.

We returned Monday morning, just in time for me to sneak into the rear rank and answer rollcall belatedly. A list of promotions had been posted. Among the new corporals I was listed. But through my name a line was drawn. For a week, with others who had been A. W. O. L., I spent spare time digging new latrines and filling in old ones.

As usual, I had done a natural and not very improper thing at the worst possible moment. In my absence, the

political colonel known unaffectionately as "Pink Whis-
kers" had been sent to a Mediterranean port to command
Military Policemen, where he would be removed from
subordinates who had been hinting darkly that he would
not survive the first day at the front.   His place was taken
by Col. John M. "Machine Gun" Parker, a classmate of
General Pershing at West Point and reputed to be one of
the commander-in-chief's most intimate friends.   It was
Colonel Parker's assignment to make us not only fighters,
but soldiers.   Loose discipline was to end.   A. W. O. L.'s
and evening champagne parties out of bounds, and potato
stealing and the filching of wood from the Frenchmen's
choice groves, and similar forbidden pleasures were to
cease—and did cease for the most part.

"I don't blame the men for running wild under that
so-and-so," Colonel Parker was reputed to have told our
officers when he arrived, "but they'd better not try it while
I'm in command."

Our unit commanders, faced with the task of making us
over into real soldiers or getting into difficulties themselves,
became hard-boiled in their own rights.   Those of nar-
rower gauge took it out on the men, and we who had embarrassed them by being A. W. O. L. when Colonel Parker
arrived were the first victims.

Although I had ranked high among the men assigned
to radio, and was in line for a course in signal school
with the expectation of a sergeancy which usually followed

such study, my connection with radio ceased with that
A. W. O. L. Thereafter I fought the war as a blinker man,
operating and observing light signals, and as a telephone
lineman and switchboard operator.

We went at the end of January to a quiet front on the
Chemin des Dames, not far from Laon, where we lived
in old chalk mines and studied the methodology of what
then was considered up-to-date warfare. The front lines
were not too close together. The sector had been used
for rest purposes by both sides, and there was something
in the nature of a gentlemen's agreement between French
and Germans that, pending any real drive to break through,
harassment would be kept to a minimum so that soldiers
wearied on other fronts could catch up on their sleep and
re-equipment.

We of the Yankee Division were not parties to the
understanding. We had come over to get a minimum of
training, go over the top, drive the Germans out of France,
capture Berlin, and go home. The idea was expressed
by a popular song of the period:

> Just like Washington crossed the Delaware,
> So will Pershing cross the Rhine.

Our artillery practiced on the German trenches and
communication areas, and our infantrymen went on raid-
ing parties, all to the dismay of our French colleagues and
the annoyance of Germans who had been sent there to

rest. The latter stood it with much patience, answering shot for shot and raid for raid but leaving the initiative to us, until the 18th of March, when they decided to impress upon us the amenities of the sector.

Starting soon after dusk, German batteries dropped 30,000 gas shells upon the division front, interspersed with enough high explosive to teach us that war was no lark. John Piper and I were occupying an observation post 150 yards in advance of our front line, on a hill crest overlooking the Oise-Aisne Canal valley. We spent the night repairing our telephone line, which ran over open ground back to the front trench. When our gas masks interfered with our work, we took them off. The next afternoon, when we woke from naps, we were both intensely sick to our stomachs, and our eyes were swollen so we could hardly see. Piper was worse off than I. We telephoned for relief, and when it came, I helped him back to where ambulances took us to hospitals. That was the last time I heard from Piper until, sixteen years later, through a mutual acquaintance we located each other on Scripps-Howard newspapers—he as financial editor of the San Francisco News, and I as reporter on the New York World-Telegram.

Rejoining my company, I was with it from early April to late June, on the "sector northwest of Toul," doing observation work in the regimental headquarters village of Beaumont. After a short rest we relieved the Ninth Infantry of the Second Division in Belleau Woods, and participated in the counter-attack which obliterated the German salient toward Paris. Just as our part in this drive was ending, an ulcerated tooth got so bad that I was sent back to have it pulled. I went to a first aid station for what seemed a simple matter, on July 24. From that time until October 1—eighteen days after my outfit had participated in the St. Mihiel drive—I was in six hospitals and one convalescent camp, trying to get that molar pulled. It was still in my jaw when I was discharged in May of 1919.

Meanwhile my service record had become mislaid in the shuffle, my pay record had gone astray, somewhere in the clerical works a note had been made that I was badly wounded, and my parents had been notified formally that I was killed in action. Fortunately, they had a letter from me written after the date of my supposed death, and took the news calmly.

Not knowing of all this confusion, I was concerned chiefly with getting back to the Yankee Division and locating a paymaster. In the first I was successful, in time to participate in the Argonne drive which ended the war. October 30, again badly gassed while repairing telephone lines under conditions that prevented use of a gas mask, I started back to base hospitals. Armistice ended the war before I had received more than emergency treatment. I never rejoined my division, which held its final parade in Boston the day I landed in Hoboken as a casual.

That winter I spent on the Côte d'Azur, in the resort city of Hyères, not far from the French naval base at Toulon. It was one of the pleasantest of my life in many ways. Four of us, from different divisions, different sections, different racial strains, different social and industrial backgrounds, formed an inseparable quartet. A Massachusetts cotton-mill Swede and I worked in the hospital office, a Minnesota Swedish house decorator worked in the hospital kitchen, and a Philadelphia medical student served as helper to the chief surgeon. With such diversified connections we owned the hospital. We could have what we wanted. Among other privileges, I was authorized to sign the executive officer's name to all documents, including requisitions for passes for the four of us to visit Toulon, which was especially forbidden to most American soldiers.

The war, and my participation in belligerency, I have deliberately covered in skeleton outline both because it is questionable whether anybody today is particularly interested in front-line experiences in a war already ancient history, and because no experiences of mine were of particular interest in themselves. I was not a good soldier or a hero; I never went over the top, bayonet on rifle and grenade in hand, nor did I ever stand on the parapet of a trench and repel attacking Germans.

My experiences during the war were experiences in

human contact, which left their imprints on me because of the unusual ignorance and inexperience with which I approached them.   I have traced in the background just enough to account for my presence in those places where personal training in the humanities was acquired.

From mid-May of 1918 to my final discharge a year later, I received exactly 75 francs in pay from the United States government.   This was one casual pay, worth approximately $15.   My service record never caught up with me, and in its absence I was unable to draw the $5.40 a month owing to me after deduction for life insurance and allotments home.

While soldiers receive food, clothing, shelter, razor blades and a certain amount of smoking tobacco, there are other things even in war time which make at least a little cash useful.   In the absence of pay days, I managed to make out some of the time through various expedients.   Sometimes I was able to run a dime or a quarter sent from home into a few francs in red dog, black jack, stud poker and crap games, and just as often I lost the dime.   Often it was possible to sell the less useful of issued luxuries, to those who did have money, for the price of a place at the penny ante blankets or the cost of cigarettes and chocolate at the Y.M.C.A.

I think the best trade I ever made was shortly before we left Neufchateau for the front.   In a package from home I had received a pound box of loaf sugar, of which

I had nibbled only a few lumps when we learned that we were going to pull out. Sugar was a real luxury to the French, but only a treat for us. I made a deal with the housewife next door. In return for the remains of my pound of sugar, she cooked from an even dozen of her eggs—which sold for a dime each—an enormous omelette, with which she provided an abundance of French fried potatoes, bread, jam, and a bottle of vin ordinaire. A friend and I stuffed ourselves on this feast until we almost burst.

At Mars-sur-Allier, waiting for a dental officer to do something about my ulcerated tooth, I did well as unofficial tobacconist to the Spanish and Chinese laborers who had been imported to relieve Frenchmen for war duty.

It started wth a nickel sack of Bull Durham issued by the Red Cross, which I sold for a franc, the price of four more sacks at the commissary. Each of these I was able to sell without difficulty, to a tobacco-starved laborer, for a franc. The profit was enormous and the sales resistance non-existent.

When I found how unlimited the market was, I went into business. For a time I did well. Now and then I would pull down enough of my profits to buy a dozen eggs at half a franc each from a French farm family. In the farmer's field I would pick a hat full of blackberries. The proprietress of a little café was glad to cook my eggs into an omelette, prepare a liberal dish of French fried potatoes, and supply bread and vin ordinaire for a few francs.

Those were feasts for the gods that I enjoyed, until my prosperity attracted attention and competition developed. Before long the market was glutted and I was out of business.

After the Armistice, when I went back to Mars in another hospital, still without income or resources, I found no market for tobacco, but a developing demand for clothing—particularly for army shoes. This I attempted with some success to satisfy. With circumspection, it was possible to pick up excellent underwear and shoes which had been turned in for replacement, and French families were willing to pay fair prices for them.

I made friends with many French peasant families in the course of these negotiations, and almost without exception I found them delightful. They were sharp bargainers, whether as sellers or buyers, but to a Yankee this is a virtue. If they had not watched the sous they would have had nothing, for the streets of French villages are not cobbled with gold.

One old couple I remember with particular pleasure. They had a son about my age who had been captured by the Germans, and when I first met them they had been informed that his release was imminent. They wanted shoes, socks and underwear ready when he should arrive in tatters. Piece by piece they acquired these items from me, selecting with care, haggling over price, but all in good spirit. Each time that I was there, after our business was out of the way, the old man would take two pitchers into the cellar and fill them. One, for his wife and him, would contain vin ordinaire. The other, for me, would brim with the finest, clearest, sweetest white wine it has ever been my pleasure to sip. Not until my pitcher was emptied would my friends consent to let me start back for the hospital.

Just before daylight on the morning of April 20, 1918, I stood in the doorway of a shell-battered house, at the junction of the main street of Beaumont with a road leading northwest to the little village of Seicheprey in the shadow of Montsec, and watched hundreds of young Americans go into battle with two unnecessary strikes against their chances of ever coming out alive.

The Germans had sent 1,200 picked shock troops against our first battalion in a surprise attack, preceded and accompanied by an artillery bombardment which the French liaison officer said was as intense, within its limited area, as anything during the great battle at Verdun. The enemy, well-trained in combat, was using trench mortars and flame throwers, machine-guns and bayonets. His men had gotten into our trenches and had broken up our forces into small isolated groups, before we knew what was happening.

These youngsters that I saw were the reserves, going up to help. They were replacement troops who had just come to the fighting front. They carried Enfield rifles into battle, though they had been trained with Springfields. They had bayonets, but many had never been shown how to get them out of the scabbards and onto their rifles. They had gas masks, but most had never been taught how to fit them onto their faces.

They gave a good account of themselves. Eventually the Germans retired to their own trenches, leaving booby traps to catch the unwary. Probably we were right in believing that we had beaten them off. But if that had been a real drive, with wave after wave of enemy troops coming over in their turns, I don't see how those replacement troops could have taken it. They were unprepared, because their country had been unprepared.

Hundreds of them died and more hundreds were wounded unnecessarily, because it was their country's traditional policy to maintain an army of petty policing proportions, and to train that nucleus in obsolete methods, and to wait until we were actually at war before even laying plans to obtain equipment with which to train the men we had not yet recruited.

At Fort Ethan Allen I saw regular army cavalry, transformed into artillery overnight, drilling with tree trunks cut into the dimensions of artillery pieces, and mounted on the front wheels of lumber wagons, and drawn by farm horses. These and scores of thousands like them, went to France and were given French guns, because we not only had no field artillery of our own, but we did not even possess the plans from which to manufacture an efficient weapon for our own use.

We have the greatest industrial nation in the world, which can turn out anything from safety pins to automobiles by the millions with super-efficiency. We pride ourselves that American inventive genius is even more superlative than American production genius and American merchandising genius.

Yet when we went to war, after nearly three years in which to consider the increasing probability that we must fight, we had to depend upon our allies for artillery, for airplanes, for gas masks, for rifles, for grenades. Without their assistance, our men might have gone into battle armed with sporting rifles and hunting knives. Throughout the World War no American ever flew an American-built airplane in combat nor, except for a few big naval guns, did any American artilleryman ever fire an American gun at the Boches.

Neither were we more alert about those things which did not involve the expenditure of money. The World War had been settled for two years into the trenches when we declared ourselves in. No longer did troops march into battle in columns of squads, and deploy "right front into line" under shell fire. War had changed its methodology completely.

Yet our division, the second to go to France, trained 35 miles from the fighting front in the disciplinary rudiments of close order drill, up to within a month of the time we stuck our necks into No Man's Land. Only then did English instructors come to show us how to catch an enemy in the groin with a rifle stock on the upswing, smash him in the face with the butt, and cut him with the blade on the down stroke while—if he had waited for us to go through the manual—he was falling.

Only then did we get out and dig practice trenches, and hide in them, and get onto our toes and go over the top at an imaginary zero hour, and learn to take advantage of cover as our forebears did a century and a half ago.

Like all of the two million Americans who got to France in 1917 and 1918 with their eyes opened, I saw unpreparedness at what I thought was its worst. But we did not see unpreparedness as the Poles, the Belgians, the Dutch, the French and the English have seen it in 1940—or as millions of our juniors in this country may yet see it if this nation is forced into another and worse World War with even more tragic unpreparedness.

In the past few years we have appropriated billions of dollars for national defense, a great deal of it during a period when the most inattentive must have realized that we might be called upon to defend American interests before very long. Yet when our president and his most trusted intimates started hurling insults across the back-yard fence at the world bullies, we had no weapons to use and no plans for getting weapons in a period short of years.

One of the few things I have admired about Franklin Roosevelt is his apparent comprehension that America inevitably would be affected adversely by defeat of the European democracies, whose armies and navies long have constituted our Maginot line. But my admiration ceases when I remember that while he was spieling truisms and bellowing bellicosely across the Atlantic, he was dissipating our defense appropriations and accomplishing little of practical value.

After freeing a paltry few hundreds of airplanes for the Allies by leaving ourselves dangerously short, we had to answer the desperate appeals of Premier Reynaud while Paris was falling and the beloved old French civilization was collapsing before modern Huns, with the reluctant admission that there was nothing more we could do.

We could not enter the war, and help to defeat the Communazi menace, because we had no soldiers. It would have been useless to conscript soldiers, because we had no equipment for them. We could not send planes, because we had just about enough for home guard duty. We could not send tanks, because we had just about enough to protect Poughkeepsie. We had a marvellous semi-automatic rifle, but there were just about enough of them to equip a metropolitan police force. We have a miraculous bomb sight, and we claim to lead the world in aviation, but we had only a handful of bombers—and when we talked of turning on the heat and building planes by the thousands, we found we lacked the pilots to handle them under war conditions. Planes waited while our factories tooled over to build English-patented streamlined motors, because we had stuck to the 40-mile-an-hour slower air-cooled type.

It is difficult to think or speak calmly about the short-sightedness which has distinguished America's attitude toward self-defense, since first Cornwallis surrendered at Yorktown and right down to this moment. It may be too late now for the most earnest haste to gird our national loins adequately for the crisis which Communazism has brought to us.

At a time like this, anything that might be said in condemnation of our historic complaisance in the matter of unpreparedness can do little more than ease the mind of the sayer. It is offered, then, with the suggestion that if there still remains something of civilization by now, we recognize the truth that mothers' little gentlemen, too nice to learn the art of self-defense, are always getting kicked around by the school bully, who seldom troubles anybody capable of beating his ears off when occasion arises.

I was discharged from the army in May of 1919, at Camp Devens, Mass.   My service record was still wandering around somewhere, so I stood over an army clerk's shoulder and told him what to put on my papers.   The paymaster handed me a $60 bonus and $95.57 in back pay, plus transportation home.

Along toward dusk, as the train rolled northward, I thought I noticed a change in the air.   It was sweeter, fresher, snappier.   I looked out of the window and there, sure enough, the grass was greener and the woods cozier and the farm-houses more friendly.   I checked the time table, and what do you suppose I found?   That's right— I was back in Vermont.

Chapter Three

EXPANDING HORIZONS

⋆ 3 ⋆

Expanding Horizons

THE World War made a capitalist out of me. By the time I returned home in 1919, discharged from the National Army, I was worth a good, round five hundred dollars in bank accounts and Liberty Bonds—more, in all probability, than any of our family had possessed at one time since the second administration of Grover Cleveland.

I might have done better if I had worked in a factory or a shipyard during those two years. On the other hand, I might have spent the much larger wages on silk underwear and automobiles, and have acquired spending habits that I could not support in the post-war slump.

As it was, I accumulated a nest-egg in the traditional Yankee manner, earning little and spending less. Our Uncle Sam, so generous to those who made blankets and ammunition and trench kits for his soldiers at cost-plus,

and to the men and women whose ever-increasing wages
went into the cost to which entrepreneurs added their
percentage, paid one dollar a day to his nephews who
were privileged to enjoy the glorious adventure of actual
warfare. To this he added ten percent for overseas service.
My pay fluttered back and forth from $1.10 to $1.21 a
day, according to whether at any given time I was a buck
private or a first-class private. Out of this, during most
of the war, I saved $25 a month by having it sent direct
to a bank without ever coming into my possession.

When I got home, I had the accumulation of these
allotments, plus a $120 bonus given by the state of Ver-
mont to its National Guardsmen and the $60 federal
bonus, in addition to almost a hundred dollars of back
pay accumulated for more than a year. By the time I had
repaid some small borrowings and bought necessary clothing, I found myself with approximately half a thousand
dollars of my very own awaiting profitable investment.

While I considered the best way of turning this capital
to good use, I went back to Groton to see whether my
old job was still open. Scott Welch proved as good as
his word. I went right to work at the old scale of $12
a week. My parents moved to Groton to be near me,
and I boarded at home.

Before long I made a deal with Welch. For $1,200 I
bought a newspaper—one-third cash and two-thirds on
mortgage.

The Groton Times claimed a circulation of 1,200 and actually distributed close to a thousand copies weekly, but only about three hundred copies were paid for. I struck the rest from the mailing list, and a howl went up. Pay in advance, for a newspaper? My subscribers had never heard of such a thing. Some of them were insulted. One very respectable business man wrote me off his speaking list for weeks. At first he read a neighbor's paper, then he bought copies at the drug store, and finally, a bit sheepishly, he came in one day and paid his $2 for a subscription.

The nominal charge for advertising was twelve cents a column inch for local merchants, and fifteen cents for national advertising. The local rate was maintained, though a considerable part of the income was taken in trade at the stores. National advertisers had been bullying us into taking their copy at whatever their generosity allowed. One agency had been sending a large space order for a famous stove at three cents an inch, minus the fifteen percent agency commission, on a take-or-leave basis, and we had been taking it. I anchored the rates at fifteen cents for local advertising and twenty for national, and I became the one to say "take it or leave it." Some left it, but the net result was to increase my income and leave more space available for local news.

The financial cream came from commercial printing—letterheads, envelopes, shipping tags, auction bills, enter-

tainment programs, advertising dodgers, record forms for
the local wood-working plant (which patronage I obtained by buying the plant's little printshop and paying for
it in printing), maple sugar and syrup labels, and town reports. These had been priced by guess and by gorry, as
we used to say, on a basis of what the buyer could be
induced to pay. I subscribed to a standard estimating
system, modified it to meet local conditions, and insisted
upon standard rates. Again I lost business because my
prices were higher than those of competitors, but again I
found my net income increased slightly, with less work
involved in earning it.

I had two assistants at the outset—local young women
who set type by hand, one letter at a time, picking each
from its compartment in a case, placing it in a metal "stick,"
and when each line was full "justifying" it by changing
the width of the spaces between words. It took a good,
fast, diligent compositor to set two columns of type in a
day. Any machine compositor who can not set a column
an hour should go back to housework or farming.

One of my helpers was a bachelor maiden who had
run the business throughout my absence during the war.
She could do almost anything about the plant fairly well,
was faithful and loyal and hard-working, and was as much
a part of the plant, in local esteem, as the press or the
paper-cutter. She had been getting $10 a week. I raised

her, by successive steps so that prosperity would not go to her head, to $12.

The other did nothing but set type for the paper, though she did this with commendable speed and accuracy. From seven o'clock Monday morning to six Saturday night she sat on a high stool, picking letters from the case and putting them into the stick, justifying, correcting, reading semi-literate hand-written copy from our local correspondents in surrounding towns. She was getting $6 a week when I took over, and I raised her in course of time to $8. Even this was not enough to compete successfully with Nature. Eventually she left to bear and care for a baby.

I was committed to paying $25 a month to a bank on my mortgage. Out of the income $20 a week went first to my help, $5 a month to rent, $3 a month for electricity for lights and power, $2.50 a month for two telephones, and $25 a month to the bank. What was left was mine. I always was able to get the $5 a week that I paid at home for board, and usually I could make a deal with one of the stores to exchange additional advertising or printing for necessary clothing, toilet articles—even a phonograph, on one occasion.

Including the amortization payments on the mortgage, I managed to take out of the business during the first year about as much as I paid the more fortunate of my two helpers. For this, I seldom worked more than sixteen to eighteen hours a day—often as few as ten. During February I worked regularly until midnight or after, getting out town reports for my own and neighboring communities, a bit of financial gravy which helped greatly. At other times, when there was work to be done I stayed and did it, but when things were slack I shot a moderately good game of pool.

After some time it occurred to me that I was working harder, for less remuneration, than before I risked my capital to become a business man. This realization was stimulated when I had to find a substitute for the helper who left.

It appeared to be impossible to get an experienced compositor for less than $12 a week, which would have left me no personal income above board and room. I tried training almost numberless local girls, in hope that I could find two who together would do what one had been doing, but while my labor costs went up, my production went down.

Later I learned from a professor of economics that mine was a marginal enterprise—or perhaps sub-marginal—which had no excuse for existence. Since I could not pay my helpers an adequate wage and at the same time get one for myself, I should have discontinued the business. In the past few years my education in economics has gone further, and now I realize that the girls who tried to learn the trade of type-setting were stultifying themselves and betraying the working class by accepting three or four dollars a week from me—that although this was more than they were worth as producers, and although they could have earned exactly nothing from any other employer in town, it would have been better for them not to work at all and live off their parents than to work for a sub-subsistence wage.

At that time I had no training at all in higher economics. I knew that those girls, living at home in a town where there was no employment for them, were glad to get three or four dollars while trying to learn a trade at which, if they made good, they might eventually earn as much as $12 a week. It is only of late that I have been informed of the grave injustice I was working upon those poor girls.

Perhaps I was slower in learning because both of my original helpers had cultivated other sources of revenue, as musicians. The one to whom I paid most was most successful in extra earning. Once a week she played the piano at the local moving picture show for $3, later increased to $4. On an average of once or twice a week she played with a local orchestra for a similar nightly wage.

Few men in our town, with families to support, earned more than she. The pay scale in our stone sheds was higher, of course. The union minimum, as I remember, was $8 a day, and a top notch stone-cutter got as much as $11 a day. But the only $11 man I knew seldom worked more than two days a week.   He found $22 enough to support his family and buy what liquor he wanted, so he spent the rest of the time fishing, visiting and playing pool. Nor did those who would have worked five days a week find that possible, for the monumental granite business, on which our section had once had a monopoly, was moving into other states where the pay scale was lower. It has recovered to some extent since the major portion was consolidated by one large corporation, which up to recently, at least, operated entirely on an open shop basis.

In any event, I did learn that my labor situation was unbearably unsound, and that I must find a different solution.   The one upon which I decided was mechanization. I would buy a linotype machine on which my remaining assistant could set all the type we needed in about half her time and have the rest to help with other work.

Even a used linotype of the most inexpensive sort would cost in excess of a thousand dollars, and I could not have mustered $50 in ready cash.   I talked with local business men.   Some were willing to buy stock to help finance the purchase, but others remembered too well that they had bought stock from the previous publisher.   I couldn't sell enough to do it.

I went to the neighboring metropolis, population 614, and talked with the president of the national bank, which held the mortgage on my plant.   I had known him since

I worked for Sherwin, who did all the bank's printing. I told him the situation frankly.

"Will you lend me up to $1,500 to buy a linotype?" I asked.

Without batting an eyelash or asking for an accountant's balance sheet or a look at my books, he told me:

"Yes. When you're ready, come in and let me know."

That was my first experience with banking, other than the maintenance of a very unprofitable checking account.

I've heard often how hard it is for an ambitious young man to get financing to set himself up in business. It may be so. I did not find it so then, nor have I found it so since outside the metropolitan areas, where banking is so impersonalized that all humanity has been squeezed out of it.

At the time I was not yet twenty-two. By any standard, I was making a subsistence rather than a living. I was operating at a loss, in a community that had little past and no future, with an enterprise which had ruined all previous proprietors. Any large metropolitan bank would have considered me a poor risk. But this small-town bank president was accustomed to lending on character and personality. He knew I worked hard and did not squander. His bank had received my monthly allotments during the war. He knew that thus far I had met each obligation as it came due. He was willing to take a chance on me, as a person. It may be that he was not a good banker. Perhaps he was not safeguarding adequately his clients' money. I wouldn't know, except that after the 1933 banking holiday, when many larger and more business-like institutions were folding up or reorganizing with heavy loss to depositors, this little institution went right on doing business.

The loan never was consummated because, while I was looking for a bargain in a linotype, I had an offer which I felt I should accept. The late Lewis P. Thayer, for years dean of Vermont publishers, who had given many ambitious young newspapermen their starts toward success, recommended me to a group of business men who wanted to start a new paper in the nearby railroad center of Woodsville, N. H. They were willing to take over my business for what I had paid, combine it with theirs, and pay me $40 a week to edit and manage their paper. The deal was made, and I became minority but largest stockholder in a $5,000 corporation.

I worked day and night, month after month, installing new equipment, lining up news correspondents, getting subscriptions and newsstand outlets in the new territory, developing commercial printing business, and trying to turn out a newspaper and commercial printing in a plant which had been poorly installed and did not function well mechanically.

I could not stand the pace. I reached a point where it was impossible to keep up everything there was for me to do. When my local associates brought in a stranger

to take over the business end I was grateful, and too tired
to consider the significance of their failure to talk the new
arrangement over with me in advance. I was glad to give
the new business manager an option on my stock so that,
in the event I should ever want to sell, control could
remain on the paper.

It should not have, but it did come as a shock when my
new associate informed me lugubriously one day, in strict-
est confidence, that he had learned the other stockholders
were going to ask me to resign. He was correct. I did not
resign, but I was removed by a vote in which I stood alone
in the negative.

Most of my salary had gone toward paying for and
operating an automobile for the new venture's field work,
and toward the unusually high personal expenses of the
development period. I was broken financially, exhausted
physically, and so discouraged that I let the new editor
have my stock for virtually nothing, and turned back the
car to the dealer.

My first business venture had ended in failure. All of
the savings of the war period had been dissipated. I had
been kicked out. And I was very, very tired.

I met a Congressman soon after I became owner of the
Groton Times. He was the late Porter H. Dale, who
when he died was senior senator from Vermont. He
dropped into my office one day unannounced, in company

with the judge of probate from Wells River, whom I had gotten to know while I worked for Sherwin.

I was properly impressed. I had seen President Theodore Roosevelt ride up the street when he made a visit to Massachusetts, while I was in Buster Browns or before. I had sat in an audience addressed by ex-President William Howard Taft in 1916, and listened with awe when the local pastor made bold in his introduction to jest at the great man's bulk, and suggest that in time of war Mr. Taft would be a good man to get behind. But never before had I been in position actually to talk, as man to man, with a member of the government of the United States.

Porter Dale was an impressive figure even in Washington. Tall, well-proportioned, with a heavy mane of white hair, he was always immaculately frock-coated. His voice had the deep resonance of the skilled orator that he was, and his manner the sincere cordiality of the gentleman he was. Vermont farmers are not like those of some states. We never ask a candidate for high office to don overalls, simulate illiteracy and grovel for our votes in the filth of our barnyards or entertain us with a hillbilly band. We like to believe, however incorrectly, that we have sent our best to Washington, to utilize there in our behalf an ability greater than we ourselves possess.

Later I got to know Porter Dale quite well. I learned that he was not one of the inner circle of congressmen who ran America. But he, rather less than most politicians

I have known at all well, developed feet of clay. The last time I visited with him in the Senate Office Building in Washington, and the last time I asked a favor of him after I had left Vermont and ceased to be of any potential use to him politically, he was the same kindly, helpful, courteous gentleman as when he walked into my office in Groton in the summer of 1920, seeking support of the Times in his campaign for re-election to Congress.

He was an ardent, last ditch Prohibitionist. I was not. Most of the politician Prohibitionists I knew left a taste in my mouth like the morning after a polluted night before. But he was a sincere Prohibitionist. His father, a one-time lieutenant-governor of Vermont, had drunk himself into his grave, I have been told, and Porter Dale hated alcoholic liquors as he could never have hated any man who did him wrong.

Anything that the World War veterans wanted, he would try to get them. He was denounced as a political prostitute who sold his statesmanship for soldier votes. That was unfair. He had two sons in France. In his attitude toward veteran legislation his errors of outlook never caught up with his sincerity of conviction.

I began learning about practical politics from Porter Dale. He maintained as effective a personal organization as I ever have known, and he did it by personal contact, personal service, friendly thoughtfulness, unswerving faithfulness to his promises.

In my first political activity as a newspaperman, I opposed Congressman Dale's re-election because I felt that the late Ernest W. Gibson, one-time commander of the Vermont national guard and until recently senior senator from Vermont, was an abler man.

When the votes were counted, in all of the towns where mine was the home newspaper my candidates had won, with a single exception. In each, Congressman Dale had a handy plurality. The people were inclined to take advice about candidates they did not know, but Porter Dale had visited every crossroads hamlet; he had friends at every four corners; he had done favors for every business man or farmer who asked anything legitimate. No opponent, to my knowledge, ever beat Porter Dale for any office he sought in Vermont.

Seldom have I enjoyed myself so much as in that first campaign after I became a legal voter and a newspaper publisher.

The town's politics were run by a little group known facetiously as the "Big Six," who caucused with their friends in the schoolhouse and chose local candidates who usually were elected, though now and then a Democrat was sent to the state house of representatives, or elected as selectman or village trustee, because of ability and personal popularity.

The law required posting of a specified minimum of caucus notices in certain places. The Big Six complied, but few outside their circle ever saw the notices. The one in the postoffice was placed, that year at least, on the inside of the entrance door, which was kept open during the summer, concealing the legally posted notice effectively. The caucus was under way when I learned of its appointed time and walked in. I was not made at home. The Democrats, perhaps because they had nothing to lose, went out of their way to invite me to their caucus.

The good folk of the town were shocked when I editorialized about G. O. P. exclusiveness and Democratic hospitality, and ventured to say, tentatively, that we voters should look the candidates over and not vote blindly a party ticket. My father was asked to talk with me and make certain that I was not going to do anything rash. I assured him that I just wanted a little good, clean fun, and did not plan to be swept overboard by iconoclasm.

By nature a non-belligerent, I spent a few days that summer in mild worry about a big man who didn't get there.

There were four candidates for the gubernatorial nomination. One was James Hartness, then head of the Jones & Lamson Machine Tool Co. and a famous industrialist, who campaigned with an airplane and promised to put a smokestack on every hill in Vermont if we would elect him. One was a paper mill owner, one an educator, and one a confessed politician who said he was running because he would like to be governor.

Before the campaign was old enough for commitments to have been made, I received from a publisher representing one of the candidates a request for the Times' support. There would, he wrote, be a good-sized appropriation for advertising, which would be placed largely in newspapers supporting his candidate.

I found it possible to read only one inference into the sequence of his remarks, so I published the letter, and said editorially that I had decided not to support this candidate, and that thenceforward the only way his name would get into my paper would be in paid advertising.

The incident created quite a bit of comment. For the first time in my life I was in a limelight more brilliant than shines on the stage of a high school play. I still consider it strange that most of my fellow editors thought I had done a heinous thing. I could almost picture one militant editress slavering with anticipation, as she warned editorially what the over-sized newspaperman whose confidence I had violated would do to me, in person or at law or both.

Hartness was elected. Vermont's hills still are green, and undefaced by factory smokestacks. The candidate who planned to advertise with his friends was an also-ran at the polls.

The American Legion was being organized the year of my return from France. I undertook to get it going in my county. In Groton, by proselytizing one eligible who was away at college, we got enough members to obtain a charter. I served variously as adjutant, finance officer, commander, and—because I paid my own way—as delegate to state conventions.

In the Legion I learned much about practical politics. A convention of any live fraternal order is a political convention. It involves the advance lining up of delegates, the trading and exchanging of promises, the nursing of acquired delegate strength, the Parliamentary jockeying. All the mechanics of a regular political convention are there. Some of our more successful state and national politicians have learned their trade as Legionnaires.

From the beginning I met at these conventions men who, then and later, were influential in state affairs. Soon I became affiliated with a small but growing group which was trying to take control of the state Republican party from the dominant organization, which for at least quarter of a century had been controlled by the late Senator Redfield Proctor and his sons, in alliance with railroad interests.

It is only slightly exaggerated to say that Vermont's Democratic party could caucus in a telephone booth without crowding. For any state or national office, the Republican nomination is as final as the Democratic nomination in South Carolina. The real election comes in the primaries. The important division is within the Republican party.

Our group of "young" or progressive Republicans started with only a single office holder, Porter Dale, whose original election was not in any way attributable to our organized support.

We built the movement up to the point where we had almost a monopoly on major offices. In this we had the assistance of Democrats, who nominated their candidates in convention and voted mostly in the Republican primary for anti-Proctor candidates. Then, in the elections, they were free to waste their votes on their own designees in full knowledge that it didn't make the slightest difference.

One of the political acquaintances I made in Legion activity was Col. H. Nelson Jackson, a Canadian-born physician who as an infantry officer won almost every decoration given by any allied nation for bravery in action, and on his return after the armistice organized the Legion in Vermont and became an important figure in veterans' affairs nationally and internationally. He had married the heiress to one of Vermont's largest fortunes, and managed his wife's investments diligently and efficiently. In common with a great many others, I admired his ability, his energy and his civic spirit.

One day the idea seized upon me that he would make an ideal candidate for governor. Probably many had the same idea and acted upon it with more finesse. I did the first thing that occurred to me—I wired him a request to run, and published the telegram. He declined courteously.

Later I learned how it should have been done, when more skillful politicians decided that Colonel Jackson should run for a vacant senatorship. He was about to sail for Europe, I think in connection with business of the Federation Internationale des Anciens Combatants, inter-allied veteran organization known popularly as Fidac, of which he was an officer.

At a series of conferences it was decided just when and how the public should be let into the secret. A cablegram requesting that Jackson run was drafted with great care. The proper list of signatories was agreed upon. The colonel's cablegram of acceptance was prepared. Then he sailed.

Colonel Jackson wanted badly for years to hold high elective office. He had the time, the money, the yen for the limelight, and both the desire and the ability for useful public service. Positive and self-assured in most things, he was timid and uncertain about this one. He could have been governor in 1920. He could have been senator in 1922. But when he got away from his friends, with an ocean between, he lost faith, and to the cable of invitation he sent a declination.

It was 1936 before he got up courage to run, and then it was too late. He was beaten for the nomination by George D. Aiken, and soon afterward sold the daily news-

paper he had owned for almost fifteen years to advance
his fortunes and those of his brothers, one of whom was
lieutenant-governor when he was drowned in Vermont's
disastrous flood of 1927, and the other of whom was several times Democratic mayor of Burlington.

As editor and publisher, and also as the working officer
of the local Legion post, I was a prominent citizen. To
raise money for the post, two or three of us used to borrow
the use of barns from the more prosperous farmers, hire
a three-piece orchestra, and hold barn dances. We hired
the local opera house, upstairs over two stores and the
postoffice, and imported an out-of-town orchestra for
modern dances. We raised around $200 a year, by sub-
scription, and brought in an outside band and prominent
state figures as speakers for Memorial Day exercises, for
which I drilled neighborhood boys with .22 calibre rifles
as a firing squad.

In most of these activities, I had to take the lead, do
much of the work, and preside as chairman when one was
needed. Up to the end, I underwent agonies each time I
had to get up before my fellow townsmen and mumble
even an introduction for my old national guard colonel.

After the debacle in Woodsville, I rested at home for a
time, and then went to Hanover, N. H., as compositor in
the shop which does most of Dartmouth College's printing.
Working overtime one night, I fainted.

The doctor said that I had a bad heart condition which required a life of ease for a time, without worry or hard physical exertion. I took a summer job at a club in the White Mountain region, printing menus and renting boats.

One of the members was the late Chester S. Lord, then retired after years as managing editor of the New York Sun. He was an ardent fisherman, who spent almost every waking hour on the lake. Consequently I saw him, on a "Good morning, Mr. Lord" basis, seven days a week during his stay. Before he left, I got up courage to ask him how to go about getting on the Sun's reportorial staff.

"Get a job on a small town paper," he told me, "where you'll have a chance to do all kinds of reporting. It is the best training school there is for newspaper men. That is what I had my son do before he started working in New York."

I was disappointed, because I had hoped that he would send me to the Sun with what amounted to a royal command to "give this promising young man a chance to show what he can do."

I took his advice perforce, because there seemed to be nothing else I could do, and circumstances gave me the opportunity to start on a small daily newspaper. It seems as though he was correct. I would offer the same advice to any young person whom I could not persuade to divert his ambition toward lusher pastures.

*

*　　*

*　*Chapter Four*　*

EXTRA-CURRICULAR EDUCATION

★ 4 ★

Extra-Curricular
Education

WITH ten dollars in my pocket, and no more in sight, I matriculated at the University of Vermont and set out to acquire some of the book learning which the war and my venture as a publisher had interrupted.

It was in the fall of 1922. I had gone to Burlington for a physical examination at the Veterans Bureau, to which I had applied some time before for compensation and vocational training. There had been no noticeable enthusiasm about my claim, and the atmosphere did not seem improved on this visit. I was given an order for transportation home at government expense.

Burlington is a beautiful city. For my money, it is the most beautiful city. From the university campus on the east, Burlington slopes gently to the shore of Lake Champlain. Its lovely tree-shaded streets are lined with single-family homes, some tastefully pretentious and others modestly comfortable, but all scrupulously well-kept. There are many perfectly preserved examples of fine colonial architecture, of which some were standing when the Marquis de la Fayette laid the cornerstone of the second "Old Mill," the main college building. At that time there was only a single apartment house in the city, and it hardly looked the part.

By metropolitan standards the Queen City of Vermont is minute. Its official population has never reached the 25,000 figure, unless in the census just completed. Nevertheless, it is the metropolis of the state, the largest city within more than a hundred miles in the United States, and the home of an ancient state university, and it enjoys advantages not vouchsafed to suburban communities of many times its size.

Across the lake, to the west, the Adirondacks rise fast in New York, and nowhere have I seen the beauty of color that can be watched from almost any Burlington street of a late afternoon as the sun, sinking over the mountains across the lake in a riot of shades and tones, is reflected manifold in the placid waters of Champlain.

Among the advantages which Burlington does not possess is frequent train service. While I waited for a train home, I wandered about the city, admiring its quiet beauty. At the top of the hill lay the broad green campus of the University, where fellows and girls little younger than I were bustling about in comradely confusion, intent, I imagined, upon learning.

It looked most attractive. Before the war intervened, I had planned somewhat indefinitely to save up some money and go to college. The idea had been lost, but now I found it again. I had no job, or anything in particular to do with my time. Besides, I remembered that a charming young lady whom I wanted to know better had been given an honor scholarship at the university for that year.

More casually than it is told, I wandered into the university offices in the medical building, obtained credit for tuition and books, went downtown and hired a room for $4 a week in the home of a physician-alderman, and became Joe College.

The morning's Free Press had carried an advertisement for a linotype operator. Having matriculated and taken a room, I answered the advertisement and got the job at $25 a week. I was to work alone from six in the evening to two the next morning, setting type for the college newspaper.

The setup would have been ideal if I had known how to operate a linotype. Unfortunately, my only experience had been punching out a few lines at lunch hour, while my operator was away, during my short time in Woodsville, and helping to get things working when some minor accident put the machine out of order.

Any fair operator can set a column of type, of newspaper width, each hour. He is supposed to do it by the touch system. I did not know the keyboard, and had to hunt for each letter. When I had a "squirt"—that is, when through my fault or the machine's a mass of hot metal squirted out and solidified in the working parts, so that the wheels could not turn—I had to clean it up.

For a couple of weeks I got along by holding my tongue and letting it be inferred that the machine was not working well. Meanwhile I was improving a little. It looked as though I might get away with it until the foreman, probably thinking to be helpful, gave me another machine that he knew was in good working order. On this linotype, the lettering on the keys was so worn away that I could not see it readily, and my production fell to new lows.

Soon we had a heart-to-heart talk, the foreman and I, in which he learned the truth about my linotype experience and told me, kindly but firmly, that it wouldn't do. If the shop had been allowed another apprentice under union rules he would have given me the chance. But since I was not up to earning a union salary and becoming a union member, and there was no apprenticeship opening, I was out of luck.

I had saved up a little toward paying for the tuition and books to which the university had staked me. This and credit carried me for a short time. Then, just as it seemed that I was through, out of a clear sky the Veterans Bureau came through with compensation—more than six hundred dollars of it in a lump sum—and vocational training. The government was ready to take over my tuition and books and incidental college fees and charges, and give me $100 a month on which to live.

I fear that I lost my sense of proportion. I decided that nothing less than Columbia University and the Pulitzer School would do for me. I paid up bills, bought luggage, acquired new clothes, said goodbyes and prepared to move to New York. Then fate, in the form of a red-headed co-ed, intervened.

A fellow freshman invited me for Thanksgiving dinner to the flat where his girl friend and three other co-eds kept house for economy and companionship.

The three other girls, as I learned later, tossed coins to see who would entertain me. The loser, after I had made a preliminary visit which included a trip to the movies, was called home for Thanksgiving. Her responsibility toward me she bequeathed to her room-mate.

A young widow who was among the girls I tried to train as compositors in Groton told my mother once that "When Burt falls for a girl, he is going to fall hard."

She proved a good prophet. I put away my new luggage, cancelled my withdrawal from the University, and went to work. At Christmas I gave my Thanksgiving acquaintance a diamond—a small one, not quite perfect and very inexpensive, but one which she still wears and declines to have replaced. She was graduated in June; and on the last day of that month, so that she could be with me when I started summer school July 5, we were married.

We were very poor. By the time I had financed a short honeymoon in my father-in-law's car, we were down to some gold pieces that were among the wedding gifts. The government increased my allowance to $135 a month when I was married, but the book-keeping held up the checks so that none came for some weeks. The University lent me a little. We scrimped as carefully as we could.

Finally on a Saturday we went to the cheapest shopping district and bought the absolute necessities, and found ourselves with exactly ten cents left. We had no bread, which then cost ten cents. Both of us loved fresh corn on the cob, which had just reached the market. We walked back and forth in front of the last store on the way home, debating whether we should eat bread or corn over the week end.

Common sense prevailed—my wife's. She went into the store to buy bread. I stood on the sidewalk, staring disconsolately into the gutter. A modest glitter attracted me. I investigated. And then, for the first and only time in my life, I found a dime.

We had corn, too, for Sunday dinner.

More than once since 1923 my wife and I have been very poor. I would not advise young men to assume the responsibility of providing for wives during their college courses. But for my own part, if I were a freshman again and could find a co-ed with the stamina my wife has shown, I wouldn't think for a moment of letting her get away somewhere to teach school. It would be too hazardous. I know the rush that small town beaux give school-ma'ams.

We worked hard those next three years. I worked for the Free Press as a reporter during vacations and in holiday seasons, wrote editorials during the editor's vacation, and corresponded for any paper that would take news from the university. The only faking I ever have done consciously, as a reporter, was in football stories I wrote at a time when I had never before seen the game played.

Emily had worked all through college to help herself, and she continued to work for another three years to help us. She taught cooking in night school and did secretarial work at the university administration office. One of her assignments there was to check the attendance records sent in by the instructors. A list was compiled of students accumulating more than five absences and this was forwarded to the dean of undergraduate men at regular intervals.

One of our private jokes was the fact that my name was on the list more frequently than any other, and I always had warning of when to expect a summons to the office. Dean Swift, who headed the department of mathematics and attended to discipline on the side, tried at first to impress upon me that even if the university were wrong I still should obey its rules. I agreed in theory but seldom found time to co-operate in practice.

I operated on the theory that I was in college to learn, and that often I could learn more in other places than at class lectures and recitations. The regulations in many departments were against me.

My attitude toward class attendance resulted eventually in a great disappointment. It prevented my taking postgraduate work as a teaching fellow.

I was editor of the college weekly, and among the steps I took to wake it up was a campaign to renovate and modernize the class cut system. Week after week I wrote blistering editorials of which the title of one, "Day Laboring for Education," typifies the theme. In course of time, running out of local material, I cited the system at Middlebury College, our traditional rival in sports and studies, as a horrible example of what never should be permitted. Within a month Middlebury had a new cut system resembling what I advocated. So far as I know Vermont hasn't followed my advice up to date.

The faculty showed a great disinterest in my ideas. So did the student body. It took all my most oppressive insistence to persuade the Student Senate, of which I was vice-president, to adopt a resolution favoring my proposals, in order to quiet me long enough so that we could discuss smokers, pep talks, and freshmen who wouldn't wear their pea hats.

I had assumed that the administration did not read the Cynic, but I was wrong. When, approaching graduation, I asked the registrar about a teaching fellowship in government for the next year, he wrapped the faculty attitude up in a neat bundle and handed it to me:

"We feel, Mr. Heath," he said, "that the University has done all that it can for you. . . ."

He paused for a moment, savoring the morsel, and added contemplatively:

". . . and we feel that you have done all that you can for the University."

That was my first editorial campaign to correct a burning social evil.

One reason for the irregularity of my class attendance was the variety of my outside interests, both on and off the campus. With no intention of belittling book learning, of which I have much too little, I feel that extra curriculum activities were of infinitely greater value to me in later life than any of the specific things I learned in books.

In my classes, I learned something of how to learn, though I have forgotten most of the things I memorized there incidental to the main purpose of study. In and through classes I made the acquaintance of the best of the faculty membership, and because I was older than most students and had outside interests, I was able to pursue that acquaintance with some of the teachers to my everlasting profit.

The University of Vermont is a small institution, whose enrollment from two-year teacher trainees through postgraduate students numbers only around 1,200.

Its faculty contains few whose names are of national note, but many who deliberately have refused opportunities at the big-name universities where their salaries would have been multiplied and their talents skillfully publicized.

In such surroundings it is not difficult for any earnest student to become the personal friend of real gentleman-scholars who, on a broader campus and with greater outside commitments, would have no time for callow undergraduate contacts. From such men, in the intimate democracy of a small college, the student can acquire something much more precious than the ability to answer examination questions correctly twice each year.

By the time I got around to go to college, I knew pretty well what I was after. I wanted book learning, to be sure, but even more I wanted to learn how to get along with people, giving and taking. I wanted to absorb some of the more urbane facets of living, such as did not exist on a farm or in a small village or in army life, and to learn why some persons seem always at ease in any surroundings

while others are like fish out of water whenever they leave
their own firesides.

Some of this I could get from my fellow students, in
class and on campus and in fraternity activities, but a great
proportion of the students came from surroundings not
dissimilar to my own. It was to the faculty that I had
to turn in large part.

From many, whose names would mean nothing outside
Vermont, I profited. To one I owe more than he will
ever know or I ever be able to tell. He was Arthur Beck-
with Myrick, erudite, urbane, tolerant, kindly head of the
department of romance languages, a genial, rotund gentleman who strolled our rustic campus with all the Gallic
aplomb of a boulevardier on the Rue St. Germaine, and
who has been famous at Vermont down the years for his
histrionic readings of Cyrano in French classes.

I was exposed to French in Prof. Myrick's class only
for a few weeks, after the instructor of my regular class
had capitulated to student irritations and the effects of war
shock, and retired to an institution for treatment. I knew
him best in the fraternity house, where he used occasionally
to spend long evenings lifting week-end bull sessions out of
their innocuous tritenesses. But I remember him best
because of an incident in my junior year, in which his
innate *savoir faire* unintentionally but very effectively
taught me how socially aboriginal I was.

We had invited Professor and Mrs. Myrick to dinner.

It was to be something of an occasion, and we had practiced stringent economies to finance it adequately and at the same time to pay for balcony seats at the Opera House, where the great Minnie Maddern Fiske was playing in The Rivals the preceding evening.

The night of the show, to which we had looked forward eagerly since the first preliminary announcement that it was coming, we were eating warmed over baked beans in impromptu fashion on the kitchen table, when the door bell rang. Emily went to the door. There were the Myricks for dinner, and there were we, half-dressed to go out, polishing off the last of the beans. Otherwise the pantry was bare.

Our embarrassment was so obvious that it could not be over-looked.

"Weren't you expecting us?" asked Professor Myrick.

We hemmed and hawed and tried to explain that we had mistaken the evening, and admitted that we had tickets to see Mrs. Fiske. Our guests rose to the occasion so simply that they put us almost at ease, although even today I couldn't swear that it was not we who had gotten our dates mixed.

Professor Myrick, himself an enthusiastic amateur thespian and theatre-goer, took a few minutes to tell us how much we were going to enjoy the play, and to reminisce about his own fond memories of the first time he saw it. They took themselves off, as amiably as though we were parting after a casual sidewalk encounter.

The incident in retrospect is trivial. Then it seemed stark tragedy. It demonstrated impressively one of the many phases of social training in which a rustic youth had left me inept and uncouth. It was another step in the process by which college gave me something more valuable than lies between the covers of any text book.

Those who come out of suave surroundings, by way of Groton or Choate, have no necessity to learn in college how to live with other men and women. To us from backwoods homes, this was a free gift from the university, uncataloged, without price and beyond evaluation.

This side of my education was pursued deliberately and everlastingly, on and off the campus. Because I had always been inordinately terrified at speaking before any group, I went out for debating in my freshman year and participated throughout my entire college course. I helped form a new local fraternity, which progressed so rapidly that six years after we received university approval for our organization, we became a chapter of Sigma Alpha Epsilon. With no alumni, and only one under-graduate who was not dirt poor, in our third year of existence we bought a $20,000 chapter house, worked out with the local bank a self-amortizing mortgage of the type popularized recently by the Federal Housing Administration, and held onto the property through the depression when older and wealthier groups failed.

Our new fraternity, formed with the avowed purpose of becoming a chapter of Sigma Alpha Epsilon, needed campus honors, and we went after them. My talents lay in non-athletic fields, where I carried as heavy a load as any member of my class and wound up as editor of the university weekly, associate editor of the junior year-book and a member of the junior and senior honorary societies.

Meanwhile I was devoting much time to the American Legion, in which I was a member of the inner group that ran the state's largest post, holding office and heading working committees. I was active in the Society of the 40 Men and 8 Horses, supposedly the Legion's play organization but actually its controlling oligarchy. I became commander of the state's largest county Legion organization, and state treasurer of the "40 and 8."

It was at this time that I became an insider in the group of young amateur politicians who were trying to take over the Republican organization in the state. At one time, at a quiet caucus in a lonely hall on a Lake Champlain island, we were ready to move into the open with good chances of success, until one of the established politicians we had expected to front for the movement, the mayor of Winooski, lost his nerve and withdrew.

Many of these things were juvenile, of course, but on top of a certain minimum of study and recitation work, and of time devoted to supplementing the family income, they aggregated an almost overwhelming grist of work from first class at 8:30 until far past midnight almost every night in the week.

I enrolled for my junior year needing a second language for my degree. I selected Latin because I had studied it briefly as a high school freshman twelve years before. The head of the Latin department agreed that I might take freshman and sophomore Latin—the equivalent of four years in high school—together in my junior year, and then take two years of college Latin simultaneously in my senior year.

Night after night for two years Emily, who had learned Latin in high school, would lie in bed helping me until midnight with Latin composition and translation, and then would fall asleep exhausted while I spent an hour or two more on other studies, or worked on the Cynic, or prepared news notes for papers for which I was correspondent.

Undoubtedly I took on a little too much. When Commencement honors were distributed, I was just on the outside everywhere. My senior essay almost won a welcome monetary prize. I was considered for the medal awarded to the senior who had done most for the university, but another won it. I missed scholarship honors by a decimal of one percentage point. I was highest of two who just missed Phi Beta Kappa in the final election.

I wanted one or more of these honors badly, as a sop

to a self-esteem which I have always had to bolster by whistling through my own intellectual graveyard. It hurt when I lost them. But now I feel differently. Given the same opportunity and the same handicaps, I would do pretty much the same things I did then. What I got out of college was of infinitely greater value to me, in the long run, than the honors that I missed.

I had learned to compete with my fellows in those affairs which were currently of importance, and to make a place for myself on my own merits in the most democratic fields I have ever known—the college campus and the American Legion.

On a brilliant June Monday I paraded into the University of Vermont gymnasium and became a bachelor of philosophy. Two days later I was a practicing politician, doing my part to resist a Coolidge *blitzkrieg*.

It is a lazy man's method to borrow such alien expressions to save brain cudgeling, and in 1926 there was no such word as *blitzkrieg*, but after some thought I can find nothing which so well expresses what Calvin Coolidge tried to do. It was his intention to purge the United States Senate of my friend Porter Dale, who had ventured to oppose the presidential will, and it was his expectation that Senator Dale would be obliterated from the political landscape with one blast from the White House.

Cautious Cal, protagonist of unstinting thrift, was Vermont's pride and joy. The second Vermonter ever to occupy the White House, he used his New England heritage as a political hall mark, and shed some of his surplus fame upon the rock-ribbed Green Mountains of his native state. So long as he remained a Republican he could have almost anything he asked from Vermont for himself.

Perhaps Coolidge had been too long away from intimate contact with his fellow Vermonters, or it may be that he was poorly advised by counsellors who never did know one of our most unalterable traits. In any event, he undertook to tell Vermont whom to send to the senate, and he was reminded that with us Yankees molasses catches more flies than vinegar.

Porter Dale was conscientiously and heartily in favor of anything that would help war veterans. This included what we called "adjusted compensation" and our opponents dubbed "the bonus." When he was elected in 1923 to an unexpired term, he committed himself unequivocally to continued support of adjusted compensation. When it was adopted he voted for it. When it was vetoed by President Coolidge his vote helped to pass it over the veto.

Deserting his general philosophy of letting well enough alone, the president gave orders that Senator Dale was to be retired. So certain was he that the voters of his native state would obey without question, that he handed his banner to the aged ex-Governor William W. Stickney, law partner of Attorney-General John Garibaldi Sargent, who had been out of public life so long that he had no claim to support except as the president's designee.

Senator Dale resisted as a matter of course. He made my former national guard commander, Col. Fred B. Thomas, his campaign manager, and I became assistant manager. Senator Dale and Colonel Thomas spent their time with key political and civic and social and community leaders. I spent mine with the state's editors, seeing that they were informed as to the issues, confirmed in their support or softened in their antagonism, providing them with occasional news items and writing editorials for any that liked ideas I suggested.

When we started our opponents were assured and we were worried. In about a month all was changed. We were assured, and the opposition was on the run. About the first of August candidate Stickney was invited to Boston to discuss things with some of the President's friends. From there, he announced that his physician had discovered that he was physically unable to continue the race.

The futility of the President's attack was evidenced when the primary vote for Dale, unopposed, exceeded the combined vote cast in a contest for lieutenant-governor and lacked only 6,000 of equalling the vote cast in a bitter three-way fight for governor.

I had bought a second-hand automobile for my campaign travelling. During the last days of the campaign I prepared it to go job-hunting.

I took the woven-wire spring from a cot bed, sawed its two wooden side-pieces in half, and hinged them so that the spring would fold small enough to stand by day in the back of the car. Around it we packed bedding, luggage, boxes of foodstuffs, and miscellaneous travelling paraphernalia. For the rivets which had fastened the backs onto the car's front seats, I substituted bolts with wing nuts.

On primary day Emily and I drove to Burlington, cast our votes, and in mid-afternoon started for Florida or any way point where work might be found. We weren't at all particular, so long as there was a living to be had. Florida was a tentative terminus only because Emily's father had talked about me with an editor of a Jacksonville paper, and we were naïve enough to suppose that this meant I could work there if I chose.

The first night, unusually tired after a hard day, we found a cottage on the shore of Lake Bomoseen, which because it was after the camping season we were able to rent for a dollar. The farmer-owner sold us eggs and milk.

We drove leisurely down Lake Champlain, over to Albany and down the Hudson. Nightfall found us in open country. We saw a sign in the yard of a farmhouse advertising camping privileges, and arranged to park there for fifty cents. We chose a secluded spot under a big apple tree. I took the backs off the front seats, removed the cushions from the rear seats, and spread my cot spring the length of the car, stuffing surplus possessions under and around. After a supper cooked on our canned heat stove, we went to bed.

It was economical, which was what we needed, but I discovered one miscalculation. I had not realized, when I transformed our two-door sedan into a perambulating one-room apartment, that the bedspring would sag under the weight of two persons onto the boxes and bags stored under it. We never were able to curl ourselves into positions in which sharp corners weren't gouging us.

In the morning, when we woke and looked around, we found that the small building at our right was not a chicken house.

The third night we slept in our car at an auto camp in Englewood, New Jersey, just across the Hudson from New York City. Our arrangements were unchanged because our equipment permitted no variation. We were happy that we had thought to bring netting, for that night we had our first encounters with those almost birdlike creatures that breed in the Jersey swamps and are euphemistically known by the natives as mosquitoes. We draped our open car windows as carefully as we could, but it was not a comfortable night.

The next day, wearied, bedraggled and badly in need of something more cleansing than the sponge baths we had been able to take, we drove into New York and took a room at a relatively inexpensive theatrical hotel just off Times Square.

Before leaving Vermont, I had written to Edward J. McKernon, then divisional superintendent of the Associated Press, reminding him that a letter of recommendation from President Guy W. Bailey of the University of Vermont had been turned over to him, and informing him that I should be there in a few days looking for work.

At the hotel, I found waiting a letter from Mr. McKernon. It said very close to this:

"We have no openings at this time, and if we did, you do not appear to have sufficient experience in newspaper work to satisfy our requirements. However, since you say that you are going to be in New York anyway, you are welcome to come in for a visit."

I went at once to Mr. McKernon's office. After a few moments' conversation, he suggested that I go to New Haven and talk with William J. G. Myers, bureau chief there. He said he would let Myers know that I was coming. We drove up to New Haven that night. By half past nine the next morning I was on the payroll of the Associated Press.

Chapter Five

THE BIG PUDDLE

The Big Puddle

ALWAYS I have preferred being a moderate-sized toad in a small puddle. I never wanted to be the big scarred patriarch, who has won his ascendancy at considerable pain and has to defend it with unremitting vigilance. I just want to be a good, respectable, respected middle-classer whom everybody knows and nobody hates or fears or envies.

During most of our first year in New Haven we were bitterly lonely, and cursed the city as a cold, inhospitable host. Then we ran across an old school teacher of Emily's. She introduced us to a distant relative of my wife's who was established in business and had a wide circle of pleasant friends. We began to feel at home just about the time we had to pack our goods for the move to New York.

I resisted jumping into the big puddle—New York—because I feared that it would be too impersonal, too callous, too cruel, too demanding, too hectic. For most newspapermen New York is the rainbow's end. All good reporters hope some day to share in its pot of gold. The competition, I thought, would be intense, and in it I could hardly escape being crushed.

When it was first suggested that I be transferred from the little state bureau in New Haven to the Associated Press' general headquarters in New York, I declined firmly, and argued it out with my wife only after the decision had been made. We were doing well enough, I felt, between my twice-raised salary and that which Emily earned as secretary to a child welfare organization. We might have been there yet if a superior office politician had not put a fast one over on me.

In the New Haven bureau were three editors, one for each shift, who were entitled to select their working hours in order of seniority. At first, of course, I had the unpleasant "lobster trick" from midnight to morning. In the course of a year I became senior editor, as others left, and was entitled to pleasant day hours. Then the latest addition to our little staff persuaded the bureau chief that it was unfair to make any one man work the "lobster trick" regularly, that there should be a rotation in which each would take his share of the bad with the good. On the general merits of his contention I have no argument, but I felt that from my standpoint it had come pretty late. I sent word to the divisional superintendent that I was ready to move to New York.

On my birthday, in 1927, I tossed my hat timidly into the center ring, and went to work in the big city, alongside those legendary figures who long had impressed us provincials with their achievements and with the cocky self-assurance of their attitudes when they dropped in, now and then, to take over some good story that presumably we could not have handled satisfactorily. Except for one rather short interval, I have lived and worked in New York ever since, never ceasing to think of it as a temporary term of indenture.

It is only fair to confess that some of my ideas about New York have undergone a change.

We had always heard of the tricky sameness of big city house fronts and apartment entrances. It is one of the whimsical conceits of small towners to imagine how embarrassing it might be to come home some early morning, presumably from a wild night of wining and dining in a girlie show night club, and mistake another's apartment door for one's own. Or, in the alternative, to have a neighbor come home similarly befuddled. We learned that it does happen here.

Emily had to serve out a notice in New Haven, so I came on ahead. She joined me for New Year's in the new apartment we had rented on Long Island. New Year's

Eve was our first night together in our new home. I had to work until two in the morning. No sooner had I fallen soundly asleep than Emily began shaking me vigorously.

"Wake up, Burt, wake up," she kept whispering loudly until I showed signs of understanding. "There's a man in the house."

I heard footsteps approaching, slowly but with no apparent stealth. I sat up in bed. The living-room lights were on. Before I could rub my eyes wide open a personable enough young man in dinner clothes came calmly to the door of our bedroom, turned on the light, and looked surprisedly at us in bed. He didn't appear at all dangerous. I couldn't think quite what etiquette might require under the circumstances. While I pondered sleepily, Emily went into action.

"Get out of here," she said sternly, pulling the bed-clothes up about her. "You get right out of here."

So far as I was concerned, that seemed as good a line to follow as any other, and I chimed in.

"What the hell do you think you are doing here?" I asked our uninvited guest. "Go on, get out."

What we would have done if he had chosen to argue I have no idea. Fortunately he didn't.

"Isn't this where the Blanks live?" he inquired calmly.

"No," we told him.

"Well, then, where do they live?" he asked. We confessed ignorance.

With all the aplomb in the world the intruder apologized, made a trifle unsteady exit, carefully locked our door behind him with a key that should not have fitted, and disappeared forever from our lives.

We were quite prepared to believe that such incidents, with enough variety of form to spice them, might be the constant diet of New Yorkers. In that we have been disappointed, pleasantly enough. Most of our other disappointments about New York have been on the pleasant side.

New York, we have found, really is a friendly, helpful place, provided one can find a samaritan who isn't in too much of a hurry to notice distress signals.

It is quite possible, and seems usual, to live in an apartment house for the term of a lease and not know the name or occupation of the neighbors who share one's six by twelve hallway or use the same self-service elevator. One can and often does learn of the mishaps of friends only through the newspapers or by accident days or weeks later.

In Vermont we had never had to make friends. They made themselves. In New York we have developed, over a period of years, a very satisfactory circle. But we have had to make them slowly, continually renewing the personnel as moving day took one after another to parts of the city so distant as to preclude frequent association.

When we first came looking for a home we were shown an attached house—one of a row, each twenty feet wide, sharing a community wall on each side with the neighbor, sharing a community driveway, sharing front lawn and back space and most of the privacy which we had regarded as necessary. We scoffed at the idea of living in such a place. We preferred an apartment. But for four years, now, we have been the contented owners of just such an attached house as we swore we never would so much as rent.

One of the strangest winters of our lives was the one when I was out of work, our finances were at rock-bottom, and we economized by living "on Park Avenue."

To tide us over Emily found a job as novice salesgirl in one of the big department stores while I answered advertisements, canvassed editors, tried to sell magazine articles, did occasional publicity bits, and kept house.

We were so poor, not for the first time in our married life, that even nickels for subway fare had to be used with discretion, and restaurant lunches were luxuries verging upon dissipation. We decided to take a single room in Manhattan, located so that Emily could walk to and from work and come home for lunch, and I could walk to midtown newspaper offices and literary agencies, for economy. It had to be unfurnished, because we did not feel we could pay hire on furnishings and in order to save storage charges on our own effects.

While I took an automobile-load of surplus belongings to Vermont and blocked the car up for the winter at the farm, Emily canvassed the midtown east side for the sort of room we wanted.

At last she found one which she thought would do, and paid in advance thirty dollars for a month's rent on a third floor room.

"I don't know whether you will like it," she told me when I returned. "The address sounds good, but it's just a row of old brownstone houses."

"What is the address?" I asked. She told me—on East 65th Street, between Madison and Park Avenues.

"It ought to do," I told her. "Franklin Roosevelt lives two doors east."

"Why, that can't be so," she expostulated. "He wouldn't live in a place like that. Wait until you see it."

"Nevertheless, he does," I assured her, and proved it by my notebook of private telephone numbers and addresses of prominent news sources.

We dickered cannily with a moving man and got his best price. We arranged to move in late afternoon. I stayed at our apartment to meet the movers. Emily went from her counter to the new room to await them, and tried to turn on the lights. Nothing happened. She complained to the rooming-house proprietor and was assured that the

current would be turned on at once.   Two friendly little
old ladies who had been watching called her aside.

"We don't want to interfere," they told her, "but we
think you should know that the lights and gas are off most
of the time.   The young woman means well, but she is
trying to operate three of these houses on a shoestring,
and apparently she can't keep her bills paid up.   Everybody in the house is planning to move out."

Meanwhile the van had arrived with our furniture.
It was seven o'clock.   Emily couldn't move in, nor could
she hold the van and men long at hour rates.   Her new acquaintances came to the rescue.

"Down on 53d Street," they told her, "there's a couple
named Allison who are just opening a rooming-house, and
haven't completed furnishing it yet.   Why don't you try
them?"

So Emily grabbed a taxicab, a form of conveyance
which we find too extravagant for frequent use even in
good times and which wrenched the budget doubly then,
and went to 53d Street, just across from the exclusive Rac-
quet Club where Mayor Walker used to hang out.   There
she found an unemployed Canadian and his wife staking
the savings of his twenty years with the Canadian Pacific
railroad on a rooming-house.   They were sympathetic.

"We haven't any suitable room left unfurnished," they
told her, "but why don't you let the movers set your furniture in here until you can find a place?   You can take the

second floor front for the time being, and we won't charge you anything for leaving the furniture in a room we are not using yet."

We took them up, after not too convincing protest. The next day they decided to move their furnishings out of the second floor front, which had a sizable dressing-room suitable for kitchenette purposes, and let us put ours in for $40 a month, electricity and gas included.

We stayed there all winter. The house was old and the heating plant worn out. The owners wouldn't spend money for repairs because they planned to sell their holdings for business use. We used to burn all the newspapers we could get, carefully wadded to make them last longer, in the fireplace. We stuffed the drafty windows with felt weather stripping.

Emily walked to her work and I walked on my job-hunting. She came home to the lunches I prepared, and suffered tolerantly the dinners I cooked.

I had a regular routine for dinners. Saturday I would buy a good-sized roast of whatever meat was cheapest. This was our Sunday dinner. Monday we would slice off of the remains. If enough remained, we would duplicate Monday's dinner for Tuesday. When the sliceable meat was gone, I would get a dime's worth of soup greens and make a stew, which usually was good for two more days' dinners. Since we invariably had oyster stew Friday

night and home-baked beans for Saturday, there never was
much mystery about our menus.

Emily still treasures as a fonder memory her birthday
that spring. She worked, of course, and I celebrated by
trying to frost a cake. In honor of the occasion I attempted
also to mop the floor. When she came home for lunch, I
had all portable furniture on the bed, the floor about half-
mopped, and cake frosting all over the extemporized
kitchenette.

She explained that I had made the frosting too thin,
and that was why I had to spend the morning dashing back
and forth between bed-living room and kitchenette—first
mopping a bit of floor, then scraping the icing back up on
top of the cake, and then mopping as much more as I could
before the frosting again got out of hand.

Because of our cooking, the neighborhood mice made
our room their rendezvous, and annoyed us at night with
rattling investigations into anything of paper they could
find. One night when friends stayed with us we gave
them our bed and made one for ourselves on the kitchenette floor, where the mice trotted around us in bold curiosity all night.

During this period of our travail, until we went to
Vermont the next summer after I had obtained a commission to edit and refurbish a book, we found our friends
standing by loyally, going out of their way to deluge us
with week-end invitations, to take us to entertainments we

couldn't afford ourselves, and otherwise to help in tactful ways which would not scarify my growing sensitivity over my inability to get work.

That period taught me pretty well to distinguish between real friends and friends of expediency. It showed me some of the factors which have gone toward breaking some millions of our unemployed so that a considerable proportion of them have become permanently unemployable. It forbade me ever to say again that anybody who wants to work can get work. It gave me some inkling of how the great mass of New Yorkers, whose incomes are even less than ours was then, must scrimp to preserve respectability.

Between Emily's and my earnings we had an income averaging $25 a week. Out of this we had to pay $40 a month for our room. We set aside $10 a week for food and petty household expenditures. Out of the remainder we had to finance the remaining costs of living and find $100 every six months to pay on the mortgage on our Vermont farm, which alone was enabling my aged and infirm parents to survive while we had no money with which to help them.

No mathematical genius is required to demonstrate that we could not go to the theatre or buy many clothes. Emily had to buy the material from which to make two dresses, because store regulations prescribed a type of garment which had not been featured in her wardrobe. Fortunately I was able to get by with what I had. If our economies had been enforced beyond the ability of my suits to hold together, the situation would have become embarrassing.

My slightly more than two years with the Associated Press, in New Haven and New York, I would not have missed for a great deal. It was excellent training. It offered wide diversity of experience, and it threw me into competition with older, keener, better-trained reporters who knew all the tricks of the trade. It brought me into contact with a more vivid, more varied and more rapidly-changing kaleidoscope of news events than I had imagined existed.

Because the Associated Press is a membership organization, whose newspaper owners are obligated to provide it with the news of their communities, it features first-hand reporting much less than do other news services. Its work is largely the interchange, in accurate digest, of news it has not gathered. Its editorial employees are largely rewrite men and sub-editors, rather than reporters.

Before I had ever gone through the regular routine of learning to gather news and write it from notes, I was doing daily the more advanced work of rewriting, copyreading, editing and scheduling news. Before I had learned to satisfy the peculiarities of a single boss, I was forced to please as bosses all the editors in the state of Connecticut.

Chiefly because at first I was the youngest member of the New Haven staff, and as such drew the undesirable "lobster trick" from midnight to morning from which an editor could best be taken for emergency duty, I had more than my share of reporting.

When a New York writer killed his house guest near Willimantic I was hauled out of bed an hour after I finished a night's work, rushed by automobile to the scene without so much as a spare handkerchief or a tooth brush, and worked twenty hours a day for a week and a half before I got back home.

That was the first story on which I ever worked under real competition. New York papers had their star murder reporters there. Our bitter rival, the United Press, sent its bureau manager. During the investigation he and I were so inseparable that we even shared a hotel room—not from affection, or for economy or because of inadequate accommodations, but merely because neither of us was willing to trust the other out of his sight. We went to bed together, got up together, ate together, and usually one rode in the other's car when we made our rounds. Once he left the room at night to get some cigarettes, and the next morning my office telephoned frantically to know why I let the U. P. scoop me on an angle of the story. The next day I got away long enough to brazen my way into the murder house yard, use my eyes vigorously while the state police were persuading me to leave, and get a scoop of my own.

I was in the New York office of the Associated Press exactly a year, working from six at night to two in the morning. Theoretically I was a reporter, but the term was elastic. Some of the time I rewrote news taken from member newspapers and from the coöperative service which covers New York for most of the papers. Often I filled in as a "wire editor," in charge of one or other of the circuits over which news is routed to and from different parts of the country. Occasionally I had opportunity to go out to a dinner or a meeting at which news or speeches of national interest would come too late for us to depend upon the newspapers.

For some months two of us had a drab routine covering four member newspapers. In early evening I would go downtown to the office of the now defunct American, and read proofs of its local news until the first edition went to press around eight o'clock. Anything of general interest I telephoned to my office. Then I would walk up through the slums of the lower east side to the old World, and watch its news for an hour and a half while Charlie Egan did likewise at the Herald-Tribune. When the World's first edition was ready for press I would take the subway uptown, and relieve Charlie at the Herald-Tribune so that he could go on to the Times. After the Herald-Tribune's first edition was ready I would go to the Times and stay with Charlie until midnight. Then we would tramp back to our own office. That was how the Associated Press covered New York.

The night hours weren't pleasant. The routine was boring. We had a night city editor who must have read about some genius who ruled his staff in the Sergeant Flagg manner, and who modeled after his hero. I learned quickly that I was never going to attain my ambition of getting into the foreign service through the AP. I obtained one raise, soon after the transfer, but my campaign for another raise and day work proved an utter failure. So I started canvassing the city's news rooms looking for a chance on a newspaper.

The general news editor, apparently sensing my discontent, went out of his way that fall to give me a really good assignment. He sent me to cover the campaign of Albert Ottinger for governor, against Franklin Roosevelt. It was one of the most arduous jobs I ever did. Because we had member newspapers from coast to coast, with edition times ranging from early morning to earlier morning the next day, we had to maintain twenty-four hour coverage. Reporters for morning newspapers could sleep late, take things easy during the day, and pick up from the rest of us in time to get their stories ready each evening. Reporters for evening newspapers had to work early and late, but had time to rest in between. I had to work without a break from the time the candidate left his room each morning until, after he had gone to bed, I sat wearily at a type-writer in my hotel room or in a telegraph office, and tried to piece together out of shopworn facts a story that could appear the next morning and look as though it were completely new.

Nevertheless, I enjoyed it. It was my first experience in the big time. I was working with and competing against the best political reporters of the metropolis, most of whom were paid at least twice my salary and all of whom had more leeway in their news-handling. They had only to please their own editors, while I had to avoid offending any of our 1,200 members. In this I was successful enough to win the commendation of my superiors. I felt that it entitled me to consideration of my request for a small raise and day work. My superiors appeared to disagree.

Learning that there were changes brewing on the New York Post, I went there and renewed my application for work.

"I am leaving at the end of the week," the city editor said, "and I don't want to make any changes now. There is an opening, however, and I will speak to my successor about you. Give him a couple of days to get settled, the first of the week, and I think you will find a job waiting."

I waited impatiently the two days, and then sought the new city editor of the Post, reminding him that his predecessor had spoken to him about me. He appeared startled.

"I'm sorry," he said. "Pop Byers told me that an AP man was coming to see me whom he thought I would like to hire. He didn't mention the name. One came yesterday—Chester Morrison—and I hired him. There isn't a thing left."

Discouraged, I started for home. On general principles, so as to leave no stone unturned, I took the long route to a subway and stopped at the Evening Telegram, then recently acquired by Scripps-Howard. It wasn't much of a paper. But for its large section of classified advertising it would have been a terrible commercial flop. It still lingered in the public mind with the bad odor of the days when James Gordon Bennett sensationalized its columns to make money to carry his respectable Herald.

There is a regular formula for getting into a newspaper office seeking work. I used it. The Telegram's star reporter then, the highest-paid reporter in New York by repute, was Courtenay "Brick" Terrett. I knew a reporter who knew him, so I asked for him at the door and was shown in. After a casual visit, the reason for which he knew as well as I, he introduced me without prejudice to the city editor, Walter Lister. Neither of them knew me from Adam. I told Lister about myself.

"When could you come to work?" he asked.

"In two weeks," I told him.

"What do you want?"

"Seventy dollars."

"What are you getting?"

"Sixty dollars."

"It is against my policy to pay anybody more than he is getting," he told me. "But if you want to come at sixty, and make good, in a month I will raise you the ten."

That is an old story in employment. It means, in most instances, changing without a raise. But at least it meant day work and widened experience, and a chance to meet reporters who could help me change again later for higher pay.

"I'll come," I agreed.

Back at the Associated Press I handed in my resignation.

"Where are you going?" asked my friend, the general editor.

"I'm going to the Telegram."

"Why?"

"Day work and a ten dollar raise," I exaggerated a bit.

"You're a fool," he said. "This is the greatest news organization in the world, with unlimited opportunities. The Telegram is a weak sister that probably will fold up soon. You can be proud to work for us. You will be ashamed every time you tell anyone you are with the Telegram. I'll give you the raise."

"And the day work?"

"We'll have to see about that," he evaded.

"It's too late," I said. "A week ago I would have taken you up. Now I've given my word."

On the Telegram I did some rewrite, and then was assigned to write the local angles for a special automobile show number. I worked hard and used all my imagination seeking novel angles on an event that had been reported from every angle that exists. The day before the edition went to press the editor called me over.

"How do you sign your name?" he asked.

"S. Burton," I told him.

On the proof of the lead story for the section he wrote

By S. BURTON HEATH
Telegram Staff Writer

That was how it appeared the next day—my first by-line. The Associated Press couldn't have had me back for $80 a week. I have had by-lines pretty regularly since then, except for intervals when I was doing policy or editorial work—sometimes on exclusive stories that led the paper under our biggest headlines. But down to this day no by-line has given me the thrill of that one on an unimportant story in a promotional section.

While I was on rewrite I was puzzled by the fact that whereas I always seemed to get rather routine stories, one of my fellows never failed to get each day at least one or two vivid human interest items, that read like pages from a novel. Reporters gave me the pertinent facts, but he always had intriguing dialog and his stories usually had a fillip at the end. I rated as a competent rewrite man, but he was fast becoming a star.

In course of time I was sent out on stories, and eventually I telephoned one to him to rewrite. When the edition came out I hunted for it in vain. At last, reading a most interesting little piece, I experienced that feeling one does, at times, of living through something that has happened before. With some difficulty I discovered the reason. The story I was reading was this chap's version of the very commonplace item I had telephoned to him. His fertile imagination had changed the facts beyond recognition. He had done no injustices, nor did his version deceive readers about anything important. It was just a triple-short story, based upon the news incident and run as news, without the editors' knowledge that it wasn't an accurate report.

It was during this period that Mary Ware Dennett was trapped by postoffice inspectors into mailing a copy of her brochure, The Sex Side of Life, to one of them posing as an ordinary buyer from Virginia. We became quite excited about it, and I was assigned to cover the news developments and simultaneously to drum up a public protest. Day after day I telephoned to liberal thinkers, getting their statements and the names of other protestants to canvass. I built up a quite imposing bonfire. The story got hot.

Then Brick Terrett moved in. He had done none of

the spade work, when there was digging without glory. When the affair grew to by-line prestige he took it over, with me still to do the work while he wrote signed stories. He kept the assignment until public interest wore thin and it passed the by-line stage, and then turned it back to me to wind up.

One of our reporters spent some weeks investigating the government's casual control over the importation of ergot, a drug used principally in childbirth to prevent excessive flow of blood. Ergot is a fungus disease which attacks grains in their embryo state, replacing the kernels with a growth which contains medicinal elements. It comes from Russia and Poland, from Spain and Portugal. Our inquiries developed that the Russian ergot of rye was reaching this country mouldy, because of careless shipping, and that the mould was affecting its medicinal qualities so that the resultant liquid extract was irresponsible. Many deaths in childbirth were resulting from the inability of obstetricians to rely upon the strength of supposedly standard ergot.

When this reporter reached a penultimate point I was assigned to complete the study and write the articles. The results caused much furore in the medical and governmental fields, and withstood all attacks from those whose culpability was pointed out.

It may have been because of this that I was assigned to my first major investigation, into the cost of electricity in our state and the vicious holding company structure which not only built up this cost but also imperilled the stability of the vital utility structure. In that inquiry and its aftermaths I met many men who have been among my most cherished friends and my most valuable news sources.

Before the results of the inquiry were printed, I resigned, to try a little business venture of my own in mistaken belief that the then young depression would be over in a few months. My departure was wholly friendly. The gloomy prophecies of my AP friend had not been borne out. The Telegram was gaining in prestige and in financial strength. The public's attitude toward it had become one of respect and friendliness. I had been treated well: better, by far, than I had anticipated.

Not long after I joined the staff Walter Lister was promoted from city editor to news editor. Late on his last day as my immediate boss he came over to my desk and mentioned casually his promotion. We visited for a few moments, and he started to leave.

"By the way," he said, swinging back momentarily, "I've put through that ten dollar raise that I promised when you came."

That is the only time in my experience that such a promise has been made good without so much as a reminder from me.

Chapter Six

THE ROOSEVELT WAY

★ 6 ★

The Roosevelt Way

MY first encounter with Franklin Delano Roosevelt was in the autumn of 1929, during his first year as governor of New York. I spent more than an hour and a half alone with him one day, exploring his mind on a subject of which he claimed to be master.

I went humbly to Albany as a supplicant for wisdom, approaching the throne as a life-long admirer of the great T. R. and a willing acolyte of any member of his family. I went also under some naïve assumptions as to the characteristics that any governor of a great state must possess.

My editors felt that the householders of New York were paying too high a price for their electricity, because the monopolistic nature of the business precluded competition and because a lax, disinterested Public Service Commission failed to protect the public interest.

Up on the northern boundary of the state, in the International Rapids section of the St. Lawrence River, a million horsepower was flowing past our back door, waiting to be harnessed and put to work. Former Governor Alfred E. Smith had long demanded that the state develop this current, and use it as a club with which to force down the price of electricity. Franklin Roosevelt took up the torch, and made this a principal item in his campaign.

I was instructed to go thoroughly into the matter of electricity costs and St. Lawrence waterpower—find out if our householders really were paying too much, and why—find out if St. Lawrence power really could be developed, and brought to New York, and whether it would result in cheaper electricity for the household.

Where I grew up, responsible men make it a practice not to promise until they know whether they can make good. I assumed that Governor Roosevelt, before he promised to bring St. Lawrence waterpower to New York and use it to reduce the cost of electricity, had gone into the subject enough to know what could be done and what should be done. Therefore I started with him. Making an appointment, I took a train for Albany.

In those days public business was not the hectic thing it has become. The busy governor of the great state of New York sat down with the young reporter, and talked graciously and patiently for an hour and forty minutes, with no interruption more than an occasional telephone call or aside with his secretary. He was charming, with that captivating camaraderie that took the nation by storm four years later. He was fatherly and tolerant and kindly. He was everything I could ask except the one thing that I did ask. He was not instructive.

The St. Lawrence River rapids are more than three hundred miles from New York City. The cost of transmission lines to carry a million horsepower over such a distance is enormous. Did he know what the cost might be—roughly? No, he hadn't checked that, but it was a mere detail. He drew a diagram, showing how he would hook up the St. Lawrence with Niagara Falls, and both with New York City.

A highly reputable study made a year later, by a Roosevelt-appointed commission of which I was secretary, placed the cost at $75,000,000—a detail, perhaps, but scarcely "mere."

Electricity leaks out of wires, over a long line, with heavy losses. Had Governor Roosevelt inquired how much of the million horsepower would be lost *en route*, and how this would increase the basic cost of the current? No, he hadn't, but it wasn't important. He had heard of some wonderful new cable in which line losses were negligible, and we could use that. He drew his diagram again. But up to this date, the wonderful new cable has never been announced or put into use.

There is a great waste in electrical production because of the fact that use is not evenly distributed over the day.

It is necessary to provide facilities with which to generate, transmit and distribute the greatest amount which will be used at any moment of any day in the year. Most of the time much less will be used, and the excess equipment will stand idle, eating its head off in capital charges. This is the problem of load factor.

For household use, at that time, it was necessary to provide facilities for roughly seven times as much current as actually would be used. Even if all other problems were disregarded, because of load factor the half-cent current of which Governor Roosevelt talked would cost three-and-a-half cents on the banks of the St. Lawrence, so far as family use was concerned. There are complications in this business of catching running water on a wheel and toasting bread or curling hair with it.

Did Mr. Roosevelt know how much these things might affect the availability of St. Lawrence current in New York City? No, he didn't, but he thought most of it was just eyewash used by the power trust to keep him from doing something for the common people. He drew his diagram again.

I spent a hundred minutes, trying to get some information from this amiable man. He took a hundred minutes from the business of the great state of New York, being nice to me. And what did I get out of it? A diagram.

I am sorry that I did not save a copy of that diagram, but it is easy to reconstruct. Substantially, and accurately to all practical purposes, here it is:

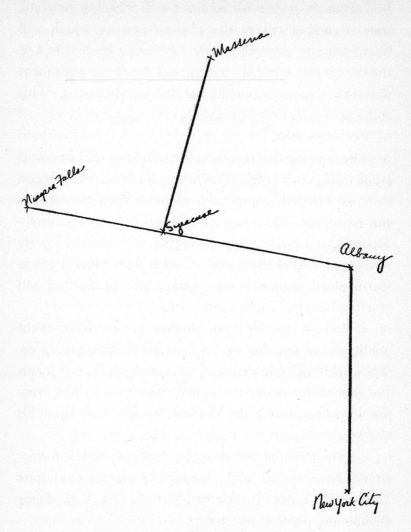

This is the diagram with which Governor Roosevelt answered
questions about his water-power program.

I spent that entire winter and spring studying the problems of cheaper electricity and the public exploitation of water power. I wrote a series of articles leading to the conclusion that while we were flooded with opinions there were too few facts available, and that trustworthy answers could be found only through honest, impartial study by competent experts.

The state legislature, controlled in both houses by Governor Roosevelt's political enemies, gave him *carte blanche* to name his own commission to make such an inquiry, and appropriated $200,000 for its expenses. The governor appointed outstanding experts in each of the various fields concerned. As chairman he named Robert Murray Haig, international authority on taxation and public finance; as vice-chairman and counsel, Julius Henry Cohen, authority on the municipal corporation method of financing public works, and for years Governor Smith's adviser on utility matters. Congressman Frederick Davenport, who was Bull Moose candidate for lieutenant-governor in 1912, provided liaison with the Washington administration and Congress; Samuel L. Fuller, a liberal-minded private banker, represented the financial group to which bonds would have to be sold; former Lieutenant-Governor Thomas F. Conway represented both the upstate rural and Democratic political interests.

The commission employed me as secretary. I directed the routine of the office, provided liaison among the members, handled newspaper relationships, and traveled all over the state for the dual purpose of acquainting newspapers with our work and obeying the legislature's instruction to ascertain the sentiment of the public.

Most such commissions hold hearings, listen to carefully selected experts or pseudo-experts whose opinions are known in advance, permit opponents of the predetermined viewpoint to have a brief day in court, and then write a generalized report recommending what they were appointed to recommend.

We operated differently. The St. Lawrence Power Development Commission retained such nationally known experts as the late Major-General Edgar Jadwin, retired chief of army engineers; the late Col. Frederick Stuart Greene, state commissioner of public works; and Col. John P. Hogan, hydroelectric consultant for many famous projects, now connected with the national defense program. Our legal staff included Charles Poletti, an ardent Roosevelt supporter who is now lieutenant-governor of New York; and our marketing staff Dr. John Bauer, a foremost critic of all utilities, who was a personal choice of the governor's.

Each of our technical staffs was told what questions in its field were posed by the investigation we were supposed to make. None had any further instructions except that it was to make a thorough, unbiased study and report.

After months of study and consultations these technical

experts reported to the commissioners, who used the facts thus ascertained to arrive at two main conclusions on questions posed to us.

They decided, as Governor Roosevelt hoped, that the International Rapids could be harnessed to provide large quantities of electricity at low first cost. The American share of the cost of such a project would be about $90,000,000.

But they did question strongly the economic desirability of constructing a state transmission and distribution system paralleling and competing with the company networks already serving the public. In raising this question they parted company with the governor.

When I first talked water power development with Governor Roosevelt in the fall of 1928 he had very fixed ideas what he wanted to do, and proved incapable of discussing any of the practical phases of the problem. After this commission of his own selection had provided answers to the practical questions, Governor Roosevelt reiterated his fixed ideas before he had so much as read the facts which the state paid some $150,000 to gather for him.

As a matter of courtesy, the commissioners went to Albany and told the governor what they had found and were about to report. Without taking time even to look at the technical bases for their decision, the governor publicly disagreed with their conclusions. He called Commissioner Conway to him, and had him draft a dissenting report expressing exactly the views they had held when there were no data to warrant any confirmed opinions.

The existing private power set-up, in the area which most needed the benefits of cheap electricity, involved approximately two billion dollars worth of lines, transformers, sub-stations, auxiliary plants, meters and other equipment. For the state to spend two billion dollars paralleling this system, and dividing the existing business with it, would be suicidal. The alternative was to buy or condemn the private system, at a cost of two billion dollars, and establish a public monopoly.

Our experts did not consider this last alternative sound. That was a matter of opinion. I was not and am not sure that they were right. As has happened so often since, I arrived at my original break with Franklin Roosevelt because he would not climb off the fence and take sides. He insisted upon giving to the state the right, at the option of an appointed commission and without further action by the legislators, to construct a multi-billion dollar system to compete with the private utilities. He said he wanted this right to use as a club to force the companies to play ball with the state. The good, sound, useful club would have been the right to buy or condemn the existing systems and to set up a state monopoly. This was too strong medicine for his political stomach. He wouldn't take it.

The issue here is almost identical with the issues which have been raised in the Tennessee Valley, in the state of Washington, and wherever the New Deal has found a chance to go into the power business in the guise of protecting navigation or providing for the national defense. It is not at all obsolete, nor is it local to New York State. It is the fundamental issue which the Democratic leadership did its best to raise against Wendell Willkie.

Our commissioners, with the exception of Conway, declined to ignore the facts and change their report to conform with the governor's ideas. The alternative was to fight. Though I was a hired subordinate, I felt that I too must choose my side. Most of my friends were sentimentally committed to the governor's viewpoint. The newspaper to whose staff I hoped to return was against us. The Power Authority which would take over our work would be appointed by the governor, and inevitably would reflect his views. The depression was getting deeper, and I could not afford to be long out of work.

The choice became no easier when I was offered a chance to go back to my old paper if I would resign from the commission's work. The decision that I made resulted in eighteen months of pretty hard sledding, but I still think it was the only one I should have made. I stayed with the commission for the remainder of its brief lifetime.

We drafted a bill creating a permanent Power Authority, to develop generating and possibly transmission facili-

ties, and directing that this Authority make effort to negotiate contracts with the power companies so that they
would distribute the current and pass on savings to the
public.

Governor Roosevelt offered his own bill authorizing
the proposed Authority to go further—to construct its own
distribution facilities, without limit to its investment, which
might easily run between one and two billion dollars if
so much money could be found.

I went to Albany to fight for our bill.

If I had been working for a private employer, what I
did would properly have been called lobbying. Because
my employer was a state agency, it passed that I was merely
placing myself at the service of the governor and the legislators. Since the governor did not choose to avail himself
of my services, I worked largely with his legislative opponents.

I went to Albany, took a room at the hotel most fre-
quented by legislators and politicians, and undertook to
see that our bill became law without too great modification.

It was not an easy assignment. The governor was
frankly hostile. He had his own bill introduced and ex-
erted his utmost pressure to get it through. He was in
position to veto any measure of which he disapproved
too strongly. On the other hand, both houses of the
legislature were controlled by the Republicans, who had
a long record of friendship with the utility companies

and who considered our bill only a little less vicious than the governor's.

It became a three-sided battle of wits—the governor and his minority of Democratic legislators working for one bill, the commission majority with me as contact man working for another, and the Republican leadership anxious to kill both but not quite hard-boiled enough to do it. The outcome was decided by the success of our strategy. We succeeded in stirring up a free-for-all in which everybody was able to claim victory but we got what we were after.

One of our commissioners suggested to the Republican leaders that they could assure sound administration of the new law, and at the same time put one over on the governor, by making the law name the investigating commissioners as members of the new permanent Power Authority. This hit the Republicans' fancy, and they introduced an amendment to that effect.

None of our commissioners wanted to serve—and, for that matter, only one of them and I knew how the proposal came to be made. The governor was enraged. He protested that his objection was not personal, but merely because the legislators were trying to encroach on the gubernatorial prerogatives. The louder Governor Roosevelt objected, the firmer became the Republicans' desire to pass the bill with the names included. Before long we had the majority leaders so firmly committed that we felt the passage of our bill was assured.

Then we had to see that it was not vetoed by the governor. We poured a little oil. The commissioners issued a public statement that since the governor did not want them, they preferred not to serve, and asked that their names be taken from the bill. I assured the Republican leaders in good faith that because of all the contention the commissioners would not serve. Their names were stricken from the bill.

The Republican leadership was so firmly committed to the bill by this time that it could hardly fail to pass. Governor Roosevelt had been led to concentrate his fire so exclusively on the matter of personnel and gubernatorial prerogative that he could hardly shift stance fast enough to justify a veto. As a result, we obtained the law we sought, intact and complete.

Needless to say, the governor did not appoint any of the original commissioners to the new Power Authority. He took care to select five personal adherents who, without previous experience in anything that had to do with electricity or water power or public administration, were in complete accord with his philosophy in the matter.

When the appointments were announced I was in the editorial rooms of the Burlington Free Press, for which I had worked at odd times while I was in college. The city editor asked what I thought of the appointees. Sitting

down at a typewriter, I interviewed myself on the subject
for the next morning's paper.

The appointments, I said, forecast the doom of New
York's ambitious program to develop St. Lawrence electricity, demonstrated that Governor Roosevelt "was interested in the St. Lawrence power project only as a
stepping stone to the presidency, and was willing to sacrifice the project to his political ambitions." I added that
the new trustees were "obviously handpicked to attempt
to carry out Roosevelt's personal ideas instead of those
which were incorporated in the state law by the 1931
Legislature."

This was not merely an assumption based upon logic,
however sound and well-informed. It happens—and this
has never before been mentioned except verbally within a
very small and select circle—that I had heard almost ver-
batim the instructions given by Mr. Roosevelt to at least
one of his new appointees.

Those instructions were, effectively, to work for a
situation in which the governor would be justified in asking the Legislature to permit the state to construct its own
duplicating competitive transmission and distribution systems—the very proposal which had been turned down on
the basis of expert engineering reports that electricity so
delivered would cost more even than the excessive rates
charged by the private companies, and that the existence
of such duplication would increase the legitimate costs

of the companies above the apparently exorbitant rates being charged.

In part because of these instructions, which I did not feel privileged then to mention, and in part because of my knowledge of the prior records of the governor's appointees, I pointed out that three of the members were so thoroughly disliked by all utility officials that their appointment insured failure of the negotiations which the law instructed them to conduct.

Franklin Roosevelt is adept at dishing it out, but he has never learned to take it. When a clipping of my criticism reached him the governor sat down with a secretary and dictated a request to the commission's quondam vice-chairman that I be muzzled, on the ground that "many of the statements are untrue."

I sent back an invitation for the governor to point out which were the untrue statements. Nothing came of it. Later that summer a mutual acquaintance told me that Mr. Roosevelt had remarked that he should take legal action against me, and was informed that in that event former Governor Smith would come to my assistance.

While I was still in Vermont I received by wire an invitation from the late Frank P. Walsh, who had been made chairman of the new Power Authority, to open its offices and serve as its secretary. I returned to New York and went to see Mr. Walsh, with whom I had been friendly, and showed him a clipping of the interview in which I criticized the qualifications of the new commissioners. It was not difficult for us to decide that it would be embarrassing for me to serve as secretary to the new body.

For eight years the commission, headed first by Mr. Walsh and later by Professor Bonbright of Columbia University, Governor Roosevelt's adviser on utility matters, devoted its not inexpensive efforts to investigating the public utility companies of the state, and issuing reports on their exorbitant rates, their watered valuations and their excessive earnings.

I would be the last to suggest that such studies and such reports are not valuable and justifiable. I devoted some time and effort to the same end, reached much the same conclusions, and publicized them. But it happens that I was being hired and paid to do that, while the trustees and employees of the Power Authority were being hired and paid to plan, negotiate, and eventually construct and operate a gigantic hydroelectric project that must, since it would be financed by bonds sold to the public, pay its own way and amortize its own cost.

The Power Authority appointed by Governor Roosevelt devoted itself to producing material which was extremely useful to Candidate Roosevelt. Although it was a state agency, financed out of New York tax proceeds, after March of 1933 it worked more closely with President Roosevelt in Washington than with Governor Lehman in Albany. It was directed by law to try to arrange contracts with the New York state electrical utilities for distribution of St. Lawrence power, but it did everything that fertile minds could have devised to antagonize and alienate the officials of those corporations.

Meanwhile, in Washington, President Roosevelt was further confirming my charges that his interest in the project was political. It was his job as president, if he was sincere in wanting to develop this power, to negotiate a treaty with Canada, which would have to participate in any development and would share in the power that was to be generated.

After he took office he was too busy to do anything about negotiating such a treaty. The Power Authority continued to shoot at the utilities. Then, in 1936, the President revived the subject. In the midst of news out of Washington about his campaign for re-election, came word that an accord with Canada was imminent, out of which a treaty would be offered soon to the Senate so that thousands could be employed on the project, directly and indirectly, and then cheap electricity would be offered to the public.

Apparently something happened to the negotiations. No accord was reached and no treaty offered. The Landon threat collapsed. Roosevelt was re-elected overwhelmingly. He turned his attention to a number of other things. Not a word was heard about any treaty with Canada for power development until, by sheerest coincidence, the campaign year of 1940.

I watched the papers carefully for word that the project was about to go through. It was to be my own private tipoff that the President was decided on running for a third term. Sure enough, it came. My friend Adolph Berle had been given the task of completing negotiations with Canada, the news story said, and at last President Roosevelt was going to complete this much discussed development.

The obstinancy with which Roosevelt refuses to let new evidence influence his attitude on major matters of public policy has been demonstrated often and discussed frequently. One illustrative episode has never been publicized.

Senator Robert F. Wagner, a Tammany man who has risen far above his background, was established as a humanitarian, a liberal and a friend of organized labor before Franklin Roosevelt had any citable record in any of those fields. He has sponsored several of the New Deal's sounder contributions to social progress, notably the well-intentioned and potentially desirable National Labor Relations Act.

With the purpose of the N.L.R.A. only the ultra-reactionary could quarrel. But like most radical departures, it was not perfect in its original form. Because its

subject matter is so enormously important and so highly
controversial, the act's errors in detail were capable of doing inestimable damage to an economic system trying desperately to resuscitate itself after a narrow escape from
death.

The N.L.R.A.'s weaknesses have been pretty thoroughly publicized by now, and still are uncorrected. In
the early fall of 1938 they were recognized but not well
publicized.

At that time a newspaper which admired Senator Wagner, had always supported him and wanted to endorse
his candidacy for re-election, sent one of the best reporters
in New York to ask the senator's views about certain specific amendments to the act. The senator conceded the
need for each of the revisions in question, agreed readily
to sponsor them at the next session of Congress, and was
willing to be quoted freely on the concessions and the
promises. He asked to see a copy of the interview before
publication, to be sure that his attitude was interpreted
correctly and stated accurately.

The reporter returned to his office in late afternoon,
labored into the evening writing the article, and took it to
Senator Wagner's office. The senator never saw it. A
partner informed the newspaperman that though Senator
Wagner still believed that the law required revision, he had
decided not to admit it or discuss the matter.

Not long afterward I mentioned the episode to an

intimate friend of the President's and the senator's who had expressed curiosity and resentment because that newspaper opposed Wagner's re-election.

"Senator Wagner telephoned the White House that night and told the President that he had given the interview and what he had said," the friend told me.

"He was told that he must stop the interview—that no matter what he thought, he must not admit publicly that any flaw existed in the act—that to agree to the slightest revision would appear to be a sign of weakness.

"I know that Bob would like to see those changes made, to silence justifiable criticism of the act and forestall resentment resulting from abuses, but he doesn't feel that he can act until the President is ready."

That was nearly two years ago. Since then the Smith committee has explored publicly the evils then under consideration, and others. The President is not yet ready to let Senator Wagner act on his convictions.

One day early in 1929, a none too prepossessing visitor came to the office of the old New York Telegram to tell us confidentially how we could get a great exposé. I was assigned to talk with him.

If I would go to an apartment building which he named, at a certain hour of any day in the near future, and would conceal myself circumspectly, said this informant, I would see certain men go into a certain apartment. He named and described the men, their customary garb, and the bags they would be carrying. These bags, he said, would contain the day's take from the slot machine racket.

Inside the room, I was told, would be James J. Hines, a Tammany district leader of increasing prestige about whom rumors were becoming prevalent, and the now violently deceased Dutch Schultz, whose notoriety as a gangster was less at that time than it became toward the close of his life. The meetings were for the purpose of dividing the swag, said the informant, and out of it a kitty was set aside to finance the corruption of law enforcement agencies.

As long ago as 1929 informed Broadwayites, newspapermen and court observers were speculating freely about Jimmy Hines and the underworld. Speculation, largely in connection with gang-operated rackets, continued to grow as Hines' power in Tammany Hall waxed greater—as one by one he pulled theoretically coördinate district leaders under his dominance, and used his power to displace leaders who declined to play ball with him.

It has never become generally known, but it has long been no secret among politicians that Samuel Seabury, who was able to get the goods on numerous important officials and to force the resignation of the popular and powerful Mayor Walker, devoted much time to a vain effort to get the facts about Jimmy Hines. Judge Seabury knew what to look for, but he never did learn where to look. Hines had no bank accounts, no safe deposit boxes, no substantial possessions. There was no single key with which to open the tight-shut doors behind which he operated.

George Medalie, United States attorney under President Hoover and for some time under President Roosevelt, gave a New York county grand jury information about Hines and other Tammany leaders, including Albert Marinelli and William Solomon, who were very close to Hines. Nothing came of it.

In 1933 we printed the fact that Hines' political club was giving relief jobs and food and rent tickets in return for votes for Tammany's candidate for mayor, John P. O'Brien. There was not even an official investigation into our charges.

These things, and others like them, were pretty generally known in the political circles in which a governor and a president move. They raised question as to the repute of Hines, Marinelli and Solomon. Yet when President Roosevelt undertook to use the power of the presidency to purify Tammany Hall, and to obtain a new political regime to carry the New Deal into New York City, the politicians he selected as his personal representatives were Jimmy Hines, Billy Solomon, Al Marinelli, and their associates.

Right up to the time that he was convicted by Tom

Dewey of taking a regular salary for his services in influencing policemen and judges and other officials to protect Dutch Schultz's policy racket, Jimmy Hines was recognized as the President's right-hand man in Tammany Hall.

Al Marinelli was not cast off until he resigned as county clerk and stepped out as district leader after Dewey had devoted several radio speeches to his activities and had preferred charges against him with Governor Lehman.

Billy Solomon was one of the Roosevelt leaders right up to the time that Dewey indicted him on a charge of accepting large sums from a printer, and passing on some of them to political leaders and public officials, to defraud the state and the city over a period going back to 1932.

Franklin Roosevelt started his public career as a state senator fighting Tammany Hall over the selection of a United States senator. He has always sought to appear an enemy of Tammany. Yet when he ran for governor in 1928, he was elected because Tammany resorted on his behalf to some of the methods it uses only when the Tiger is very anxious to win.

That year I traveled for the Associated Press with Roosevelt's Republican opponent, the late Attorney-General Albert Ottinger, who lost by 26,064 votes while Herbert Hoover was carrying the state by more than 100,000 plurality. A switch of 13,033 New York City

Jews, who at that time usually voted Republican in presidential years, would have elected Ottinger and have effectively stopped Roosevelt's start for the presidency.

Political reporters learn many things which for one reason or another do not get into their news stories. Because the Associated Press required that its men report only the overt campaign activities, I never did write about the cute Tammany tricks by which many more than 13,033 New York Jews were induced to vote against Ottinger.

The Republicans had nominated him because of his appeal to his own race, by virtue of which he had succeeded in being elected attorney-general when Governor Smith was carrying the state for all the rest of the Democratic ticket. If Roosevelt was to beat him, Ottinger's Jewish vote had to be reduced. Tammany wanted Roosevelt to win badly enough to see that this was done. For my own curiosity, though I could not write it, I checked upon some of the devices used. One is typical.

Albert Ottinger, the bachelor candidate, used as his "official hostess" the charming wife of his brother Nathan, who was not particularly Jewish in appearance. Near Albert Ottinger's home was a Presbyterian church. These would not seem to be particularly pertinent to an election —but they were made so. The report spread, so fast that nothing could catch up with it, that Albert Ottinger was married to a Gentile and had chosen his home so as to be able to attend the Presbyterian church conveniently.

Jews are race-conscious and race-proud. They have no use for apostates. This alone, of half a dozen similar reports which were spread early enough for wide dissemination but too late for effective disproof, was enough to account for Ottinger's defeat.

This is not mentioned with any implication that such methods were approved by Franklin Roosevelt, or that he knew about them at the time. It does suggest that his long career of anti-Tammany pronouncements did not convince the sensitive Tiger leaders that he would do them any injury, if he were to become governor. On the contrary, they expected to profit by his election enough so that they did everything in their power to help him.

Chapter Seven

FUSION MAYOR

★★★
* 7 *
* *

Fusion Mayor

FIORELLO LaGUARDIA'S is the first reform administration that has ever succeeded in New York because LaGuardia is probably the best politician who has ever led a reform movement.

He has an uncanny feel for the public pulse, and a remarkable talent for transforming hostile darts into boomerangs. He is not afraid to fight fire with fire, or to play the demagogue when demagoguery is needed. He knows when to compromise and when to walk a chalk line. He is not a party man, but neither is he afraid to use political parties to advance his program. By playing clever politics day and night, he has given a remarkably non-political government to an intensely political city.

In New York the Democratic enrollment is double that of all other parties combined, and the Democratic party has long been closely controlled by a highly efficient machine. There have been three reform administrations since the metropolis was formed just before the turn of the century. LaGuardia's is the first that succeeded in winning a second term, because he was the first reform mayor to recognize that good works are no substitute for votes.

I was in on the ground floor of the fusion movement which led to LaGuardia's original election in 1933, his re-election in 1937, and the success of some of his more interesting experiments. Never close to him personally, I have numbered among my good friends many of those who have done the work of reform under his direction, and I have been privileged to sit in as reporter or as unofficial consultant upon many of the more important projects which have contributed to the administration's success.

In the fall of 1932, after a period of free lancing, I was called back to join the World-Telegram's bureau of municipal research, newly created for the purpose of destroying Tammany Hall and building up a reform movement by turning a pitiless spotlight upon the waste and inefficiency and corruption of the Tammany regime.

LaGuardia did not dominate the picture then. He was just a congressman running for re-election, with every prospect of success. The hope of reform then was Acting Mayor Joseph V. McKee, who had succeeded James J. Walker when that erstwhile favorite resigned under charges and fled to Europe. Tammany had refused McKee its nomination, but a newspaper campaign was under way which resulted in a phenomenal write-in for him exceeding 300,000 votes. Nobody was naïve enough to believe that he could win by write-ins; it was hoped either to force Tammany to accept McKee as its candidate the next year for the full term, or to put him in position to run as an independent fusion candidate against whomever the Tiger chose.

LaGuardia was caught in the Democratic tidal wave that fall. Though his entire career had been devoted to battling the very evils which the voters were rejecting, he lost to a Tammany hack with no record of any sort except in political ward work. He was a victim of that same unreasoning mass psychology, that same "vote every star" complex, which the reform movement had to overcome if it was to get anywhere.

Meanwhile John Patrick O'Brien had been swept into the mayoralty as part of the same Democratic landslide. O'Brien had been selected as an antidote for the bad taste left by Walker. He was chosen carefully as an exact antithesis to Walker in all except two vital qualifications: he was from Manhattan, the old New York, and he was an Irish Catholic.

Walker had been a man about town, so his successor must be the very symbol of domestic respectability. Walker was a raconteur and a wit, so his successor must be stolid and unimaginative. O'Brien satisfied these re-

quirements to a T. He was always making asinine statements and giving inept answers to questions. Alvah
Johnston described him in the New Yorker magazine
as "the genius of unconscious humor, the prince of foot
swallowers, the master of the faux pas, a creative artist
in the malapropos. Nobody turns out an inappropriate
phrase so neatly," Johnston added.

In politics it is desirable to have a candidate whom the
public laughs with, but suicidal to have one the voters
laugh at. O'Brien was the latter. In his slow-witted
responses to questions he was always letting cats out of
bags. The payoff came early in his brief term, when he
was asked who would be his new police commissioner.

"I haven't had any word on that," he replied, with
a malapropism remarkable even for him.

There was a howl of derision. Anti-Tammany elements lost no opportunity to publicize the mayor's apparent admission that he couldn't appoint a police commissioner until he got word from Tammany Boss Curry.

When he discovered the cause for the levity, somewhat tardily, Mayor O'Brien retreated to that last ditch
of public officials who have stuck their feet into their
mouths.

"I was misquoted," he declared. But the damage had
been done.

In mid-summer Welfare Commissioner Frank J. Taylor
warned publicly that there was no money for relief, and

that unless some was found there might be food riots. The mayor was asked about it.

"Oh, now, don't let us get to brass tacks," he answered. "I don't know about these payrolls. You'd better see Taylor."

During that tragic period it was my job to keep the public informed of its government's power dive toward bankruptcy. It was not an easy assignment, for several reasons.

Not only was I a complete greenhorn in anything but the most superficial aspects of municipal government, but the sort of work we were trying to do had never before been done by a newspaper, to our knowledge, and we were forcd to chart our course as we went along.

I was on the outside, looking in: fighting with Tammany commissioners who were reluctant to give the least crumb of information, though legally we were entitled to it; forced to put together bits from here and bits from there, in order to learn what actually was being done with the almost a billion dollars a year that our city spends; working in the knowledge that each time I scored a telling point I would be challenged, and would have to sustain my accuracy against the dicta of Tammany's big name "experts."

Although I had never studied accounting, and had betrayed no talent in my one-year study of high school book-keeping, I began keeping a running account of New

York's huge income, outgo and capital obligations. It took some time to set it up, but it proved invaluable. Through it I predicted in December that the city was threatened with inability to pay off more than $150,000,-000 worth of bonds maturing by May. Mayor O'Brien, Comptroller Berry and their associates said that not only was I wrong, but that I was injuring the city by malicious statements. On the last day of March the mayor confirmed my three-month old prophecy, in a general press interview.

Regularly I pointed to forthcoming defaults, of which nobody else was aware except the city administration, which would not tell, and presumably the bankers who did not tell. I learned from a shocked contractor, and informed the public, that the city's own school board refused to accept the city's bonds at face value. I had Joseph D. McGoldrick, one of the President's original brain-trusters, discuss for publication why the city's maturing bonds were of no more value than the current tax collections, which were terrible.

Day by day and week by week new brush strokes added to the horror of this financial picture until the reading public, which seldom gets the implications of a single episode in the financial field, became upset by the cumulative weight of evidence.

Through all this period I was in continual contact with the reform and civic leaders who were trying to coagulate dozens of impotent anti-Tammany groups into one effective army which, by fusion with the Republican organization behind an appealing candidate, might defeat Tammany that fall.

At the outset we took it for granted that McKee would be our candidate. Because he was so close to the Bronx county organization, whose chairman was President Roosevelt's intimate and man Friday, we counted upon nothing worse than neutrality from that Democratic stronghold and from Washington.

McKee had a hard time making up his mind. At last he decided not to buck Tammany. We had to go into the open market and find a new candidate who could be built up fast. There were plenty of reputable enough men who actively or passively wanted the nomination, but none was of sufficient stature.

Always the search led back to one man, who had announced unequivocally that he wanted to run and intended to run, and that we could make the best of it with him or, in the alternative, we could have him run independently and make of the election a free-for-all. He was the ex-Congressman, Fiorello LaGuardia.

He had fought courageously and effectively for many liberal causes, but always with a strong taint of the demagogue. He had made his best fights against some evil, seldom in favor of a constructive proposal. The great affirmative monument to his career was the LaGuardia-

Norris law curbing the injunctive powers of the courts in labor disputes, and even this was negative in the sense that it forbade a vicious practice but did not create positive machinery for good.

In his last term in Washington, when he was supposedly anathema to his fellow Republicans and their leadership, the ultra-reactionary G. O. P. leader Bert Snell had quietly appointed him an unofficial committee of one to study all bills on the unanimous consent calendar. This was a supreme tribute to his astuteness, his raw courage, his honesty and his diligence. The unanimous consent calendar is made up of private bills, claims, and matters of legislative courtesy—favors for the folks back home—which either go through without objection or, in case a single member objects, go back to committee and usually die there. There were hundreds of such bills. It was LaGuardia's assignment to study each on its merits, and on the majority which had no justification to shake off personal pleas and log-rolling suggestions from their sponsors, and take upon himself the responsibility of killing them with his sole objection. Only a very industrious man, with no axes of his own to grind, would accept such a task.

He was the congressman who made liquor in a store show-window and defied the police to arrest him, to demonstrate his disrespect for national prohibition. It was he who took a raw steak into the House and waved it to dramatize his attack upon the spread between what the farmer gets for "beef critters" and what the housewife pays for beef roast or round steak.

His term as aldermanic president right after the World War had been notorious for the violence of his public brawling with Comptroller Craig. He had been defeated overwhelmingly by Jimmy Walker four years previously, after a campaign devoted to scandalous charges which the voters obviously had not believed.

Short, squat, dark, shrill-voiced, arbitrary, excitable, undignified, he neither looked nor acted the part of mayor of a great city. He possessed a talent for friendship, but also an infinite capacity for spontaneous abuse and vilification.

When he was in Congress he occupied Room 150 in the House Office Building, on the ground floor near the elevators. His associates, waiting to ride up, used to listen aghast to the maledictions upon Marie Fisher, his secretary, that came through his opened door. Occasionally one, bolder or better acquainted, would venture to expostulate.

"Get the hell out," LaGuardia would roar, if his voice could accurately be called a roar. And sometimes he would add, a bit sheepishly:

"She knows I don't mean it."

She must have known, for she married the fireball.

All this made LaGuardia interesting, and beyond doubt he was praiseworthy, but in it there was no indication that he possessed the tact, the sagacity or the administrative genius necessary to boss successfully an army of 125,000 servicing a city of seven millions, or the financial acumen to pull a twenty billion dollar corporation out of virtual bankruptcy.

This latter was one of the chores which confronted New York's next mayor. The city's bankers, tired of throwing good money after bad, had put down their collective foot. The time had arrived, as my studies had shown five months before that it would soon, when the city had to find some $200,000,000 of new financing or default on its bonds, its payrolls and its pensions. In return for funds with which to avert such complete disaster, Tammany Hall had arranged on behalf of its puppet officials a consent receivership, confirmed by the state legislature and effective for a period of four years, tying the city's hands tight in all matters of financial discretion.

I came very near to stopping LaGuardia's progress at this vital point. Among my friends were the leaders of several of the reform groups which would be needed for effective fusion. Each time LaGuardia's name came up in our discussions I convinced them anew that he was quite impossible. If there had been any real alternative he might not have been nominated. Because there was not, we went more deeply into his record, and became convinced that while he might not make too good a mayor, he would be a good candidate—and that even a poor anti-

Tammany mayor would be superior to any creature of Boss Curry.

My friends withdrew their opposition. The few remaining objectors were brought into line. LaGuardia was nominated, and I was assigned to handle my paper's bitter-end fight to assure his election.

For my purposes as a campaigning reporter, he was perfect. His long record provided ample material for use. He had fought, years before there was a New Deal, for the same liberal causes which the public had just discovered and demanded. In his previous campaign for mayor he had made apparently wild charges against Tammany Hall and its leaders, and these had been corroborated in detail in the Seabury investigation.

After passing up the opportunity to be elected as the anti-Tammany candidate, McKee had obtained support from New Deal leaders and entered as an independent. The Bronx organization, which always contributed heavily to Democratic majorities, went with him, and so did many leaders in other boroughs who hoped thereby to win presidential favor and federal patronage. The Democratic ranks were split wide open.

Day by day throughout the campaign, I prepared simple, easily-understood "deadly parallels" for the voters. Some days I took texts from LaGuardia's 1929 indictment of Tammany, and showed from the record their accuracy, to establish presumptively the accuracy of his current charges. Other days I offset McKee claims that he was the reform candidate by citing the records of his managers and his supporters. We devoted little of this attention to O'Brien. It was obvious early that Tammany was out, and that the race was between LaGuardia and McKee.

It was LaGuardia who won, and it was the men with whom I had spent much of my time for the past year who were in line for important jobs in his administration— Adolph Berle, Jr., and Joe McGoldrick of the original Roosevelt brain trust; Rufus McGahen of the Citizens Union; Russell Forbes, expert on governmental purchasing; Paul J. Kern, the new mayor's assistant in Washington and New York; Maurice Davidson, chairman of the City-Fusion party; Bernard Deutsch, new president of the board of aldermen, and Raymond V. Ingersoll, new president of the borough of Brooklyn, among others.

Because of my acquaintanceships among these men who would be running the city for four years to come, I spent the first couple of hectic months as city hall reporter, and the next two years circulating among city departments looking for the sort of news that is not generally available, but which comes from intimate continuing knowledge of the city's business plus the helpful thoughtfulness of friends in high places.

During that period we had so continuous a flow of exclusive stories about the operations of city departments that other papers were aggravated, and complained to the mayor, who already was perturbed because so many of his pet announcements had their edge dulled when we printed their gist in advance.

During the past seven years I have watched LaGuardia corroborate a pet theory of mine—that the best radicals usually are sobered by responsibility and become liberal conservatives. It is easy enough to stand outside the factory and criticize the product. When one is handed the task of getting production with the materials available, if he is honest and fundamentally sound he ceases to be a perfectionist and does the best he can under the circumstances.

So far as LaGuardia is concerned, this is best illustrated by the sales tax, of which for years he was the most vociferous and effective critic and opponent. One of his most spectacular successes as an independent in Congress was in the spring of 1932, when President Hoover and the Democratic majority in Congress both favored a national sales tax, and Congressman LaGuardia organized a petty minority opposition into a revolt that killed the proposal.

When he became mayor, however, LaGuardia found it necessary to place unemployment relief on a pay-as-you-go basis, and for that purpose to raise some $75,000,000 a year. Whatever his will, it could not be levied upon real estate because of statutory and constitutional restrictions.

Adolph Berle told me that the city's bankers forced

the sales tax onto the mayor by refusing to lend for relief against any other source he could suggest.

LaGuardia proved political genius by accepting the burden, assuming the responsibility, and making effective capital out of his enforced decision to pay for relief out of current income and for that purpose to tap the only source available, however unpopular.

It has been LaGuardia's frequent boast that he forgot politics when he went into City Hall. If that were true he would be out of a job now.

There are exceptions, but they are few, to the rule that he never makes an appointment without giving it political consideration. He has given the Republicans just enough patronage to be able to point to it when that party threatens to stop playing with him. When he ran for re-election it was touch-and-go whether he would have the Republican line on the ballot. He cut the City-Fusion party so short that it has died out. He has kept a few of the better Tammany men in jobs. All that looks non-political, and might be called non-partisan.

On the other hand, few appointments have been made without due regard for their effect upon racial, religious, fraternal or other self-conscious communities. Tammany, which knew quite a few tricks of the sort itself, went out of power leaving one appointive court in particular heavily dominated with Irish Catholics, with only a single Jew out of sixteen judges though the city's Jews outnumber its

Irish at least four to one. It took some time, because he could move only as vacancies occurred through promotion or retirement, but LaGuardia has seen to it that the judges now include three Jews, a Negro, a Pole, an Italian, a German—even, unusual as that has become among New York jurists, one member of English extraction. The men he appointed were able lawyers and have made good judges.

English stock seems to have little political race-consciousness, and no possible quota of Italian appointments appears to satisfy that group that an Italian-derived mayor has been liberal with his kinfolk. But the Jews, the Poles, the Germans and the Negroes are appreciative—the more so when a mayor is so thoughtful as to select the head of the American Jewish Congress, the head of the leading Polish society, the favorite of the anti-Hitler German organization, and similar established communal favorites.

The LaGuardia flair for timing appeared when Soviet armies invaded little Finland, which suddenly acquired sympathetic importance out of all proportion to its negligible voting strength. Long before the Finns' courageous resistance had been broken by the weight of Soviet numbers, LaGuardia had a Finn on the court bench where no Finn had sat for years, if ever.

Almost since the day he was first nominated, LaGuardia has been kicked about from time to time by President Roosevelt. Although he is notorious for his fiery nature and his reluctance to hold anybody's bag, he never has whispered a protest where it attracted public attention, and he has gone out of his way frequently to support Roosevelt and the New Deal commissariat. Nobody who knows the mayor supposes that is because he likes being slapped by Roosevelt better than by others. On the contrary, for every kick he has extracted some balm.

Thrice, at the request of Roosevelt, he asked his famous parks commissioner, Robert Moses, to resign as chairman of the Triborough Bridge Authority. On that one I locked horns with P. W. A. Administrator Harold L. Ickes, who was the President's whipping boy for the occasion, and created such a popular furore that Roosevelt and Ickes backed down and left Moses in possession of the field. The mayor was willing to sacrifice Moses at Roosevelt's request, just as later he sacrificed his almost equally efficient Housing Authority chairman, Alfred Rheinstein. But only at a price—nice, fat allocations from the P. W. A. for the benefit of New York.

On the other hand, he was the first mayor in recent times who plunged over city lines in his efforts to get for key departments what seemed to him the best men available, even though they controlled no votes. He went to Connecticut for a health commissioner, to Washington for a commissioner of correction, to the army for a sanitation commissioner, to Tammany for a man to build and run the city's subways.

The fact is, and it should not detract in the slightest from the credit due to Fiorello LaGuardia for a lifetime of public service, that his intolerance of politics is an attitude adopted at the beginning of his political career, with full consideration.

He and his friend Nathan D. Perlman, now a justice of special sessions court, went into public life in the same district at about the same time. Neither was sufficiently thick-skinned to join Tammany Hall, through which they might have been assured of political preferment.

"I decided that my only hope of accomplishing anything under the circumstances was to work with the Republican organization, weak as it was," Judge Perlman told me once. "I couldn't see how an independent in New York could accomplish anything or get anywhere.

"Fiorello disagreed. 'I'll manage to get along all right as an independent,' he assured me, and while he took the Republican label he played his own game without regard for party lines. Eventually Fiorello, who was supposed to be handicapped by his independence, went to Congress, and I did not get there until he retired temporarily and left a vacancy. I attended assiduously to my congressional duties, including the errands a congressman is supposed to run for his constituents. Fiorello came back to Congress, from a different district, and declined to be bothered with such personal assignments. He was too busy legislating for the nation as a whole.

"I followed the rules and LaGuardia violated them all. Yet I had to wait until he became mayor, before I attained my ambition and became a judge."

One of LaGuardia's campaign promises was to give the city a new charter to replace that which had been growing ever more archaic since it was first tossed together at the turn of the century. After some vicissitudes, in which for a time Tammany appeared to have beaten him, he obtained legislative authority to name his own drafting commission. He put on it such men as former Solicitors-General Thomas D. Thacher and Charles Evans Hughes, Jr., and Joseph D. McGoldrick.

The new charter had to be submitted to a referendum in the presidential year of 1936. At the same time the commission submitted, without recommendation, a question whether members of the new city council should be selected by proportional representation—a radical-appearing proposal which the politicians hated.

While I was in Vermont on vacation that summer Joe McGoldrick telephoned, asking me to handle publicity for the campaign. I told him I could not. Then the late George Brokaw Compton, who was to manage the fight, wired that he and George H. Hallett, Jr., foremost authority on municipal affairs and advocate of P. R., were driving up to see me. I had a good idea of their mission when I met them at the Hotel Barre, and I was resolved not to yield. But the two Georges were persuasive, and had been good friends when I needed them.

For thirteen weeks I went through one of the most hectic periods of my existence. We had to buck both the Democratic and the Republican organizations except for the Manhattan G. O. P. led by Kenneth Simpson, later national committeeman. Our funds being limited, we had to rely largely upon volunteer help. Because so many who favored the proposed charter were bitterly against proportional representation, we had to conduct two separate campaigns.

It was understood that I must carry on my regular newspaper work, which during the election season involved overtime. When I quit I would go uptown, dine over campaign plans with the managerial staff, and then work until anywhere from midnight to two o'clock. Saturdays and Sundays I devoted from morning to midnight to the campaign.

In order that our readers might not suppose wrongly that my employment in the campaign had affected the paper's attitude, and so that other newspapers might not imagine erroneously that our paper had an inside track on campaign news, I had to work behind closed doors in an office removed from visitors, and under a pseudonym. Paul Windels, the mayor's corporation counsel and political adviser, facetiously suggested for me "Mr. Schiff," which was adopted. To this, to satisfy the elevator operator when I signed out in his book at late hours, I prefixed "Mortimer Zacharias." I had constantly to explain to persons who inquired in good faith that I was not related to *the* Schiff family.

That campaign was fun, notwithstanding the trying hours. It was a campaign of wits, of harassment and bedevilling and opportunism. When we started even Chairman Thacher of the drafting commission conceded us no chance to put across the charter, and considerably less with P. R. In the end the charter won by a 350,000 majority and P. R. by an even greater margin. The victories were not won by orthodox methods. We seized the initiative, dug in, and thereafter made a business of shooting the head off anybody who ventured to look askance in our direction.

As an opening gesture of defiance, we went into Tammany Hall and got as our campaign chairman the now late Morgan J. O'Brien, a venerable brave who had been the intimate of such Tiger bosses as Dick Croker and Charlie Murphy, and who even while he gave his name to my blasts against the opposition chiefly run by Tammany, was a sachem of Tammany Hall. After that, it was pretty hard for the Tiger to convince his whelps that all good Tammany men were against the charter.

We scored another ace when we made a deal with the organized firemen which broke the backbone of Tammany's most dependable nucleus, the great body of city employees.

The firemen had a pet question on the voting machine that fall, a referendum on the eight-hour day for them. In principle there was little question of its justice; in practice, there was the city's financial stringency to be considered. We weighed benefits against liabilities, and made a trade. In return for the organized firemen's support of the charter and P. R., we agreed to use all of our prestige to urge everybody to vote "yes" on all questions at issue. We found most of the newspapers willing to coöperate. The firemen, canvassing every friend and acquaintance and all the powerful organizations of city workers, urged "yes" votes for us to help their cause, and we reciprocated among the citizenry generally.

By this one arrangement alone, it is probable that we corralled enough votes, which otherwise would have gone as Tammany dictated, to put our proposals across.

Meanwhile we concentrated upon every opponent who dared come into the open. When Tammany clubs tried to interfere with our meetings, as they long had with impunity those of other reform moves, we blasted them with publicity. When Tammany packed a labor meeting and obtained resolutions condemning our projects, we exposed the methods used. When a radio station censored a speech I had written for one of our orators, we raised such a row about freedom of speech that our next offering went untouched—and we got into the papers biting bits from the censored talk which reached many more than would have heard the speech as planned.

We were reformers, but there was no starry-eyed idealism in our methodology. We aimed for the kill with every shot, and we aimed straight much of the time. The supreme tribute was paid us late in the campaign by Borough President George U. Harvey of Queens, a Tammany Republican with his own repute as a master of vilification.

"Damn them," he told a fellow oppositionist, "a fellow can't open his mouth against their charter without getting himself branded as a cheap, crooked politician. How can we beat such a set-up?"

Election night we held a victory party at headquarters. Chairman O'Brien, Windels, Thacher, Hughes, and most of the great and the small who had contributed to the campaign waited for the news that proved to be good. I had to work on election tables, and left before the count was far enough along to be assuring. When the result became certain, I had telephone calls from almost all of the leaders in the campaign. The only one I remember who has never mentioned the affair, to this day, is the mayor.

Twice, since then, I have worked with much the same group, headed first by Samuel Seabury and now by Judge Thacher, attempting to elect reform majorities to the council. Though we made creditable showings, we lost both fights. These failures have led some to question the efficacy of proportional representation to defeat political machines. Such pessimism seems to me very shortsighted. Our worst failures in council elections were glorious victories for the principle of proportional representation.

Under the old district system in general use, the Republican party used regularly to poll around a third of the votes and yet elect only from one to three of the 65 aldermen. The greatest anti-Tammany bloc ever elected to the board under that system was 17, in the year of LaGuardia's first victory, with the Democrats split wide open.

Proportional representation did not prove to be a cureall, by which a minority voting the reform ticket could elect a majority of the city's lawmakers. Such a result would hardly have been democratic. The best the reform elements had ever done in an off-year was to elect approximately five percent of the aldermen. With P. R. at its least productive, in an off-year featured by a European war which distracted attention from home affairs, antiTammany voters put across seven out of 21 councilmen, of whom five were from our non-partisan slate.

The new method of election, together with the new spirit that a decade of reform evangelism has brought, has considerably improved the personal calibre of most

Tammany legislators, although there still remain some who, in the parlance of my youth, could walk erect under a snake's belly.

Government always has been and still remains a thing of men, and not of forms. An honest, courageous, intelligent administration can give reasonably good government with a charter more antiquated than any I have ever seen. A dishonest, grafting, pusillanimous, ward-heeler administration could utilize for corrupt purposes the best charter that man can devise. A good framework of government makes it easier for good men to give good government, but it is no guaranty against popular lethargy and unrestrained politicalism.

Tammany's notorious Boss Tweed got some fun out of proving this seventy years ago, when reform elements begot the idea that a new charter would curb Tweed and his ring. The reformers outlined the changes they wanted made in the charter. Tweed went to Albany with a liberal supply of cash, and bought newspapers and legislators, and forced adoption of the reformers' new charter. Then he used the machinery of that document to facilitate new and theretofore unheard-of depths of knavery.

Nevertheless, the victories of the new charter and proportional representation in New York mean more to politics-ridden communities everywhere than any of the more sensational upsets achieved by the election of reform leaders. Charters and voting methods are impersonal; they have no sex appeal. Their success against dominant machines' opposition is clear-cut demonstration that when the people are sufficiently aroused and skillfully led, they do not need Galahads on white chargers to whip up courage and strength. They can win on something as unintriguing as the dry-as-dust legal verbiage that makes up a city charter.

But somewhere, in foreground or background, there has to be one or more men with the intrinsic qualifications of Fiorello LaGuardia—swashbuckling fellows, with a flair for the dramatic, keen ears to the ground, an instinctive intuition for popular reaction, and the ability and willingness to take off their silk hats at the sound of a hiss and whip all politicians with their own dirty weapons.

It is New York's misfortune that it has only one LaGuardia. The future of good government in the metropolis rests with him. It is doubtful if Tammany can beat him in an election next year. That is why Tammany is pulling for President Roosevelt to take him to Washington—as secretary of war, or of labor, or of anything else that might tempt the mayor.

There is no crown prince to the throne in New York. Tammany doesn't care how far LaGuardia is kicked upstairs, so long as the promotion takes him out of City Hall.

Chapter Eight

GANG BUSTER

Gang Buster

FOR sheer, unadulterated brain power, there have been few in public or private life who could rival Thomas E. Dewey, the young Michigander who rose in nine short years from the obscurity of a little known law firm to the side door of the White House.

The side door proved to be locked, and Tom Dewey had to come back to New York sadly disillusioned, badly disappointed and pretty bitter. He had counted heavily upon being nominated by the Republicans last summer, and turning the bitter edge of his heavy sarcasm upon the manifold errors of Franklin Roosevelt, and—if the fates were just enough to reward intelligent, assiduous, belligerent effort—to celebrate his 39th birthday in the highest office in the gift of the people.

I wonder if Tom Dewey has remembered, since Philadelphia, that day two years ago in a pullman compartment en route to Syracuse, when I got him away by ourselves and made a suggestion. He was running against Governor Lehman that fall. One damaging argument against him was the suggestion that, if he were elected, he would desert the governorship in 1940 to run for president, just as he had scorned the district attorneyship of New York county, in its middle, to run for governor.

"I can suggest one short, simple statement that might very well elect you, Tom," I told him.

"What?" he asked.

"Give tomorrow afternoon's papers a flat statement that if you are elected governor you will stay in office the full four-year term—that you will not pull out in two years to run for president."

"Why should I?" he inquired noncommittally.

"Because 1940 will not be your year for the presidency," I told him. "You can't win the presidency in 1940, but you may be able, with such a statement, to win the governorship in 1938 and build yourself up for the presidency in 1944."

Dewey considered briefly. It never takes him long to make his mind, however long he may keep his own confidence about the result. It seemed a minute, and probably was no more than thirty seconds, before he said:

"You're right. I'll do it. How shall we stage it?"

Inside of five minutes the plan was completed, down to the exact wording of the questions I should ask in his compartment that night after the Syracuse speech, on the way to Buffalo, and the exact answers he was to give.

The afternoon newspaper correspondents were called in soon after we left Syracuse. I asked my questions. Tom Dewey made his answers. By mid-morning of November 1, 1938, he stood committed unequivocally to staying in Albany for four years if he was elected governor, which by any possible construction of phraseology meant he could not run for president in 1940 without breaking a public promise.

He made a great campaign for governor. He cut Lehman's plurality from 520,000 to less than 90,000. But he lost. Many of us, who admired his enormous intelligence and his tremendous energy, hoped that the setback would trim him down to human size without breaking his spirit, and that its result would advance his public career by fitting him temperamentally to render greater service in a field where top sergeant methods are not effective.

Unfortunately, Republican politicians seeking fine feathers to line their own nests decided that he was too good to pass by. Without undue difficulty, they persuaded him that 1940 offered his glorious opportunity. The great popular interest in his exploits they interpreted as eagerness to vote for him; the widespread newspaper and magazine exploitation of his personality and prosecutions they persuaded him was tantamount to support.

There is real doubt whether they ever had any idea of

using him for more than a favorite son stalking horse, to improve their trading position at the convention. One of his "sponsors," in a moment of confidence, put it bluntly and probably accurately:

"We drafted him, and my God! He took us seriously!"

Until Wendell Willkie came into the picture, Dewey made tremendous progress because he was all but alone in the anti-Roosevelt field. Nobody took very seriously the candidacies of Vandenburg, McNary, Martin, Bridges, and their like—not that they are not worthy men and faithful public servants, and not that any of them might not have made a good run-of-the-mill president, but rather because any of them would have been so eclipsed by the Roosevelt shadow as to have been lost in the shuffle, like Landon in 1936.

Senator Taft, because of his late father's position and prestige, had to be considered seriously. To him the politicians flocked because they wanted a regular who would always keep his neck in the party collar. He was Dewey's only real opponent.

Given a colorless candidate like Taft, who hired a special "publicity man" to keep him from making mistakes, and a vivid, active, vocal candidate like Tom Dewey, the public fell for Dewey. His relative popularity curve rose sharply as the convention neared. Now he knows what most unattached political observers realized all along

—that the popularity registered by polls was not absolute and inalienable, but only by contrast with the voters' enormous disinterest in any other Republican aspirant before Willkie.

Until there developed that amazing wave almost of hysteria over Wendell Willkie, Dewey was the Republican people's choice perhaps two to one, but Charles Taft probably would have been nominated by the politicians in convention assembled. When the people adopted Willkie, Dewey was lost, and—it developed to the amazement of some of the nation's most astute political observers, who announced the collapse of the Willkie boom the morning of the night he actually was nominated—the practicing politicians were sunk, too.

The politicians climbed aboard, of course, in spite of rebuffs, and in many instances came to realize that amateurs and the general public had done the party a service. Politicians always do mount the band wagon, as soon as they are able to tell which band is playing loudest.

I had met Willkie twice, long before his most admiring intimates had any idea that he was bound for so high a top, and had come to admire him.

In early 1932, before he became president of Commonwealth & Southern Corporation, I was in negotiation for a time with a group of utility executives who were purging the National Electric Light Association of the Insull influence. It was the tentative idea that when the cleanup came, I should take over the reorganized association's public relations. Willkie, then one of the Commonwealth & Southern's legal representatives, was a power behind the movement. I met him casually. By the time the change came, I was back in newspaper work and immersed in the anti-Tammany fight.

Two years later I obtained from Willkie one of the first interviews he ever gave on the Tennessee Valley Authority controversy. To one who had dealt with many utility executives, the atmosphere was delightfully informal. There were none of the evasion, equivocation, defensive sensitiveness and reticences to which I had become accustomed with such interviewees. Nothing was off the record. There was no attempt to steer the interview toward what Willkie might prefer. He answered my questions frankly and convincingly. He did not, like many in his position, ask for a chance to see the interview as written, so that he could edit out anything which on second thought seemed indiscreet. The result was a powerful and effective statement of the case against the government's unfair competitive methods.

By the time a few enthusiasts began urging that the Republicans nominate Willkie to oppose Roosevelt, I had lost touch with him, and nobody was more amazed than I at the wildfire spread of his boom.

If Dewey had been nominated, I had hoped to travel with him for my paper, because I felt that he would be a

remarkably colorful campaigner and because I am one of
the few newspaper reporters who has ever been able to
get on with him, for long, on friendly terms.

For one of his intelligence, Tom Dewey has an amazing ability to alienate that little group of men who have
made him what he is today, the newspaper reporters.
From time to time one of these gets along with him temporarily, and then joins the great majority who are Dewey-
haters.

I met Tom Dewey during the last week of 1933, when
I went by appointment to the office of the United States
Attorney for the Southern District of New York. I found
him cleaning out his desk, preparing to return to private
practice after a month and four days as the youngest United
States Attorney in history.

Dewey, then 31, had served for two years and a half
as chief assistant United States Attorney under George Z.
Medalie, and in that capacity had convicted the notorious
gambler "Legs" Diamond of operating a still; the Tammany district leader James J. McCormick for failure to pay
income taxes on some $90,000 received as tips from bride-
grooms while he was deputy city clerk; the gangster
"Waxey" Gordon on income tax violations. He had
failed to convict the banker Charles E. Mitchell of income tax fraud, but did obtain for the government a
$1,000,000 civil judgment against him for unpaid taxes.

When Medalie resigned, the federal court judges named

Dewey as United States Attorney until the president should decide which deserving Democrat had greatest claim to the honor and emoluments.

Meanwhile, starting with an anonymous postcard tip, I had built up a removal case against a municipal court justice named Harold Kunstler, and had taken both our printed stories and much complementary material to the city's leading bar association. Their inquiries substantiated my allegations. Justice Kunstler failed to give any convincing explanation, and the Association of the Bar of the City of New York voted to file formal removal charges with the Appellate Division of the Supreme Court, which has power of discipline over lawyers and non-constitutional judges. The bar association appointed one of its members to prosecute. While he was preparing the case, he was injured badly in a taxicab accident and had to step aside. Tom Dewey, then retiring with a splendid prosecuting record, was named in his place.

My visit was to offer Dewey, in connection with the Kunstler prosecution, my own assistance and the use of the material we had gathered in our inquiry. He was courteous and gracious, and obviously competent to row his own boat in heavy seas.

For the next six months I was in frequent contact with Dewey, and with the junior office associate and the accountant who assisted him with the case. I was impressed with the skill and care with which he prepared the charges, so as to limit controversy to a minimum of issues, and then bulwarked himself on each of those issues with a mass of documentation that no court could refuse to receive and give credence.

In June, Dewey prosecuted Kunstler before an Appellate Division referee. As the trial drew near its close, with the judge already condemned in every eye as a cheap, chiseling, financially involved discredit to the bench, notorious in legal circles as the intimate of a courthouse hanger-on known as "Kunstler's fixer," the defendant resigned. Later, on charges prepared by Dewey, he was disbarred.

The last time he came into the public eye was when he drove to California with "Billie" Schieble, who at the time was under $10,000 bail as the convicted madame of about the swankiest houses of prostitution that Pittsburgh and New York have known in recent years. She swore that she went with Kunstler because he professed great love and promised to marry her, and that when they quarreled in a Stockton hotel, he left with her $1,000 gold meshbag. Later she withdrew that charge.

I have watched quite a number of prosecutions from behind the scenes, and admired some, but I had never seen one so competently prepared and so devastatingly presented as Dewey's action against Kunstler. The World-Telegram, naturally, was greatly impressed because of the paper's interest in having its campaign against a crooked judge completed successfully.

Tom Dewey is a very self-confident young man, who has never indicated willingness to give any credit for anything to anybody else if he happened to be in the picture in any way. I could hardly expect him to agree, therefore, with my contention that I started the rally that sent Dewey to third base where, if he had not tried to steal home too soon, he might have won the big game on which his heart was set.

If Dewey had stepped from the United States Attorney's office to private practice, without a public service prosecution in the immediate offing, he would have become one of New York's most successful and prosperous lawyers, because he combines great legal talent and indefatigable energy with superior showmanship. The Kunstler prosecution not only solidified his position as a prosecutor but won him the support of our paper because our inside position had given us opportunity to observe his methods minutely.

In 1934 the New York legislature decided to investigate public utility lobbying methods, after it was disclosed that the chairman of the senate public service committee had been on the payroll of one of the biggest holding companies over which that committee had statutory jurisdiction.

Ascertaining that Tom Dewey would like the chance to further his fame as counsel to that committee, and convinced that he would do a superior job, we did our best to get him the appointment. We failed, because President Roosevelt wanted former Supreme Court Justice John E. Mack of Poughkeepsie, his political godfather, whom he selected twice to nominate him for the presidency, to have the buildup.

Judge Mack put on a good show, which lasted two years, cost the taxpayers $550,000, and never got around to checking up on the lobbying situation which it was created to investigate.

The intention of the resolution creating the committee was as clear as words could make it. That was one of my pet projects, to which I was assigned by the editors for the duration. On the way to Albany one Monday morning Charles Poletti, then counsel to Governor Lehman, called me into his pullman compartment.

We were old friends. He and my wife had gone to high school together in Barre, Vermont. I got to know him when he was on the legal staff of the St. Lawrence Power Development Commission, on leave from the noted law firm of Davis, Polk, Wardwell, Gardiner & Reed, where he was John W. Davis' favorite assistant.

"What is it your paper would like to see in this resolution?" he asked, showing me a preliminary draft. I scanned it hastily.

"I believe," I told him, "that it should be expanded so that no possible corruption of legal verbiage can stop the committee from following any clue to the absolute limit, in any direction."

We discussed language. The resolution was revised. When it was adopted, it did exactly what Poletti and I had agreed upon. It told the committee to look into lobbying, and it gave the committee—merely to forestall any such jurisdictional entanglements as once threatened to wreck the Seabury investigation into the New York City government—almost unlimited scope supplementary to its prime authorization.

With his $550,000 Judge Mack investigated thoroughly everything that was incidental, and ignored completely the main purpose of the inquiry. He presented entertainingly and convincingly material which had been explored fully by the Public Service Commission, but ploughed no new ground.

Judge Mack's personal charm, considerable as it is, does not exceed his integrity of purpose. He just was not a digger, a groper, a ferret, a prosecutor born to the chase; and more than once he was stopped by his legislator employers when he was on the scent of game that might have proven sensational.

We wanted Tom Dewey for that job, because he would have recognized malefaction where to Judge Mack's trusting naïveté all was sweetness and light, and because, having recognized it, he would have refused to recognize any power in the political committee to stop him from following evil to the bottom of its woodchuck hole and digging it out, and shaking it in the sight of God and man until it didn't have even any pelt left.

We failed to get him for that job, and in the long run it proved fortunate. While Judge Mack was playing around with the utility situation, a county grand jury ran away in New York.

It long had been known to the informed, though none was in position to prove, that there was a definite alliance in New York City between organized criminals and politicians, through which politicians in some instances received regular salaries for their services in protecting criminals, but more often took their pay at election time, when gangs moved *en masse* where they were needed, registered and voted—sometimes several times per person— and in certain districts saw to it by strong arm methods that anti-Tammany votes were kept to a minimum.

This was particularly true in Manhattan, which is New York county. There Tammany had long regarded the district attorneyship as more vital to its purposes even than the mayoralty, an office which generally is considered second only to the presidency. It has not been seriously contended that any recent district attorney was personally corrupt, but only that they were inactive, and easy to persuade of the most charitable interpretations, and willing to place on their staffs political appointees whose first duty was not to the people but to their district leaders.

There seldom was any investigation into matters affecting politicians or politically-allied crooks. When the police brought such in, they seldom were convicted.

After much agitation a New York county grand jury set out to investigate rackets. A reporter for the New York American published stories about racket matters which all reporters knew, but none had been able to prove sufficiently to print. Whether or not this man was able to prove them I do not know. Many of us have believed that he could not, but took the chance of printing them in full confidence that they were true, and in trust that the crooks affected would not dare sue. The grand jury called him in and asked the source of his information. He declined to name it, and was jailed for contempt of court.

Meanwhile there had developed one of those little side plays which so often never are publicized. A member of the grand jury, on behalf of jurors who wanted to get to the bottom of the situation and felt that they could not get adequate aid from Tammany's district attorney, William Copeland Dodge, got in touch with us. Without violating his oath by revealing any of the grand jury's business, he asked questions about its rights which indicated that a runaway was developing. We covered the obtainable news with increased assiduity, and continually urged editorially that the grand jury take the bit into its own teeth and ask Governor Lehman to supersede Mr. Dodge with a special prosecutor.

This raised the question of who, by temperament and training and by demonstrated achievement, could be trusted to push so tremendous an inquiry to the limit, without fear or favor, without permitting anybody or anything to stop him, and get convictions wherever guilt existed.

I knew the man. No sooner had the situation developed than I suggested to Lee Wood, our executive editor, that Tom Dewey had demonstrated in the Kunstler case the exact qualities that were needed for probing into the alliance between crime and politics.

The grand jury shut District Attorney Dodge and his assistants out of its deliberations and voted to ask for a special prosecutor. Governor Lehman accepted its recommendation. He sent to Mr. Dodge a list of four eminent lawyers, none of whom could have devoted the time and energy and enthusiasm that were needed, and ordered Mr. Dodge to select one from the list.

We demanded that Tom Dewey be appointed. The four men suggested by the governor declined to serve, and unanimously urged Dewey. After a month of maneuvering, Governor Lehman sent Dewey's name to District Attorney Dodge with instructions either to appoint Dewey or be superseded. The appointment was made.

As special prosecutor, ranking technically as an assistant to Mr. Dodge but functioning independently in his own offices, with his own staff, his own budget, and a salary equal to that of his nominal superior, Dewey opened up.   He sent thirty-six loan sharks to jail for long terms and broke up their ring.   He was about ready to indict the gangster Dutch Schultz when that worthy was shot to death in a New Jersey bar room.   He convicted Lucky Luciano as head of a nation-wide syndicate controlling compulsory prostitution, and sent him to prison for 30 to 50 years, and with him eight of his henchmen. He broke up a restaurant racket and sent ten of its members to prison.   Over a period, he prosecuted 73 racketeers and convicted 72.

He made a marvellous record, and gained nation-wide publicity.   His success was tremendous.   But he had not yet achieved his real ambition.

The day of his appointment, reporters visited his law offices on the erroneous report that he planned a press conference.   I remained after the others, and talked with him for a time, alone and off the record.   We discussed the general situation, the salary he might properly expect without limiting too much his style of living, and the task that confronted him.

"May I make a suggestion?" I asked.

"If you get Jimmy Hines, your investigation will go down in history as a complete success, whatever else happens.   If you don't get Hines, you will always feel, as I think Judge Seabury does, that you left something undone that you should have done."

"You are right," he said.

In August of 1937 he had not got Hines. The closest he had arrived, publicly, was incidental mention of the Roosevelt leader's name along with that of Dutch Schultz in the restaurant racket trial. He indicted Dixie Davis, mouthpiece for Dutch Schultz and attorney for Harlem's $20,000,000 a year policy racket, together with several other Schultz subordinates. Out of this case arose his successful prosecution of Hines.

The day before I left for a vacation on my Vermont farm in August, 1937, I spent some time with Dewey in his offices in the Woolworth Building. In the course of a general discussion he inquired whether, in my opinion, he should accept the Republican-Fusion nomination for district attorney.

I said he should. He appeared to demur, though rather as if he were thinking aloud than as though he were expressing a conviction. I think he was quite honest and frank that day, with me and with himself.

"I would like to be district attorney," he said, "and have opportunity to go after crime in Manhattan generally. I think I could do much good. But on the other hand, I might be defeated."

This was the only time I have ever heard him express uncertainty as to the success of any enterprise of his own.

"If I were defeated," he went on, "I doubt whether I could properly continue as special prosecutor, or whether I should not be bound to regard the defeat as a popular mandate to turn over the rackets inquiry to the new district attorney.

"I have a lot of important matters under way." (He did not mention the possibility of pushing through to get Hines, though without a doubt that was in his mind.) "I wonder whether I have the right to hazard the complete success of this job on an election, in which I should be the candidate of the minority against a strong organization fighting for its very life?"

He was more indecisive about that than about anything else I ever discussed with him, and we lingered over it for what, with him, was a long time, I arguing that defeat for the district attorneyship need not mean his resignation as special prosecutor, and he leaning to the other viewpoint without committing himself finally. Before I left, he had expressed a tentative decision that he would refuse the nomination.

Pressure on him was great. All the reform and anti-Tammany forces of the city were anxious for him to run, and convinced that he could win. At last he asked Lee Wood to attend a conference of anti-Tammany leaders, and support his declination to make the race.

"I'll go," said Wood, "but I won't promise which side I'll take in the argument."

As a result of that conference, Dewey accepted the Republican-Fusion nomination. He asked if I might have leave of absence to handle publicity for the campaign, and was told that election time was the one season of the year in which the paper could least spare me.

I did see that Dewey cancelled tentative commitment to a radio publicity representative closely allied from youth with Tammany, and found for him probably the ablest free lance in the campaign radio field, Reynolds Brooks, who had produced amazing results for me in a campaign the previous fall.

Dewey became district attorney January 1, 1938. He indicted Jimmy Hines in May, charging him with being a paid employee of Dutch Schultz's policy ring, hired to influence judges and prosecutors and police officials to protect Schultz and his gang from successful prosecution.

In July of 1938 a person whose identity is known to less than half a dozen persons up to this day, came to our editorial rooms in a strange manner with a strange story.

He had gone first to a business executive of a rival newspaper, who for reasons I have never learned sent him to one of our business executives, instead of to the editor of his own paper. What he brought was the missing link that completed a chain of damning evidence against Martin T. Manton, senior judge of the second circuit court of appeals and, next to the Supreme Court justices, ranking jurist in the United States.

On the strength of his story, I was assigned to spend as much time as necessary verifying and expanding the proof of Manton's crookedness, so as to build up a case on which we could demand and obtain his impeachment and removal.

The next day, coincidence brought back to our office a money broker who also had a scandalous story about Manton. Automatically he was referred to me.

His story he offered for sale. He wanted $10,000. I laughed at him. He came down to $5,000, and I still laughed. As routine, I told the executive editor of the offer and what went with it, and he laughed. But he knew something I didn't. In his files was the record of a previous visit from this money lender, and evidence that the previous visit had been used to force Manton to pay part of an alleged debt arising out of extra-legal transactions between the two.

We seldom, if ever, buy anything outside our organization. When we are offered something and refuse it, we promptly forget it, feeling obligated not to use even the lead to further inquiry. In this case, however, we felt that Jacob Handelsman's previous use of us as a collection agency raised a doubt as to his good faith and affected the extent and character of our obligation to him. While we did not feel free to use his story for publication, and never did print it until the coöperative City News Agency obtained its essence from court records and broadcast them to all New York papers, we did feel privileged under the circumstances to take the story to Dewey.

At the moment the trial of Hines was pending. It opened less than a month later. Handelsman's story quoted Hines as agreeing to assume Manton's indebtedness, because "we can't afford to have Manton in trouble. He's the only federal judge left in New York we can use to get people out of jail." It seemed to us that Dewey might like to check this story for possible leads to further evidence against Hines.

Dewey has no telephone in his private office. The understanding is that he will not talk on the telephone during his business day. As a matter of fact, he sometimes goes into another office to answer calls from persons of sufficient consequence to him. For most of us, it is necessary to see him in person, by appointment with his assistants.

He has always been a very difficult person to see. Frequently, during his service as special prosecutor, I had tried to reach him, and often I had given up after going through more red tape than the effort seemed worth. Yet whenever I met him, on the street, in his office, at cocktails at Adolph Berle's, he expressed regret that we met so seldom, and asked me to drop in whenever I could.

"But I can't get through to you," I would expostulate. "It takes too much trouble."

"Of course you can," he would say. "My secretary will put you through any time when I'm not tied up. I've told her to. I'll tell her again."

So on this occasion I telephoned and asked for Mr. Dewey's secretary. A woman's voice answered.

"Is this Mr. Dewey's secretary?" I asked, and was assured that it was.

"Will you ask Mr. Dewey if he can see me today, and at what time?" I inquired. She promised to talk with him and to call back. Soon she telephoned.

"Can you be here at 11 o'clock sharp?" she asked.

At eleven, minus a minute or two, I had broken through the outer fortifications and was sitting in the otherwise vacant office of Dewey's press secretary. For three-quarters of an hour I sat there, alone except as assistants of various grades passed through. Ultimately the press secretary, Harold Keller, a former Hearst legislative correspondent, arrived and inquired my errand.

"I had an eleven o'clock appointment with Tom," I told him, "and I've been waiting here since before eleven for word to go in."

Keller scoured around and discovered that Dewey's secretary had not even yet told her employer that I had asked for a chance to see him, though she had made the appointment with me and had been informed of my arrival from the ground floor before I was permitted to enter the elevator. She had let me cancel other appointments, and come over and wait nearly an hour, so that when and if Keller arrived—without knowledge that I was there—he might determine whether Dewey should be told that I had asked to see him.

In view of our long and frequently close acquaintance, and his repeated assurances that I would never have difficulty in getting into his office, and the sequence of events in this attempt, which I had explained to the secretary was for the purpose of giving him useful information and not in any way for my benefit, I was thoroughly angered—not, then, at Dewey, but at his secretary.

Keller saw the point, checked at once with Dewey, and took me in.

I told Dewey about Handelsman's story, as it bore on Hines, and told him about my plan to follow through on convincing evidence against Manton. He considered briefly.

"I don't want it against Hines," he said. "I have an air tight case against him, and there wouldn't be time to work this up properly for use at the same time.

"But I am interested in the Manton angle. I have been planning for some time to have Murray Gurfein (head of his rackets bureau) begin an investigation of Manton. Can't you hold up your Manton investigation until Murray has cleaned up some other things he has under way, so he can work on it at the same time?"

I could not agree to that, but I did agree that I would do everything possible to see that my inquiries did not frighten Manton into covering any trail that Dewey's office wanted to follow.

Then I told Dewey of my experiences in trying to see him. He listened courteously, leaning back in his chair and grinning amiably at my indignation. When I was finished:

"But, you know, Burt, I'm a busy man, and I can't see everybody who wants to see me."

"I hadn't supposed that in this office I was just anybody," I retorted.

His grin broadened. He looked as angelic as though he were listening to a jury saying "we find the defendant Hines guilty as charged."

"That," he said gently, "is how you feel about it."

Perhaps this sequence will suggest how Tom Dewey makes enemies needlessly, and why one of the brightest, ablest men who has sought the presidency in generations would have made a historic failure if Tom Dewey had been nominated and elected this year.

Because I have been able to give him more than I asked and have been completely independent of him, I stand today as one of the few reporters who know him well and do not dislike him actively and ardently. Others have to accept his snide attitude, and smoulder with frustrated desire to hit back, because he is their news source of bread and butter.

Therefore, though I should have passed up my presidential vote for the first time since I attained majority, if I had been forced to choose between Roosevelt and Dewey, I feel toward Dewey only a real regret that one of such great potentialities should have let conceit and unrestrained independence ruin his future, by making it impossible for him to work with those who are, in the eyes of the world and in their own esteem, his equals.

Tom Dewey came too far too fast. It is not true, as one critical magazine writer alleged, that he has "no foundations." His foundations are deep and sound. The structure that he has erected on those foundations is excellent, if he would just take an axe and chop off some of the poison ivy that he has permitted to cover the essentially attractive framework.

Dewey lacks any real sense of humor, and any sense of restraint—and in spite of his almost flagrant appreciation of his own abilities and his analytical powers, he is too impatient to combine these two and make proper allowance for the fact that few of those with whom he must work are his mental equals. Those lacks explain most of the enemies whose grievances I have analyzed in an effort to understand Dewey's uncanny ability to create enmity.

For example, my closest friend is Charles E. Egan, expert in foreign trade matters on the New York Times, recognized in his circles as a thoroughly sound, intelligent, informed and reliable reporter, and one of the most amiable men it has ever been my pleasure to know.

While Dewey was special prosecutor, I suggested to my friend that an excellent Sunday feature could be written about the beneficial effect on business of Dewey's racket busting. It would have had national distribution in the most influential circles. Charlie liked the idea, admired Dewey's record, and at his request I made an appointment for him to see Dewey.

The appointment was kept. Dewey recalled his rule that he must not be quoted directly, and gave some background information to assist in interpreting the factual data to be obtained elsewhere in the office. Charlie, who has not covered crime news in many years, asked a question to which no reporter who had not been in touch with Dewey, personally, could have known the answer.

"That's a stupid question," snapped Dewey, sharply.

"Is it?" asked Charlie. The story never was written, and nothing I could ever say would make him write a line about Dewey unless by direct orders from his editors.

For another example, we were riding to Elmira on a campaign trip in the fall of 1938, with a speech scheduled for Binghamton the next night. Clarence L. Chamberlain, Republican chairman of the rock-ribbed Republican county of Broome, from which Dewey needed part of a big upstate majority to overcome Lehman's New York City lead, boarded the train to discuss plans for the Binghamton talk.

Attached to the rear of the train, behind our party's

pullmans, was the private car of Paul Block, newspaper publisher friend of Jimmy Walker who received publicity in connection with the Seabury investigation charges that resulted in Walker's resignation. Block, a Binghamton native, had suggested that he would like to preside over the Binghamton meeting and introduce Dewey.

I saw Dewey and Chamberlain talking alone in a seat out of hearing of the others. Dewey caught my eye, called me over and introduced me to Chamberlain.

"What would you think of having Block introduce me tomorrow night?" he asked. I had learned of the publisher's idea when he entertained the reportorial entourage that noon at luncheon in his car.

"I'd consider it most unwise," I told him. "While there were no charges against him in the Walker matter, or so far as I know any grounds for charges, his beneficences to Jimmy have not yet been forgotten, and I don't think you could afford to have him so actively in your corner."

"That's what I thought," said Dewey. He turned to County Chairman Chamberlain.

"He's out," he said. "What else?"

"I didn't suggest him," Chamberlain started to remark in the casual way that one might. "Your New York office passed on to us——"

Dewey interrupted, his voice a trifle higher and very cold.

"I said he's out. We needn't discuss it further."

Without another word he arose, went to the end of the car, taking me with him, and started talking with me about another matter.

Candidates ordinarily do not treat county chairmen that way without severe provocation. Yet I do not suppose that in either of the incidents I have mentioned Tom Dewey felt at the time, or would feel now, that he had been anything other than incisive and justifiably brief in busy moments.

His mind is so much faster than most of ours, that by the time we are half through digesting a problem he has canvassed its every angle, weighed its every element and come to a decision that most often is correct. It simply doesn't occur to him that men who relatively are quite bright may be several jumps behind his hair-trigger mind, and that for ordinary courtesy—not to mention kindliness or the desirability of avoiding unnecessary animosities— he might wait for us and be a bit patient.

So far as newspapermen are concerned, at least, he has another bad habit which has led many to feel that they can not trust him. I go along with this only part way, because I am a Yankee, and I grew up in the tradition of horse-trading.

In Vermont we are inclined to admire a man whose word is better than his bond, but whose words have to be examined microscopically to determine whether he has given his word, and if so what word he gave.

We have a stock story which goes something like this:

An old-time professional horse-trader was showing a fine-looking steed of which he wanted to dispose, sound in wind and limb, clean-cut, fat and glossy and trim, but priced so reasonably that the prospective buyer knew there must be something very wrong. He asked every question he could think of, and all the answers were satisfactory. The horse-trader's word was of finest repute.

"Is he scary?" asked the potential buyer at last. "Does he shy?"

"He hasn't seen anything in five years that could make him shy," assured the trader, casually whipping his cap across in front of the horse's eyes without provoking so much as a blink.

The deal was made. When the trader came through again the buyer hailed him indignantly.

"That horse you sold me—" he shouted.

"Yes?" inquired the dealer.

"He's blind as a bat—in both eyes."

"Well," said the trader, "you didn't ask me that. I said he hadn't seen a thing in five years that could make him shy—and he hasn't—has he?

"Giddap," said the trader to his own nag, and drove on.

I don't believe that Tom Dewey has ever told reporters anything that was false by the code of "on the record" and "off the record," but he makes a practice of saying things which to slower, less informed minds than his seem to be what they are not. How deliberate this is, only he can tell, though others can guess and do.

As a result, he has more than once embarrassed reporters by leaving them hanging in the air with stories they can't follow through, and which, until their editors too came to know Dewey, left the reporters holding the bag.

In June of 1936, at a press conference, Dewey charged for publication but not for quotation, that unnamed persons had offered one of his assistants a Supreme Court justiceship, which would pay $25,000 for each of fourteen years, if he would supply the defense with all information in Dewey's possession against Lucky Luciano, the racketeer convicted as a vice monger and generally reputed to have had his finger in most of the baser rackets, and with the prosecution's plans for its use.

He charged that the offer, made before the trial, included posting of a $250,000 guarantee to cover the deal, and that "two reputable business men" had told another Dewey assistant it would "be worth his while" to help the defense.

The charges were made after the conviction. A dozen reputable reporters were present. The story was printed as from a responsible source. The next day our reporter, and I imagine others, was sent back to get more information. Who offered the bribe? To which assistants? Would there be indictment and prosecution?

"I don't know what you mean," said Mr. Dewey. "I never told you about any such thing." Nobody has yet been indicted or prosecuted.

Technically he was correct. Off the record disclosures, newspapers must use or ignore on their own responsibility. But public officials who value newspaper friendships and want a "good press" don't start snowballs rolling down hill and walk away.

A similar incident followed the Philadelphia convention last June, when Dewey held the first press conference after his return.

For the record all was sweetness and party harmony and no hard feelings. Off the record, however, he told the assembled reporters that Willkie's nomination was forced upon delegates by Wall Street banking interests, which threatened to embarrass them by calling loans and mortgages unless they voted for Willkie.

A new afternoon publication departed from accepted newspaper practice by using this off-the-record discussion, attributing the charges directly to Dewey. Reporters for the other papers, scooped because they had observed the proprieties of their profession, had a conference with Dewey as soon as they could reach him.

"Unadulterated bunk," he said for publication.

Then, off the record, he added:

"And if anything that I say off the record is used again, I'll stop talking off the record."

It was in that same press conference that he made one more unnecessary break which embittered the assembled reporters. He had been asked about his future plans, concluding with the question:

"Will you run again for district attorney next year?"

"No," he said flatly, and then snapped:

"And if any of you prints that, I'll bar him from this building as long as I'm here."

Chapter Nine

TO THE HIGHEST BIDDER

★ 9 ★

To the Highest Bidder

MARTIN THOMAS MANTON is probably as un-
regenerate an old reprobate as it ever was my
misfortune to come upon. He is the only crook to whose
downfall I have contributed for whom I have never felt
the slightest twinge of pity, in the moment of his misfortune and after he had been emasculated of his potency
for evil.

The whole story of Manton's anti-social activities will
never be told, the complete roll of his crimes can never
be called, because after more than two years of probing
there are indications that only the surface has yet been
scratched.

Today he sits in the federal penitentiary in Lewisburg,
Pennsylvania, vicious, uncoöperative, unrepentant.

John Edgar Hoover, head of the Federal Bureau of
Investigation, has said in print under his signature that he

and his agents exposed Manton and cleaned up the federal judiciary. They did it all themselves, says he, and he tells how.

Nowhere in his writings have I found any mention of the part that Tom Dewey and I played. Neither, as yet, has he mentioned that his original inquiry was completed and rested for a year unused in the desk of a high Department of Justice official, until I outlined to one of his agents the case on which ultimately Martin Manton resigned, was indicted, was convicted and went to prison.

Parts of the story of Manton's downfall have been told, from time to time. G-man Hoover has told how he did it. Tom Dewey has said that he did it. I have told part of how Dewey and I did it. As a matter of fact, all of us were in on the chase, independently, and there is credit enough to go around.

Martin T. Manton was the senior and therefore the presiding judge of the federal court of appeals for the second circuit, which, in addition to Connecticut and Vermont, includes the whole of New York state with its highly litigious metropolitan district, where Wall Street produces a constant flow of cases involving both large sums of money and principles of widespread commercial and industrial importance.

The circuit courts of appeals rank immediately behind the United States Supreme Court. In theory, all circuits are equal. In practice, the second circuit is infinitely the most important. Its senior judge is generally recognized as the nation's highest jurist behind the Nine Old Men.

In 1916 Manton, then known as a prosperous ambulance chaser, was appointed by President Wilson to the federal district court. An ambulance chaser is a lawyer who solicits personal injury suits, usually for a fee which is fixed as a percentage of what he is able to collect for the plaintiff. It was common report that Manton was made a judge because he threatened to run for Congress against a member whose presence in Washington seemed desirable to the President. In 1918, a year and a half after his original appointment, he was elevated to the circuit court bench. In time, as his seniors dropped out, he rose to the top through length of service.

He was an ardent Catholic layman. His donations to the church and its agencies appeared liberal in the light of his salary, which was only $12,500 a year, but might have won him less acclaim if it had been known that his actual income attained a top as high, in at least one year, as $200,000.

As a practicing attorney, handling negligence and criminal cases, he prospered. He told a jury under oath that when he went on the bench he was worth a million dollars. His personal balance sheets for the period do not show anything like this wealth, but they do show that he was not a poor man. He owned equities in considerable real estate, as investments. He had a $150,000 summer place on the aristocratic south shore of Long Island, part of which he acquired as fee for defending a bucket shop operator who went to prison. His house there was well furnished with personal effects accepted from the mother of another client, to complete Manton's fee for unsuccessful defense of her son.

While he was on the bench his holdings expanded rapidly. At one time he computed his net worth, with little exaggeration, at approximately two million dollars.

To his growing business affairs Judge Manton at all times gave close personal attention. His private secretary Marie D. Schmalz, paid out of an allowance made for the purpose by Congress, served as an elected officer in some of his corporations, kept their books, and handled business matters for them. When Dewey tried to obtain possession of some of the books, they were in the government safe in Manton's office in the federal courthouse, where the State's authority did not extend and the judge's business secrets were safe.

At the time when I began delving into Manton's affairs in July of 1938, no living man other than the judge and his attorney, Emanuel Harris, had any idea of the scope of his activities at a time when the United States was paying for his exclusive services, and unless it was Mrs. Manton, no woman knew except Marie Schmalz.

For six years I had been convinced that Judge Manton was dishonest, and was using his high office in an illegal and immoral way. I knew that a few lawyers thought likewise. Later I learned that many lawyers and at least some judges were very sure, though few had legal proof and none ventured to do anything about it.

Two high judges were riding from Albany to New York by train, as early as 1934, when the conversation turned to Manton. Said one, a man of highest probity and, often, of much candor and courage:

"Manton is a thorough-going crook."

"Why don't you do something about it?" asked the other.

"How can I?" inquired the first. "I have to work with him every day."

Soon after Manton's resignation I was guest of a state court judge at a political dinner at the Astor Hotel. At his table was a young lawyer whom I had not met before. When I was identified to him as the reporter who had exposed Manton, he remarked:

"I don't see why you fellows didn't find him out sooner. Most of us lawyers knew about his crookedness."

"Why didn't you do something about it—if only to come to me, or some other newspaperman, and tell us confidentially what to look for and where to look?"

"Oh," he laughed, "we wouldn't do that. We preferred to use our knowledge."

There was little secret about Judge Manton's venality,

it developed, but those who had evidence couldn't or wouldn't use it to stop him, and those who wanted to do something lacked the necessary clues to specific, probative evidence against him.

"Almost every newspaperman in New York has taken a crack at Manton some time or other," wrote a friend on the New York Times in congratulation, when at last he was forced from the bench. The statement was exaggerated, but sound in principle.

Manton was convicted, legally and properly, of offering his judicial position and his decisions for sale to the highest bidder in case after case, and selling them, and taking the money.

Some cases in which he had a financial interest were decided wrongly by all the rules of logic, and some were decided wrongly by decision of the Supreme Court of the United States. But judges often make mistakes. That is one reason why higher courts are maintained to review decisions. In some instances Manton's erroneous opinions were shared by two judges whose integrity has never been questioned.

Manton had available a method of selling decisions which themselves were equitable and proper. It was possible for him because, as senior judge, he handled the court's decisions and made them public when he chose.

After the court had decided an important case according to the evidence, sometimes, Manton would send his bagman, William J. Fallon, to the litigant who had won but did not know of his victory. The conversation would approximate this:

"You have a case before the circuit court," Fallon would remark. The litigant would agree.

"It is a pretty important case to you," Fallon would insinuate. "Wouldn't it be worth something to win it?"

If the litigant appeared interested, Fallon would go on:

"I know somebody in the court who could see that you win, but he would have to distribute some money in the right places."

I have been told of instances in which litigants rejected such advances indignantly, but held their own counsel so as not to offend the court. In such cases the decision might be held up over a considerable period, to give Fallon opportunity to try again and again. Ultimately it would be handed down as it was voted.

Those who paid, however, would get their decision promptly, and would assume falsely thereafter that if they had refused to pay they would have lost.

It was only when there was an honest division of opinion between Manton's two fellows, sitting on a particular case, that he could actually sell his own decision to whichever litigant was able and willing to pay the most.

These things I did not know in the summer of 1938, when I began this inquiry. I started with a firm, reasoned conviction that Judge Manton was venal, and a feeling that I would find that he had sold out for a large sum in the infamous receivership of New York's largest subway-elevated system, the Interborough Rapid Transit Company.

The information that set me off on the successful hunt, however, did not appear to concern the Interborough receivership very closely. Instead, it indicated that while Manton was sitting on a $10,000,000 case he borrowed through his business partner, with the lawyer for one litigant as intermediary, from the advertising agent for that lawyer's client, the sum of $250,000, which he never repaid.

If this accurate expression of the mechanics seems involved, the interpretation with which I started work was very simple.

I began inquiring whether Manton had demanded and received $250,000 from a litigant in return for his agreement to decide a $10,000,000 case in that litigant's favor.

If that was the deal, he had made good, for he had decided four cases in favor of the litigant through whom he obtained the $250,000, and in every fundamental matter the Supreme Court had declared that he was wrong.

Briefly, the story was this.

The law firm of Chadbourne, Stanchfield & Levy was counsel for the American Tobacco Company and its high executive officers in a stockholder's suit seeking to make the officers repay more than $10,000,000 in cash and stock bonuses. Louis Samter Levy was a member of that law firm. The advertising agency of Lord & Thomas handled the tobacco company's biggest account, for Lucky Strike cigarettes. In the year before the loan was made, this firm placed almost $3,000,000 of American Tobacco Company advertising, from which its gross profit would approximate $450,000 for the year.

While this suit was pending, Manton asked Levy to obtain a $25,000 loan for Manton's business partner, the late James J. Sullivan. Levy went to Paul M. Hahn, then assistant to the president of the American Tobacco Co., one of the defendants before Manton. Hahn went to Albert D. Lasker, then president of the advertising agency. Lasker lent $250,000 to Sullivan. I had cancelled checks proving that Sullivan used at least $228,000 of the loan for Manton's benefit.

Thereupon, Manton's court decided each case in favor of the American Tobacco Company, and in all but one secondary matter was reversed by the Supreme Court. Eventually the suits were settled out of court. Later Hahn admitted under oath that the complaining stockholder was paid $520,000 by the company when he dropped his suit against the officers.

In the end, it developed that Lasker had supposed he was lending the $250,000 to his important client, was very indignant when he learned it had gone to Sullivan, and learned only from Dewey's staff that it had gone from Sullivan to Manton.

This did not clear Manton, however. His part in it was perfectly obvious, as was that played by Levy, who for his connection with the deal has been disbarred by the federal court after years as one of New York's most prominent lawyers. A referee has recommended his disbarment in the state courts for the same reasons.

While I was working on this, I began obtaining possession of what came to be a large and valuable file of original documents bearing upon Manton's financial operations over a period of twenty years—the first such file ever collected outside his own control, and the magic wand that interpreted one phase after another of his crooked dealings.

Mentioned casually in a list of his securities was a little block of Interborough bonds, which established a tenuous connection between the judge and the notorious receivership he had seized so outrageously that, although the legal correctness of his procedure was sustained, the Supreme Court chided him in what for its dignity were harsh words, and suggested that he would be wise to give it up.

Manton had sat, in 1928, on a special statutory court that granted the Interborough the right to charge seven cents a ride, although by contract embodied in the state law the fare was limited to five cents. The Supreme Court reversed this decision.

During the very month that he was named to sit on this case, Manton disposed of $10,000 worth of the railroad's bonds. But he did not hold them when he sat, and he sold them for $7,653.61, representing a loss so far as I could determine, so the impropriety of his sitting was ethical rather than legal. I had to look further.

I learned of the existence of an exhaustive study made by a highly reputable accounting firm, in connection with the Lord & Thomas loan, into the National Cellulose Corporation, of which Manton was half owner. Eventually I managed to obtain a copy of the report. In it I found verification of what I had known, but could not prove— that when Louis Levy appeared before Judge Manton in the $10,000,000 American Tobacco case, and when Manton seized the Interborough receivership, Levy and his partner, the late Thomas C. Chadbourne, were fellow stockholders with Manton in this National Cellulose Corporation.

The association was carefully disguised. When Manton and Sullivan formed the corporation in 1927, they sold $75,750 worth of the stock to Levy and Chadbourne. Levy's stock was carried on the corporation's books in the name of a stenographer in the law office, and Chadbourne's in the name of a clerk. Dividend checks were sent in care of a junior lawyer in the office.

The paper company never earned profits with which to pay dividends, but by writing up the value of its assets a bookkeeping surplus was created, out of which dividends were paid.

The Interborough, a $250,000,000 railroad property, was thrown into bankruptcy on a $25,000 claim, at a time when it had more than a million dollars in its treasury with which it could have paid. The details were all worked out with Judge Manton before the petition was filed.

At that time Manton had been a fellow stockholder with Levy and Chadbourne for four years and a half. Chadbourne was one of the largest stockholders in the Interborough. Levy was his law partner. Three months previously Levy had arranged the $250,000 Lord & Thomas loan for Manton's benefit.

When the bankruptcy petition was filed it was supposed, according to the rules of the court, to be taken to the district judge sitting in Part I, who was to assign it to whatever district judge he saw fit. This rule had been adopted specifically to prevent Manton from seizing another receivership as, earlier that same year, he had grabbed the huge Fox Theatres Corporation case.

But the Interborough's lawyer went to Manton, because, he has explained under oath, Manton had presided four years before over the statutory court that granted the Interborough a seven-cent fare. And Manton rose to the occasion, for the railroad in which his friends were interested, by an ingenious maneuver.

In order to meet emergency conditions, the senior judge of the circuit court was authorized to appoint a circuit judge to sit in district court. He assigned himself.

Then, the bankruptcy petition having come to him as a district judge, though none of the other district judges knew that there was such a petition Judge Manton disagreed with them as to who should handle it. Having created a controversy, he exercised his authority to settle such controversies by reverting to his *alter ego* as senior circuit court judge long enough to assign the receivership to himself as district judge.

When all was settled thus completely, the other district judges learned to their surprise that there was a petition, that there had been a disagreement, and how it had been resolved.

Thereupon Judge Manton appointed, as one of two receivers for the Interborough, the late Victor J. Dowling, partner of Levy and Chadbourne, who in turn named his law firm—Chadbourne, Stanchfield & Levy—as his attorneys.

There was such a public clamor over these appointments, though not for years was Manton's financial tie known, that the law firm resigned. Dowling kept the receivership until his death nearly two years later.

During his receivership Dowling received fees of $67,500. Receivership fees, when last I checked, totalled $307,500, of which at least half would have gone to

Dowling if he had lived. The law firm which acted as counsel to the receivers has received at least $415,000— which would have gone to Manton's friends but for the popular revulsion.

In most big law firms it is the practice for earnings to be pooled, and then divided according to a predetermined percentage system. More than $600,000 would have gone to the firm of Chadbourne, Stanchfield & Levy, if Manton's original plans had been carried out, and the men who would have benefited from it most generously would have been Thomas Chadbourne, Manton's business associate, and Louis Levy, who in addition to being his business associate had helped him to obtain $250,000 shortly before.

The ramification of this investigation was prodigious. Each episode tied closely into another, and all interlocked like a particularly complicated picture puzzle. Often it was hard to keep to the main highway, because so many intriguing byways were continually inviting entertaining excursion.

During the period in which I was most interested Manton was the dominant factor in twelve corporations, of which most were in operation simultaneously. Eight were real estate companies, of which five were intertwined so closely that the most skillful investigating accountants now think of them as five money pockets in one pair of trousers. One was the paper company, one a carpet cleaning concern which had a carpet-selling subsidiary, and the twelfth was a short-lived coal company. Whichever one tried to analyze, its finances were intermingled with all the others. In each venture appeared, as partners or lenders, the names of persons high in the civic, political, industrial and commercial life of the city and the nation, judges of low and high degree, criminals and churchmen, financiers and promoters, all the assorted types that go to make up our body politic, and many of them strange bedfellows for a high and mighty federal judge.

District Judge Grover M. Moscowitz of Brooklyn has explained his connection to the satisfaction of the F. B. I. On the recommendation of Judge Manton, Judge Moscowitz had appointed a banker named John M. McGrath as one of three trustees for the $110,000,000 Prudence Bonds reorganization. McGrath, in turn, had made Manton's bagman, Bill Fallon, his confidential investigator. Out of his activities in that capacity, Fallon was indicted and convicted by Dewey for commercial bribery. I learned that McGrath, after his appointment as a trustee, had "lent" Manton $12,000. Manton's records showed other loans from McGrath's bank, which the bank denied having made and which later turned out to have been from McGrath himself.

Then there was the matter of the Kings Brewery insurance, which opened up when I obtained possession of a letter from a broker named Charles A. Rogers threatening embarrassment for Manton unless he received either the insurance on the brewery or the return of a "certain sum of money" he had "loaned" to Manton's business partner.

The Kings Brewery was known throughout prohibition as a mob-operated source of illegal beer of high alcoholic content. The Levy brothers, Nat and Dave, its owners, were named publicly among the city's prohibition racketeers. After repeal Sam Rosoff, millionaire immigrant contractor, bought in to the extent of around a million dollars, but soon the enterprise was in federal reorganization.

The case was handled by District Judge Clarence G. Galston. There was no apparent connection between it and Judge Manton. Yet Manton's partner, Sullivan, was made one of the receivers, and one of Manton's minor business employees was put on the payroll, and Manton's bagman, Fallon, obtained a loan of $10,000 from Rogers in return for the promise that Rogers would have the insurance business. Rogers, unlike some victims of this racket, went to the trouble of talking with Manton and getting his personal assurance of delivery.

Nat Levy, whose interests include a Brooklyn hot spot known as the Bedford Rest, and who had ideas at one time of operating a dog track on a Queens airport in which Manton owned half interest, lent Manton $25,000 on each of two occasions, the F. B. I. discovered.

I lingered for a time over Manton's $60,000 borrow-

ings from one J. Rich, easily identified as "Jack Sullivan—
King of the Newsboys," who was one of those indicted
for the notorious murder of the gambler Herman Rosen-
thal in 1912. Rich died before I was ready to show my
hand by talking with him.

It took some months to identify "a man named Lynch
from Chicago," who paid Manton face value for $50,000
worth of not very valuable paper company stock, estab-
lishing a realized profit of more than $30,000 which did
not show on the judge's income tax returns. The man
named Lynch proved to be president of Standard Gas &
Electric Company, but the inside story of the transaction
is still locked in Tom Dewey's files.

I spent some time on Basil O'Connor, law partner of
Franklin Roosevelt until after the 1932 election, who
represented Manton's principal real estate corporation
during 1932 in negotiations to adjust taxes due to the state.

O'Connor was given two jobs as special master in the
Interborough receivership, by Manton. For the first he
asked $14,000 for thirty-two and one-half hours of work.
For the second, which he reported had taken forty hours,
he asked $21,000. By the time his fees were fixed Manton
had been forced out of the case, and Judge Mack allowed
$13,500 for the two assignments.

Basil O'Connor showed up again in the Fox Theatres
receivership, one of the major episodes which I studied,

which Manton seized early in 1932 and ran for the benefit of his friends up to the very moment of leaving office.

Manton's first appointments as receivers included the president of the corporation and the late John F. Sherman, who had made certain informal inquiries about buying Manton's two hotels, as a result of which Manton was enabled to borrow $345,000 on the hotels. When Sherman died Manton appointed a lawyer named Milton C. Weisman, who later took into his law firm Emanuel Celler, a member of the house judiciary committee. Soon afterward the Fox Theatres president resigned, for reasons which to investigators appeared quite unexplanatory, and Weisman became sole receiver. Not long after that, the highly reputable bankruptcy expert who had been acting as solicitor to the receivers resigned, after some disagreements, and O'Connor was appointed by Manton to succeed him.

The appointment of Weisman came the day after he had completed settling more than $400,000 of Manton's debts to closed banks for less than $160,000, at a time when Manton by his own sworn statement was insolvent by more than three-quarters of a million dollars.

Manton's last official act, before he left the bench, was to appoint as Weisman's co-trustee Kenneth Steinrich, the husband of Senator Robert F. Wagner's niece, the former Evelyn Wagner. Steinrich guaranteed the premiums on a life insurance policy on which Manton borrowed $50,000. An associate of Steinrich in the Kips Bay Brewery had lent Manton $25,000. Mrs. Steinrich was partner of Edward Sullivan, brother of Manton's partner, in an insurance business with which the Interborough, while it was under Manton's direction, placed a considerable part of its business.

And finally, to mention only the distractions which were most intriguing, there was $22,500 worth of stock in an insolvent Manton corporation which Thomas E. Murray, Jr., bought at par and tucked away shortly before he was made co-receiver of the Interborough. This money helped Manton to stave off for about two years the collapse of his real estate empire.

The implications would have been quite clear except that Murray's financial and professional standing were so well established that he did not have to buy a job from any judge, and his reputation for integrity made it unlikely that he would have done such a thing. It appeared as though Manton had made use of a church connection to save himself and then, unsought, had paid the debt. I wanted to use it against Manton, but after I had explored it thoroughly I decided not to.

Perhaps I got most innocent enjoyment out of Manton's chicken farm, which appeared up to the time I turned it over to the F. B. I. for development to be about the cheapest sell-out that any judge on any bench ever made. I should have known that Manton was not passing up his opportunities in any small way.

In October of 1935 Manton decided to go into the broiler business on his Fair Acres Farm at Bayport, L. I., buying six hundred baby chicks a week and raising them in brooders and pens. Good chicks should cost about 12 cents each. Hall Brothers of Wallingford, Conn., charged 15 cents. Manton told his foreman not to buy until the judge could talk with Almon B. Hall, who was coming to New York to discuss a patent case before Manton, which, unless the lower court was reversed, would cost Hall Brothers up to $1,500,000.

"Perhaps," said Manton modestly, "I can get their price down."

After he had talked with Hall, the judge was certain. He told his foreman that Hall would sell him the chicks for 10 cents each. Soon afterward Fallon, the judge's salesman of justice, and Forrest W. Davis, a small-town Long Island banker and crony of Bill Fallon, were at Fair Acres, visiting Manton.

"How did you get the price down to ten cents?" Manton was asked. Fallon answered for him.

"We used a little pressure," he said.

Manton's tribunal reversed the lower court, and decided for Hall Brothers. It was, remarked Manton casually, the first of 118 suits in which the patent-owner who sued the Halls had been beaten in court.

To that point, it appeared that for a saving of two cents on each of 600 chicks, or $12 a week, Manton had sold out a $1,500,000 case. The F. B. I., working from these leads, found differently. In addition to the discount, it developed, Hall Brothers paid $60,000 in cash to Manton for that decision.

When he had difficulty selling his broilers, Manton sent representatives to the hotels owned by the Prudence company, which were operated by the Moscowitz-appointed trustees, including Manton's benefactor McGrath and his confidential agent, Fallon. The Prudence hotels bought Manton's chickens, just as they bought $50,000 worth of carpets from Manton's Oriental Carpet Company.

Except for the story of the chicken farm, and a few interesting but unimportant details, I had all of this and much more when word came that Manton, alarmed by Dewey's insistence that Manton's secretary appear before the grand jury with the books of a key corporation out of the judicial safe, was preparing to resign.

We wanted to begin printing our findings while Manton was still on the bench. We felt that it would be harder to obtain official action against him once he had retired. Also, we wanted to strike while he was at the height of his power, so that no question could arise whether we had waited until he shed part of his armor, and then kicked him when he was only partially protected.

We felt that the job was ours. It was something that

Dewey, with all his resources, could not do so well. There was a real question whether Dewey had or could get evidence of any major crime against the state of New York which had not outlawed. Unless he could, he had nothing to prosecute, however heinous the offenses. It has turned out that this fear was justified. Nothing proven against Manton could have been prosecuted by Dewey. While I had urged that he find some method of making public his charges, even though he could not prosecute, I had no idea whether he would do so.

When I left Dewey, the day that I told him I was ready to investigate Manton, it was assumed that his rackets bureau would not begin on the matter for some time, if at all.

Dewey's interest in Manton was founded fundamentally upon a case in which he was convinced that the judge had sold out to two of the cheapest and most vicious gorillas New York rackets have bred, the thugs popularly known as Lepke and Gurrah.

While Dewey was special rackets prosecutor, Murray Gurfein, then one of his chief assistants, and Victor Herwitz, an able young member of his staff, had devoted more than two years to building up an airtight case against Lepke and Gurrah. When they were ready to indict, they found that the thugs were fugitives by grace of Judge Manton.

Lepke, whose real name is Louis Buchalter, and Gurrah, who is known more formally as Jacob Shapiro, had an income estimated officially at $4,000,000 a year from the fur, trucking, flour, clothing and prostitution rackets, which they had ruled with bombs, fists, clubs, acid, and general mayhem and alleged murder carried out by some two hundred strong-arm assistants.

They were convicted by John Harlan Amen, son-in-law of the late President Cleveland, in a racket involving the $10,000,000-a-year rabbit fur industry.

Senior District Judge John C. Knox refused to fix bail for them on appeal. They went to Judge Manton, in chambers. Over the request of Amen for bail of at least $25,000 each, Manton set them free in $10,000 each, which was the exact amount of their fines, with no allowance for the two years each had been sentenced to serve in the federal penitentiary. The bail was provided, and of course they skipped. Later Gurrah surrendered. Lepke remained at large until, when the combined federal-state search grew too hot, he surrendered to G-Man Hoover by way of the Hearst gossip-monger, Walter Winchell, in hope of escaping Dewey's clutches.

Dewey wanted to look into Manton's motives in this peculiar case, and also to follow up clues arising out of his quizzing of Bill Fallon.

The day after my talk with Dewey, Murray Gurfein asked me to his office, and invited me to give him the leads

I had. I was willing, so long as I could be protected against any chance that my own story would be taken away from me. We decided on a basis of coöperation, subject to confirmation by Dewey.

It was arranged that I should turn over to Gurfein anything he asked for or that I felt would be of value to him. He could not promise to give me anything in return, except that when my stories were written, he would look them over and tell me if anything in his possession disproved my findings or made them seem dangerous to use.

Neither of us was to make public anything about the investigation, without the other's permission, before January 15. If either was not ready then, we were to consider setting a later date. Whenever we were both ready, we were to have forty-eight hours in which to print part of our own findings before Dewey's office made any public move, or permitted other newspapers to have any material.

This understanding was discussed with Dewey. Gurfein and Keller reported that it could not be done.

"Mr. Dewey has never made such an agreement," they said, "and won't now."

"That's quite all right," I agreed. "You go ahead with your inquiry, and I'll make mine, and when we are ready we will print what we have."

"But you'll let us have what you find?" I was asked.

"No," I replied. "Not unless the agreement is okayed by Tom substantially as it has been outlined."

Before the week was up, I had this agreement. From that time on, Herwitz was continually in touch with me for more than six months. When my records outgrew the space I had, and contacts from the outside world interfered with my concentration, Lee Wood turned over to me a large room on an upper floor, with files and desks but no telephone, and hired an accountant to help me trace the devious records.

To that room, day after day, sometimes for a few minutes and sometimes for the most of the day, came Herwitz, other Dewey lawyers, accountants, and one other person—the mysterious source of my original clue and the invaluable tipster on Manton's life history and most of his current thoughts and actions.

During the next six months I was a lone wolf. On our staff only three of the principal editors and two of my closest personal friends and daily luncheon companies had any idea what I was doing, that kept me so busy and appeared to produce no results. The reception clerk and the telephone operator were intrigued by frequent calls from a person who, if I were out, would leave word only that my "federal reporter" had called. All working papers were kept closely under lock and key when I left my desk, however briefly. This was partly from natural caution, and partly because when I was studying industrial life insurance abuses, earlier the same year, a file containing confidential information from employees of a famous life insurance company had mysteriously left my desk and never returned. The harm was not great, for the more valuable material even then was locked away, but from then on I took no chances.

When I began using a private room the tumblers in the lock were changed, and new keys made of which I had the only copies. Whenever my helper and I left the room, every paper was locked into a steel file to which we had the only two keys.

From the day I first was authorized to begin the inquiry until I was ready to begin writing, none of the editors asked what I was doing or how I was doing it, or what I was finding, or why it took me so long. Now and again, when I ran into a juicy morsel, I would mention it to one or other as a matter of interest. Throughout, they followed the policy which has made it a pleasure to work for them—to hire trustworthy reporters, to trust them, and to hold them accountable for results.

A few days after the New Year, Wood told me that Dewey had asked for a luncheon appointment to discuss the progress of the inquiries. On his return, he said that Dewey was not ready to go to the public with his findings, and had asked that we hold off. It was left that neither would take any action without the other's concurrence, unless we were forced by some exigency to begin publication.

This proviso was made because of persistent reports that President Roosevelt was considering naming Manton to the Supreme Court. Those rumors seemed absurd when, later, I learned that a report by the F. B. I. on one of the episodes which led to Manton's conviction had been resting for a year in the drawer of a Justice Department desk. They were very persistent, however, and the sources from which they came had proven worthy of credence in other connections.

By mid-January I was ready to begin writing for publication at any time, though I could use a little more time to advantage filling in details. Before publication, I wanted two or three days' notice, so that reporters could make a fast round of those who would be discussed in my articles, asking for their answers to the stories I would write. This had to be left to the end, because up to that moment neither Manton nor any of his associates had the slightest idea that I was interested in them, and I preferred to leave them in happy ignorance to the last possible day.

Then, on Tuesday afternoon, January 24, I received a telephone call from my "federal reporter" that Manton was planning to resign. He had asked John W. Davis and Theodore Kiendl, the latter chairman of the leading bar association's disciplinary committee, to represent him in case of need, I was told. I must act fast, if I wanted to hit him while he still was on his feet.

I went immediately to Gurfein, and told him I was going to begin writing and why. He scoffed at the reports. On Wednesday morning, however, he telephoned me.

"You were right," he said, "only it is closer even than you thought. We have no time to lose. I have a plan. Come right over."

I went with him to the Criminal Courts Building, where Dewey was conducting the second trial of Jimmy Hines. Dewey approved.

That afternoon, Gurfein took before County Judge George L. Donnellan a witness who had been refusing to produce some subpoenaed records. It was Gurfein's plan, in explaining to the judge why he needed the books, to mention that it was in connection with an investigation of Judge Manton. This, we felt, would place the judge in such position that he could not step out with clean robes, and might force him to await further action and give us more time.

Judge Donnellan was not coöperative, however, and would not permit Gurfein to mention Manton's name. The only recourse was for me to begin writing. Thursday I wrote, rewrote, edited and wrote again until after midnight. Mr. Wood, B. O. McAnney, the city editor, and our libel lawyer, Harry H. Van Aken, planned the first article with me, and went over each step. Van Aken went home in the evening, but returned early the next morning to go over a proof. The story was torn to pieces and put together again and again. At last, when we were satisfied, it was sent by messenger to the Scripps-Howard general offices, where Roy Howard and Paul Patterson, general counsel, went over it and approved.

At 2:30 that Friday afternoon a final okay came by telephone, and the waiting type was locked into the front page of the last important edition of the day, under two eight-column lines of inch-high type. I went back up-stairs and began writing Saturday's article.

Up to the day before first publication only the World-Telegram employees I have mentioned, a few members of Dewey's staff, and three high state officials in whom I had implicit confidence, had any slightest idea of what I was doing.

I had been very anxious that Manton should not know, lest he find means of shutting me off from information I needed. He was boss of the federal courthouse, to such an extent that he placed employees as far down the scale as telephone operators. He could have done much to interfere with my work.

A reporter has no powers at all except what his intelligence, his personality, his pertinacity and his skill may give him. He can not demand the production of key documents under penalty. On our paper, at least, he can not obtain such documents by shady methods, however good the cause in which they are to be used. He can not compel witnesses to talk—or even to meet him. He is barred by law from certain of the most fruitful sources of information, such as bank accounts and income tax returns. He can not use information from federal income tax returns even, as was the case in the Manton inquiry, when he possesses them.

There was another and better reason why I wanted Manton kept in ignorance of my inquiries. I was confident that Dewey would find nothing to prosecute. I believed than Manton would feel likewise, and would expect that when Dewey found himself unable to indict he would drop the matter without publicity. Manton would know, however, that I could give ruinous publicity to things which Dewey could not use, and I believed that if he learned that I was finding out his crimes he would retire, in hope that I would drop the investigation and permit him to return to private practice and business unbesmirched.

The day I began writing, two of our most competent reporters, Allan Keller and Fred Woltman, were sent with carefully prepared questions to be asked of Louis Levy and of Milton C. Weisman, who had received the lucrative Fox Theatres receivership from Manton. These two, though they did not see our reporters or answer the questions, learned then what was going on. I have no

reason to doubt that Manton himself was informed at
once.

The first copy of the edition containing the first article
was handed to Allan Keller, who went at once to Manton's
chambers to show it to him and ask for his comment. In
all his years as a reporter, Keller said afterward, he had
never seen a man so stricken in appearance as the judge.

Later, federal courthouse reporters saw John W. Davis
go into Judge Manton's chambers. From a source which
has never yet played me false, I am told that Manton said
to Davis:

"I'm advised by the attorney-general to resign. What
should I do?"

To which, I'm told, Davis replied:

"If the attorney-general advises it, I certainly should
resign."

When he left, Davis denied that he had been retained
by Manton.

I learned later that he was representing Louis Levy,
the lawyer friend of Manton who had been examined
closely about how he happened to negotiate a big loan
for Manton while Levy's firm was appearing before the
judge in a ten million dollar suit.

Levy made a practice, whenever he was questioned by
Gurfein or, later, before the federal grand jury, of preparing detailed memoranda describing his experiences and
the questions and answers. When Levy was being tried

for disbarment United States Attorney John Cahill and
his chief assistant, Mathias Correa, tried to get access to
these memoranda. Davis, who was defending Levy, refused to produce them.

"I do not propose to have the privacy of my office
and my professional relations invaded, no matter what
the occasion may be," Davis informed the court cavalierly.

John Cahill, who by that time was more than a little
irritated by Davis' patronizing manner, deflated his eminent adversary to the glee of many spectators.

"Mr. Davis has no privilege," he said curtly. "These
high phrases of professional responsibility and the like
leave me cold."

Saturday is a bad day for good news stories, for afternoon newspapers, for two reasons. Department stores
being closed on Sundays, there is little advertising Saturday and therefore little news space. Moreover, because
of the half-holiday devoted, often into the night, to recrea-
tion, few papers are sold. It is customary to hold stories
that can wait over the week-end.

For my Saturday second story, therefore, I presented
a general picture of Manton's business operations, which
would serve to give background for those readers who
like to know all there is, but the lack of which would not
interfere with understanding of the successive counts in
the indictment I hoped to present daily over a period of
perhaps two weeks.

For Monday, I prepared a story reporting that Dewey and the State Tax Department, under Deputy Commissioner Spencer Bates, were investigating, and giving such of the background of their studies as I was permitted to tell.

Meanwhile Dewey had been busy. Late Saturday afternoon, on a sudden decision, he called Gurfein and other assistants into the office, and had them work most of the night and Sunday preparing a report to Hatton Sumners, Congressman from Texas and chairman of the House Judiciary Committee.

His report outlined eight charges against Manton, on which he said he would be glad to provide the committee with full information if it chose to act against the judge. This was the committee which would have filed impeachment charges for trial before the Senate, sitting as a court.

Dewey's charges were printed in Monday morning's papers. I had been given my forty-eight hours. It was my hard luck that circumstances brought them at a weekend, and deprived me of full use of one day. Now Dewey was in action.

That day Manton resigned.

We held hasty consultation. I was prepared, even if time did not permit the gathering of minor details to complete other allegations, to write from ten to a dozen articles each describing a criminal or unethical or unjudicial action by Manton which should contribute to a removal action. Dewey had included six of my charges among his, adding two of which I knew nothing except what I had gleaned from observation of his investigators. But I still had plenty more.

We decided, at last, to stop where we were, to cover future developments as news, using our complete files and intimate knowledge of the record only to enable us to handle the news more accurately, more fully, more intelligently and more interestingly than other newspapers could or would dare.

I sat back, then, and wondered when the Department of Justice would begin the sweeping inquiry that Attorney-General Murphy promised from Washington. I assumed that they had no case, or they would not have waited for me to force Manton out. I knew they had not asked Dewey for his information. Nor did they come to me for something like a week.

At long last Gregory F. Noonan, acting United States Attorney, sent word that he would like to talk with me. It was decided that I should be discreet in my disclosures for a time, in view of the fact that Noonan appeared on the books of Manton's topmost real estate holding company, the Alamac-Esplanade Corporation, as a substantial stockholder and a director.

I knew that he held the stock as nominee for the State Banking Department, as liquidator of a bank to which one of Manton's corporations had pledged it for a loan, and that he had no personal financial interest. I could not quite see, however, how he could have been a director of the corporation without noticing a peculiar and rather fetid odor about some of its affairs—particularly about the manipulation of a $345,000 loan from the Ungerleider Financial Corporation. Eventually it developed that Noonan had not even known that the stock was placed in his name by the banking department and that he had been made a nominal director. Therefore he had not been in position to observe the corporation's affairs. When his attention was called to the situation he explained it to me, and gracefully stepped aside and turned the inquiry over to others.

On this first visit, I found that Noonan had nothing at all except what had appeared in print. This was some time after Attorney-General Murphy took office and, according to Edgar Hoover, had found on his desk the F. B. I. dossier which convicted Manton. I outlined a number of episodes, which I felt could serve as starting points for inquiry until we satisfied ourselves about Noonan.

Present with us was the New York head of the F. B. I., who took complete notes of what I had to tell, checking on the spelling of names, on dates and amounts and similar things so frequently that there is no doubt in my mind that he had never before heard details of the episodes. If a report such as Mr. Hoover describes was in the hands of the attorney-general, it appears that no duplicate had been provided to the agent in charge in New York, where the crimes were committed and investigation made, and where, after I had broken the case, Manton was indicted and tried.

When we had become convinced that Noonan was on the level, and especially after John Cahill was made United States Attorney and took over the case, we became completely frank with his office and with the F. B. I., one of whose best agents was in frequent touch with me until the trial was over. To him I made available everything we had, lending source documents for use and for photostating, obtaining information from sources I could not disclose to him, and eventually putting his office in touch with my "federal reporter."

The fact of the matter is that the report to which John Edgar Hoover attributes Manton's resignation, indictment and conviction, covered only one out of more than a dozen of the judge's malfeasances—the matter of John L. Lotsch, a patent attorney and president of the defunct Fort Greene National Bank in Brooklyn, who arranged loans from his bank to Manton in return for decisions from Manton in favor of his clients and for deposits made by Receiver Milton C. Weisman out of Fox Theatres funds.

From the time that Dewey and I opened up the case, and I outlined its far-flung ramifications to Noonan and the local head G-man, Mr. Hoover's agents did a fine job of going after Manton, and while they did not explore everything, they did as complete a job as the situation demanded.

I am in complete accord with John Cahill, who is as fine, clean, aggressive and able a prosecutor as ever I have worked with, that there is no use piling up a mountain of earth on a man who already is well buried. The F. B. I. gathered and Cahill used enough to break Manton for life, to strip him of any semblance of respectability, to deprive him of his liberty, his robes, his membership at the bar and his citizenship. There was no point in going further.

I have never yet reported on a successful investigation without receiving a flood of complaints, inquiries, tips and comments, by mail, telephone and in person, from sources ranging upward from the lunatic fringe to persons of the highest standing in business, professional and public life.

Far from being an exception, the Manton case produced an enormous mass of such communications that has not yet stopped completely. Much of what came in was worthless. Occasionally there was something worth while.

Within a week after Manton's resignation I received a telephone call from a casual acquaintance from west of the Hudson, who said that if I cared to investigate Senior Judge J. Warren Davis of the third circuit court of appeals I would find him involved with some of the same persons who had appeared on Manton's books.

Our paper confines itself rigidly to metropolitan New York. The third circuit includes Pennsylvania, New Jersey, Delaware, and the Virgin Islands. My editors did not feel that I should undertake to investigate that court, particularly in view of the amount of unfinished business remaining in our own neighborhood.

I turned the lead over to the federal department of justice early in February, 1939. Later in that month agents seized Judge Davis' bank records. On April 21 Judge Davis retired, on the plea that because of his health he was not able to do his share of the court's work.

Soon afterward he visited Washington and had a heart-to-heart talk with Attorney-General Murphy, in which he offered to resign if Murphy felt he should. The attorney-general declined to advise him. Davis has remained in retirement, eligible for recall to active service and drawing the same $12,500 a year salary that he would receive if he were working. Resignation would have stopped the salary and removed him from the roll of judges subject to duty.

I kept getting reports from a number of trustworthy sources about the progress of the F. B. I. inquiry into Judge Davis' affairs, and from a volunteer investigator across the Hudson I continued to receive specific material which kept me ahead of the F. B. I. This I turned over through United States Attorney Cahill, who has a special designation as deputy attorney-general of the United States to investigate and prosecute judicial malfeasance, and through agents of the F. B. I. in whom I have confidence.

The case which built itself up in my desk, without effort on my part beyond an occasional telephone call and some visits to law libraries, raised serious questions about Judge Davis' fitness to continue on the bench. But the F. B. I. never seemed to tie up isolated incidents into a case. On more than one occasion, from sources which any cub reporter would have consulted, I was able to provide tie-ups.

Judge Davis had borrowed money with which to buy stock in a bank dominated by Albert M. Greenfield, and had borrowed more money from Samuel Ungerleider, and thereafter had participated in decisions favorable to William Fox. It was a matter of common gossip that Fox, Greenfield and Ungerleider were closely associated in a business way, but the F. B. I. could not prove it.

I had a free lance reporter in Atlantic City, who is more familiar with society and resort doings than with court files, spend about five dollars' worth of time in the office of the United States court. He sent me proof from official court records of the connection that the F. B. I. had not found. When I passed this on, agents went to Atlantic City and verified it.

A prominent Scranton lawyer, Morgan F. Kaufman,

lent $10,000 to Judge Davis' cousin, Charles Stokley, and Judge Davis lent him $5,000 more with which to save his equity in a fifteen-acre property at Mt. Dora, Florida. A year later Davis lent Stokley $4,000 to take up a mortgage on a seven-acre orange grove in Mt. Dora.

The general outline of these transactions was in possession of the F. B. I. by mid-1939, yet at the end of the year Mr. Hoover's agents had not troubled to look over land records there to find out whether these properties were the same, whether the net effect was that Kaufman held a mortgage on Davis' property at a time when Kaufman appeared before Davis and obtained a decision, later overturned by the Supreme Court, freeing the notorious poultry racketeer Joseph Wiener from the federal penitentiary in Lewisburg.

I kept hammering at the Department of Justice for action, and Attorney-General Murphy protested to our Washington correspondent that I was rushing him unduly. That may be so. Edgar Hoover says now that his staff is so inadequate for the spy-hunt he must conduct that he can not spare agents to press the Davis inquiry. There was no spy hunt during the first eight months after I turned in the original tip, and by that time I had written, and laid aside temporarily, three articles which were printed in December outlining Judge Davis' dealings with Kaufman, Ungerleider, Fox, Greenfield, and the Associated Gas & Electric Corp.

The F. B. I. now has developed certain angles which, as I knew them, already demanded submission to the House Judiciary Committee. It has obtained further information, also, about the affairs of District Judge Albert W. Johnson of Scranton.

Johnson had been investigated once before, and a report filed. When an agent began looking into his part in the Wiener case—it was he who first granted to Wiener a writ of habeas corpus which Judge Davis' court upheld but the Supreme Court reversed—the report of the original inquiry was not given to him. An alert Pennsylvania newspaper reporter discovered that it was not where, in the usual course of events, it would have been, and called the agent's attention to it. Later another agent questioned this reporter about his knowledge, but never did say what had happened to the document.

Up in Connecticut, too, the trail led, to District Judge Edwin C. Thomas. My first information about him was part of the story I originally took to Tom Dewey, involving Jimmy Hines. Jacob Handelsman, one-time Chicagoan who later set up as a money broker in New York, brought it to me. Key portions were verified by Manton when he was on trial. Because the extent of their knowledge of what was done and planned has not been established, it seems only fair to withhold the names of some persons connected with the episode.

A major figure in the moving picture business resigned

when his corporation was about to go into reorganization, and sought to become a trustee. He had Handelsman ask Manton for the appointment. But Manton was then under heavy fire for the seizure of two other receiverships, and decided to duck this one. He turned it over to a district judge so unapproachable that the movie magnate and Handelsman gave up their idea.

Meanwhile, in the Fox Theatres receivership it was desired to liquidate the old Poli Circuit of theatres in New England, owned by a Fox subsidiary in ancillary receivership subject to Judge Thomas. The movie magnate decided to buy these theatres, if he could get them cheaply enough. It was suggested that a friendly trustee would help. Handelsman told me, and later the F. B. I., that the Hollywoodite promised him $300,000 and an interest in the chain if he would arrange the matter of the trusteeship satisfactorily.

Handelsman turned over $10,000 to Manton's Forest Hills Terrace Corporation. Manton telephoned to Judge Thomas and recommended the appointment of the movie man's attorney as a trustee. Thomas made the appointment. Then another Hollywood personage decided he must have the Poli theatres, and gave the first magnate a fine-paying job in return for his inside track on the purchase.

This left Handelsman out in the cold. He asked Manton for his $10,000, which was ostensibly the down pay-

ment on a contract by which Handelsman was to buy
Manton's Alamac Hotel for $300,000. Manton told
Handelsman to collect from the trustee whose appointment Handelsman had arranged, who up to that time was
entitled to one-third of $75,000 allocated as fees. The
trustee declined to share his emoluments.

Manton telephoned to the trustee to come and see him,
and was turned down.

"All right," said Manton, "I'll see that he gets nothing
out of that receivership."

Manton called Judge Thomas, and the trustee lost
about three quarters of his fee.

By degrees Handelsman collected $5,250 from Manton,
and then threatened to sue. After Fallon had failed to
dissuade him, two New Jersey "liquor men" took Handelsman to visit Jimmy Hines, who promised that if Handelsman would accept the $3,150 which Fallon was ready to
pay, and give a release for the full $10,000, Hines would
care for the remaining $1,600.

Six months later Hines refused to pay, and claimed he
had never met Handelsman. The broker sued him, but
withdrew the suit after he had been informed that, if he
persisted in suing, District Attorney Dodge would indict
him for blackmail.

Another trustee for the Fox New England Theatres
was Benjamin Slade, who fifteen years previously was
counsel to one Joseph Weissman in a criminal case arising

out of a million dollar bankruptcy, in which Judge Thomas, instead of dismissing the indictment, impaneled a jury and directed it to acquit Weissman, so that he could not be prosecuted later. The Supreme Court in an opinion written by the late Justice Oliver Wendell Holmes upheld Judge Thomas' right to follow such a course but criticized his wisdom.

When the notorious McKesson & Robbins scandal broke, Judge Thomas handled the court phases, Benjamin Slade maneuvered them, and Joseph Weissman's son, Abraham, was appointed by Thomas as one of two trustees.

Judge Thomas occasionally sat in New York, by direction of Manton. On one such occasion Manton demanded and received $10,000 in cash from a criminal defendant before Judge Thomas, with the explanation that it was to pay Thomas for freeing the defendant.

John L. Lotsch, who confessed freely to bribing Manton, had been arrested for soliciting a bribe while he was a special master representing the federal court. He had been caught red-handed by an F. B. I. agent. Lotsch talked to Manton, who talked to Thomas. Lotsch delivered $10,000 in bills to Manton's chambers and saw them go into the safe there. Manton brought Thomas down from Connecticut and assigned him to the criminal part, in which Lotsch was to be tried. When the case came up, Thomas impaneled a jury and directed a verdict of acquittal on a technicality.

Immediately, agents rearrested Lotsch in the courtroom, on another form of charge based on the same offense. Lotsch obtained a writ of habeas corpus, claiming that he had been twice placed in jeopardy for the same acts. District Judge Goddard dismissed the writ. Lotsch talked with Manton, who advised him what points in the government's case to answer. Then the circuit court reversed Goddard and freed Lotsch. Eventually Lotsch was convicted of other offenses, but the net result of Manton's arrangements was that from the bribery he escaped scot-free.

All of these, and some other matters, would have been presented to the federal grand jury, and an indictment asked against Judge Thomas, if he had not been found mentally incapable of answering in court.

Called back from a vacation in Panama, a week after the Manton charges were published, Judge Thomas resigned after preliminary questioning. Soon afterward, he was put in a private asylum in Hartford, where he tried to commit suicide. He has since been released, but can not stand trial.

Chapter Ten

THE ADMINISTRATION OF TRUE JUSTICE

★ 10 ★

The Administration of True Justice

GROUPED about Foley Square, just north of New York's beautiful City Hall and skyscraper Municipal Building and just south of the famous old Tombs and the office of the county prosecutor, is a small but impressive group of federal, state, county and city buildings.

At the left, in an office building which is devoted otherwise to the use of relatively inconspicuous counsellors-at-law, is the Municipal or "Poor Man's" court, in which once sat Harold L. Kunstler, who resigned in disgrace and later was disbarred as a result of my first judicial investigation.

Across the square is the imposing new federal courthouse, until recently dominated by that austere old hypocrite, Martin T. Manton.

Next this is the beautiful county courthouse, in which

sits New York's highest trial tribunal, the Supreme Court. High across its front, above the Grecian pillars, carved deep and true in enduring granite, are these words:

The True Administration of Justice Is the Firmest Pillar of Good Government.

Probably every large community in the land has a courthouse where those words of George Washington would be equally out of keeping, but it happens to be in the most imposing spot in New York's civic center that I have seen them flaunted day after day, week after week for eight years, while I wondered how long even poor democratic government could survive the type of administration that justice receives in this land of equality.

The forced resignation of a Kunstler, the criminal conviction of a Manton, the flight of a Crater, the impeachment of a Ritter may be more sensational, but the daily flouting of true justice by respectable judges, who live and die with the esteem of their fellows and their communities, does infinitely greater harm to the democratic processes to which we are always protesting devotion.

"This seems to be the open season on judges," said Presiding Justice Francis Martin of New York's Appellate Division recently while Manton was on trial, County Judge Martin of Brooklyn was under indictment, and Magistrates Rudich and Capshaw had just been removed.

"There may be an odd black sheep found. This is to

be expected in every line. But that presents no reason why all our courts should be condemned."

I would not condemn all our judges, for I know many who are honest when nobody is looking, and courageous, and competent intellectually and temperamentally for the high positions that they occupy.

Not long since a Brooklyn attorney, as representative of the Appellate Division, was examining a class of applicants for admission to the bar.

"Should we respect the judge or his office?" he asked each in turn. To those who answered "Both," naïvely or with malice aforethought, this official representative of Brooklyn's highest court would retort scornfully:

"How can you respect a judge? Why, I could be a judge myself."

The repute of judges, as a class, has fallen low. I doubt if anybody has stated the reason better than John V. Mahoney, a Boston Irishman who served Governor Curley as secretary and then was made by his employer into a justice of the Superior Court of Massachusetts.

"To tell you the truth, a judge is only a lawyer who knew a governor," said this informed and unusually frank gentleman from the bench.

Sometimes it is enough to know a governor. In our state, for some time it has been the custom of governors to appoint their counsel to fourteen-year terms, at $25,000 a year, on the bench of the Supreme Court. On the whole we have gotten quite able judges in this manner—such men as Samuel Rosenman, who has not been accused of failure to carry his official burden, yet finds time to visit Washington frequently and help President Roosevelt, his judicial creator, with the burdens of the New Deal and its oratorical responsibilities; or men like Charles Poletti, who stuck to the bench while he drew its pay, but resigned its relative ease and long tenure to take a four-year term as lieutenant-governor at a mere $10,000 a year.

On the other hand, it is better to know the county chairman of a major political party, or the boss of a state, for such are easier to satisfy than are conscientious governors, and some governors regard bosses' recommendations as equivalent to training and experience and demonstrated ability.

Governor Moore of New Jersey looks no further than the muttered word of Boss Hague of Jersey City, who made Governor Moore and could break him with the snap of a finger.

"This will make his dad happy," remarked Governor Moore, as the New Jersey legislature confirmed his appointment of Frank Hague, Jr., the boss' 34-year old son, who had been a member of the bar for only two years, to the state's highest court, which finally determines the rights of all Jerseyites to life, liberty and the possession of property.

The state Law Journal, intrigued by the appointment,

reported that there is no reason, if Boss Hague saw fit, why Governor Moore should not appoint as chief justice of this highest court of appeals the extremely personable Shirley Temple.

In order to create a vacancy so that young Hague's ambitions might be satisfied, Thomas Glynn Walker was pleased to resign from the high court and serve temporarily on a lower bench until President Roosevelt could please his fellow liberal, Frank Hague, by giving Walker a life term on the district court of the United States.

Nor was Hague the only person who had a protégé and knew the President. Not long since Mr. Roosevelt had appointed to the district court in Louisiana, for life, Gaston L. Porterie, who was Huey Long's attorney-general, and who was expelled by the state bar association for the high-handed manner in which, by Long's orders, he fought against an inquiry into election frauds and punishment of the offenders.

While he was attorney-general, and these appointments were in the making, Supreme Court Justice Frank Murphy had a survey made of 270 federal, state, county and municipal judges, of whom he found that 207 had been promoted from frankly political offices and that most of these were highly sensitive to political considerations.

Soon after I came into New York newspaper work the Democrats and the Republicans on Long Island got together to care for some of their party lawyers. There was a dinner, at which the highest judge in the Island's state court discussed the need for more judges. The Republican leader of Brooklyn dropped over to the table of the Democratic leader of Brooklyn.

"Let's get together," proposed Meier Steinbrink.

"Any time you say," agreed the late John H. McCooey.

Matters of such moment seldom are delayed. The leaders got together. It was necessary for them to agree, because the Democrats controlled the votes to elect the new judges but the Republicans controlled the legislature that must create the vacancies.

At first they thought that six new jobs would do—six fourteen-year judgeships at $25,000 a year each. But why be niggardly with taxpayers' money? To be certain, they decided on eight. Then came the problem of distribution.

Steinbrink asked for one judgeship for himself, and got it. McCooey had no ambitions in that line, but "my son Jack," 32 years old, must have one. Some had to go to Democratic Queens county and some to Republican Nassau and Suffolk.

When it came to a showdown, it appeared that eight jobs would not go around.

"Not," said Mr. McCooey, "if the Republicans were given a share."

So the number was raised to an even dozen—seven to the Democrats for having the votes in Brooklyn and

Queens to control the election, and five to the Republicans for having the votes at Albany to create the judgeships.

This deal was investigated by the Seabury Committee, then probing the government and affairs of New York City. Judge Seabury was only counsel to that committee. Its chairman was State Senator Samuel Hofstadter of Manhattan.

Next year, in the judicial district which includes Manhattan, the Democrats and the Republicans got together to fill two vacancies. The Democrats had ample votes to snow under the Republicans, and had never before been hesitant to use them. But this year they graciously gave to the Republican, Chairman Hofstadter of the troublesome investigating committee, an uncontested fourteen-year term. In return the Republicans, who couldn't have elected a party member in any other way, were glad to endorse the Democrat Aron Steuer, son of Tammany's greatest lawyer, the late Max Steuer.

By all the rules of logic and common decency Justices Steinbrink and McCooey, Hofstadter and Steuer—and Justice Charles C. Lockwood, a recently defeated Republican candidate for lieutenant-governor who received another of the Brooklyn deal positions—should have proven inferior judges. As a matter of fact, these five rank very high among the city's 95 judges of highest courts.

The same John Theofel who was the Democratic chairman of Queens involved in the Supreme Court deal feathered his own nest well in another court, before he made the mistake of tying his political wagon to Al Smith's star just before Franklin Roosevelt won.

Theofel was deputy county clerk at $6,000, which did not befit the leader of the dominant party in a community of Queens' size. He asked the surrogate, or judge of probate, to make him clerk to that court at $8,000. There was a little hitch, and the surrogate died.

Mr. Theofel recommended that Governor Roosevelt appoint to fill the vacancy John Hetherington, an active Democrat. The governor acceded. That fall the new surrogate had to compete at the polls for a fourteen-year term of his own. He could not be nominated without Boss Theofel's okay, and he could not be elected without the Democratic nomination. The position pays $25,000 a year.

Sixteen days after he ascended the bench, Surrogate Hetherington made Boss Theofel clerk of his court. Two weeks later he tried to raise the salary to $10,000. He was nominated and re-elected. While Clerk Theofel was under treatment in an asylum for a condition which never permitted him to return to work, Surrogate Hetherington increased his salary to $12,000 a year.

Charges based upon this sequence have been dismissed several times by two governors of New York.

Occasionally a judge is selected for his ability, temperament, training and judicial potentialities. Surprisingly often men selected in frank reward for party services turn out to be excellent jurists.

It is a wonder, perhaps, that our courts have not proven more venal, more corrupt, more political, more intemperate, more ignorant than they are.

It is no wonder that it is the rule, rather than the exception, for judges of high and low degree to permit politicians to "speak a word" for their friends and election workers, when they have gotten into trouble, and to submit lists from which it is almost obligatory that lucrative court appointments be made. Such lists are supplemented in many instances with the judges' own indigent or demanding relatives, friends and business associates.

As far back as 1933 I spent a summer studying the practice of paying personal and political debts, and supporting relatives and friends, on court patronage, at the expense of those who in distress have thrown themselves on the courts' protection. This is what the late Chief Justice William Howard Taft once described as "vicarious generosity."

Going into a year's file of the daily Law Journal, I spent many days laboriously listing every receivership and reference given by the Supreme Court in our jurisdiction. In the end I had a tabulation showing who were the favored beneficiaries of each of the Supreme Court justices. Then I spent weeks in the court clerk's office, going through the complete files of cases handed by the favorites, noting how much or little they had worked, what were their fees, how successful was their administration, how lax was the supervision of most judges over their work, and how futile were the protests of those who saw the salvage they had hoped for being dissipated in receivership expenses.

Even then the study was not complete. I searched newspaper files, and queried lawyers and politicians and reporters and all my acquaintances who have access to political gossip, to learn why certain men and women of no apparent distinction were so favored by judges, even after they had given evidence of incompetence as receivers. I learned of relationships of blood, or marriage and of lust; I uncovered business and professional connections, current and discontinued; I learned of lawyers who earned their receiverships by writing judges' decisions in difficult cases.

Much of this material was unprintable because it would have been too expensive and troublesome to prove in court, if we had been challenged. Enough was clearly established so that the articles I wrote in the fall caused much disturbance in political and real estate circles. The State Chamber of Commerce was so impressed that it hired a staff, headed by a competent young lawyer and directed by prominent members of the legal fraternity, to check my findings. This staff took the year succeeding that which I had studied, and went thoroughly into every record, waiting until most cases were completed so as to have final information. Nearly three years later the Chamber made public a complete verification of my report, and filed in its storeroom an elaboration of it.

No possibility of patronage and pap is overlooked. Orphans must have special guardians, and only political workers seem fitted to protect the interests of orphans. Accused murderers, if they can not afford counsel, are entitled to attorneys appointed by the judges and paid by the state, and clubhouse lawyers divide such fees. The allegedly incompetent must be examined by lunacy commissions, and these are made up from patronage and nepotism lists.

A revealing illustration of this latter practice was explored by Prosecutor Amen. It concerned Judge Algeron I. Nova of Brooklyn, and his brother, Dr. Jules M. Nova. Until he went on the bench of the Supreme Court recently Algeron Nova was a judge of the County Court, which is New York's highest criminal tribunal. During the last seven years of Judge Nova's county court tenure his brother earned $46,570 in fees for sitting on lunacy commissions. Otherwise, he is not notable as an alienist, though New York has many who are.

President Roosevelt said while he was governor of New York:

"It is repugnant to our sense of the proper administration of justice that judges should be permitted to engage in business during their terms of office. This principle admits of no doubt and should be applied throughout the state."

Judge Nova, his party's creation, then was partner with Alexander Cohen in the Cova Real Estate Company, of which the judge was president and with his wife half owner. This enterprise was sufficiently active that Nova lost some half million dollars in it. By 1934 he was insolvent to the extent of $550,000. In the next three years he lopped $170,000 from that indebtedness, though his only known income was $25,000 a year, of which he swore he could not live on less than $20,835 and continue to eat at restaurants.

During that same period County Judge George Martin, the Democratic party's creation in Brooklyn, was engaged in a variety of business ventures, in some of which investors lost everything. For one of those corporate enterprises, in which humble citizens invested because this high judge was a director, Martin negotiated a $275,000 mortgage loan, though he swore he did not know the identity of the directors! This was no secret. A federal grand jury spent three months mulling it over while Franklin Roosevelt was governor, and dropped it because no federal crime had been committed. Governor Roosevelt did nothing about it.

The Kings County bench long has been a particularly sore spot in the judicial system. It was so in 1930, when Roosevelt was governor, and it is so today. I learned early to confine my inquiries to Manhattan and the Bronx, where there was a bar association alert and courageous enough to act, with some probing, and an appellate division from which disciplinary action could sometimes be obtained.

Up in Catskill lives a county judge named William E. Thorpe, who gave a pistol permit to the notorious gangster Salvatore Spitale after New York police had broadcast his record of arrests for unlawful entry, homicide, felonious assault, violation of the prohibition law and carrying concealed weapons. Thorpe explained that Spitale was a respected member of the Catskill community, though he had been widely publicized as a racketeer when he volunteered to serve as Colonel Lindbergh's liaison with the underworld during the search for the famous flier's kidnapped baby.

Six years later, when Kings County Judge Martin was on trial before the Senate for removal and business piled up, this same Judge Thorpe was invited to Brooklyn to help dispense criminal justice. I wrote a story about the Spitale pistol permit, and about the time a Democratic attorney-general from Brooklyn moved a trial to keep it from Thorpe's court. An acrimonious dispute broke out among the judges as to who had invited him. One judge was away, besides Martin. Two others declared that a third had issued the invitation without asking them. This third asserted loudly that his associates had agreed in writing, though he could not find the writing and insinuated that it must have been spirited away.

A convict told Mr. Amen recently that in certain Brooklyn courts there is a standard price list by which criminal sentences will be reduced for fees ranging from $3,500 downward to $1,500.

"There is a sliding scale of prices," said this man who said he served time because his fellows did not pay, "and God help the guy who doesn't meet the price. The mob always figures that it's got to meet the price, and that's easy. The hardest part is maneuvering the case into the court of the right judge."

For those who contemplate committing crimes in Brooklyn, and are not certain of not being caught, here is the schedule:

Suspended Sentence $3,500
One year 2,500
Eighteen months 1,500

Some of these things I have had a part in disclosing, while others have come out of inquiries which I contributed toward procuring but did not cover as a reporter.

In one way and another, probably I have devoted more time and effort to cleaning up the courts than to any other single branch of civic improvement.

As intriguing as such things are, and as exasperating as it is to see such conditions continued year after year notwithstanding all efforts to eradicate them, I do not believe that they are more damaging to the courts' reputation than the less sensational but much more prevalent problem of patronage.

Mr. Justice Martin, the highest state court judge in New York City, who complained about an open season on judges, has two brothers and a son-in-law. During the single year which the State Chamber's staff studied, in the single field of foreclosure patronage, these three relatives of the eminent judge received sixty-four appointments from which they earned $11,562.43. None was given by Justice Martin, who does not handle such matters, but who does exercise administrative control over the trial judges.

During that same year, in that same court, 413 appointments were given to eleven persons closely associated by blood, by marriage or by business ties to Edward J. Flynn, now national Democratic chairman after years of service as President Roosevelt's chief spokesman in New York state. Mr. Flynn also is county chairman in the Bronx, and as such placed his imprimatur upon the nominations of the Bronx justices before they could run for office.

One of the coziest little businesses I ever looked over was run by the brother of one Supreme Court justice and the son-in-law of another, under the name of George A. Hammer, Inc.

George Hammer is the Republican brother of Ernest E. L. Hammer, a Democratic judge. Abraham Held, son-in-law of Justice Aaron J. Levy, was Hammer's partner. Held was agent for the National Surety Co., which bonds foreclosure receivers and other public officials. He also had an exterminator company. The firm of George A. Hammer, Inc., was in the business of managing real estate. It also sublet an office in its suite to three lawyers.

In one year Justice Hammer's brother was remembered by Justice Hammer's fellow jurists with fourteen receiverships, and two of George Hammer's tenant lawyers were remembered by George's brother with thirteen receiverships.

When anybody in the office of George A. Hammer, Inc., was given a receivership—or, for that matter, when others were given receiverships by Justice Hammer or Justice Levy—it was their cue to procure a bond from Abraham Held; to retain the services of George A. Hammer, Inc., as managing agent; frequently to engage as his counsel one of the Hammer-Held lawyer sub-tenants; and sometimes to hire Held's exterminator company to clean any vermin from the distressed property.

There is a maximum scale of court allowances for services rendered to foreclosed real estate, which has been placed under the court's protection to salvage for the mortgagee whatever is reclaimable of his investment. The receiver is supposed to get up to five percent of the funds he handles. He is supposed to hire a managing agent only by permission of the court, in cases where a property is too large for one-man supervision, and to retain counsel only under similar conditions. The standard fee for managing agent, if approved, is five percent, and for counsel three percent.

By grouping in one super-market all of these functions, plus the surety bond business, the judges' relatives were able to divide approximately fifteen percent of the income of foreclosed properties assigned to members of their staff, and nine percent of the income of properties given by their jurist relatives to others.

Bonded agents of a high court would be expected to conserve every possible asset of a distressed property entrusted to their protection. The court would be expected to require such conservation. The frequent failure of receivers to live up to such fundamental obligations emphasizes the hollow mockery of those impressive words engraved over the building where these trusts are administered.

It is not uncommon knowledge that many receivers saddle insolvent real estate with wholly unnecessary expenses for repair and maintenance, and split the profits made by carpenters, plumbers, electricians, supply houses, decorators and other workmen whom they hire. I have studied court records of receiverships which contained convincing evidence that some receivers do not even go to the trouble of splitting such fees, but short cut to profit by charging the books for services never rendered.

Case after case appears in the files in which, occasionally because of flagrant dishonesty but more often because of the incompetence of the receiver or his lack of interest in economy, little or nothing was left for the poor mortgagee after the receiver got through.

Justice Aaron Levy, the same whose son-in-law shared in George Hammer's business, had a habit of appointing as receivers such persons as his dentist brother-in-law, his secretary's husband, his chauffeur's wife, his boyhood playmates and his adult cronies.

Once upon a time Justice Levy received a request from a leading bank to appoint a receiver. At noon the next day the bank, whose lawyers had heard *sub rosa* that Herbst was to be named, asked to withdraw the application. Neither the clerk of the court nor the judge's secretary could find the petition, which could not be withdrawn until it could be found. The second day Herbst telephoned to the bank's lawyers that he had been appointed, had qualified, and had bought his bond from the judge's son-in-law for $60. He refused to quit, until the matter had been taken to another judge.

On another occasion Herbst was named by his brother-in-law to a receivership which produced $42,000 of gross income. He bought a bond and some insurance from Held for $1,234; he hired Hammer and Held to manage the property, for $2,545; his own commission was $2,110.

The total cost of the receivership ate up twenty percent of gross income.

George Hammer himself got a receivership, which produced a gross income of $3,477.50. He paid Held $213.46 for bond and insurance, his own firm $174.78 as managing agent, one of his lawyer tenants $200 as attorney, himself $175.87 as receiver, and had so many repairs and so much servicing that only $65.62 remained for the mortgagee! The court cut the attorney's fee to $75, which left $190.62 for the owner.

Reputable members of the legal profession do not hesitate to make what seem the most outrageous demands upon insolvent estates thrown upon the courts' mercy and consideration. Consider, for example, the fees asked by Basil O'Connor, the president's one-time partner, from the Interborough for services as special master mentioned earlier.

When lawyers ask allowances in such matters, they provide a detailed accounting of every minute they have put on the job. Such accountings are studded with notations of five minutes spent on the telephone, ten minute conversations in court corridors, and fifteen minutes devoted to thinking about the case with feet on desk.

By such accounting, O'Connor's asking price for one special mastership was at the rate of more than $400 an hour, and for the other reference at the rate of $525 an hour. The laborer is worthy of his hire, and a professional man is entitled to pay for what he knows equally with what he does. But $525 an hour! Judge Mack trimmed it to less than $200 an hour before he approved.

Only once, to my knowledge, has a high judge been removed for gross misuse of his control over receivership patronage, though a few others have been accused formally. The one victim, guilty of bringing the court into scandal and disrepute by granting exorbitant receivership fees to his former law partner, was removed by the margin of a single senatorial vote, after it appeared that he had further transgressed by taking a kickback from his old partner. The judge was Halsted L. Ritter, of the southern district of Florida. The deciding vote was cast by Senator Sherman Minton of Indiana, whose explanation was virtually a mandate to federal judges to go in peace so long as they exercised a minimum of discretion.

"There is," remarked Senator Minton conservatively, "a somewhat general tendency for federal judges to get too cocky. Judge Ritter went beyond all bounds."

My experience has tended to corroborate the advice given me early in my investigating career:

"The only way to get a judge off the bench is to catch him red-handed taking money in the presence of witnesses who are not confederates in the bribery."

When Harold L. Kunstler was being prosecuted for removal, before an Appellate Division referee who himself was a former judge, Tom Dewey produced evidence that other judges in New York courts had borrowed from "Kunstler's fixer." I have no means of knowing whether those loans were corrupt or innocent. Neither has anybody else. The records were sealed, and nobody who had the right to see them has ever considered it worth while to ascertain whether other judges should have been disciplined.

A lawyer friend who now occupies a position of responsibility was delegated by a leading bar association to ascertain whether there was any chance of removing two high judges, who were notoriously sodden victims of personal indulgence. One used to preside in court so far in his cups that he had to hold himself erect in his judicial chair. The other, almost as bad, also was notoriously indiscreet in amorous liaisons.

Both were learned enough and honest enough, and both stood very high with Tammany Hall. My friend reported to the bar that he could substantiate charges before any jury except the one which would sit on them—the Senate of the State of New York. The matter was dropped.

One further unfortunate condition was impressed upon me when a careless youth backed his automobile into mine, at considerable speed, with substantial damage. His father rushed to the scene, and agreed to pay the repair bill if I would go to a body repair shop of his choice. When the time came, he refused stubbornly and with exasperating impudence to make good. I decided to sue. But, I found, the jury calendar in the poor man's court was so far behind that I could not count upon a trial in less than three years, even if my opponent's lawyer made no dilatory motions. I paid for the repairs, and when I had opportunity checked somewhat into this matter of judicial delay.

The Supreme Court, with more than sixty Justices, was more than a year and a half behind in Manhattan and more than two years and a half in Brooklyn. One court was a full 44 months behind with its work. The county courts were lagging almost as badly, while prisoners languished in jail or awaited trial under bail, while witnesses forgot or were intimidated or moved away.

I became convinced, and in this I am supported by the confidential opinions of officials who work in the courts, that most of these delays result from the lackadaisical negligence of judges and the deliberate obstructionism of attorneys.

A defendant who has a bad case does not want to go to trial. He has nothing to gain, and his liberty or his money to lose. A plaintiff who has filed a spite suit or a strike suit, designed to inconvenience or intimidate an innocent defendant, likewise does not want trial. In either case, ordinarily there is nothing to prevent his attorney's stalling off trial for months or years and then, by appeals, keeping the matter open more or less indefinitely.

Such deliberate procrastination, added to the normal

and legitimate delays in the chess game known as justice, clog the courts almost beyond endurance. They could be eliminated largely by energetic, tactful, fair but stern judges, who would insist upon few excuses and good ones. But the judges do not mind. If the ready calendar is clear, it's off to the ball game, and a long summer vacation.

Our courts have been made into debating societies, rather than the instruments of sure and impartial justice. Attorneys, whose prestige and fees depend upon winning their cases, right or wrong, play a game in which plaintiffs and defendants are mere pawns. Judges sit as umpires or referees, to call balls and strikes, aces and footfaults, offsides and illegal passes.

I have never had this admitted more freely than by a one-time United States attorney, a man of superior intelligence, high integrity and notorious cynicism, who drifted into the corridor where newspapermen were snatching a hasty smoke during a recess in a widely-publicized trial. This attorney was representing a defendant.

"What do you think of my client's chances?" he asked.

"I think his guilt has been proven beyond any doubt," I told him.

"I'll make you a nice bet he isn't convicted," said the lawyer.

"If he isn't," I replied, "he'll go through life with the stigma of guilt upon him."

"Sure he will," conceded the defendant's lawyer. "All I'm saying is that under the rules of evidence, I can get him off."

He did.

In criminal matters, sometimes an energetic prosecutor can cut red tape and get cases tried. Tom Dewey has done it in New York county and John Cahill in the southern district. Yet even an alert and insistent district attorney sometimes finds himself against a stone wall. Cahill is there now, on the important mail fraud case against the Phoenix Securities Corp. group.

A number of corporations and individuals, including the dashingly handsome "Major" Philip De Ronde, were indicted December 1, 1938. While he was being questioned in a hearing-room after his arrest De Ronde, a socially prominent banker who claims to be a retired Marine Corps officer, left the room to talk with his lawyer. The next report of him came from Paraguay, where he appeared to be a captain in the army.

The defendants are represented by Martin Conboy, a great friend of the President, who made him United States attorney early in the New Deal. Mr. Conboy is thoroughly familiar with the legal rights of his clients, whose defense, it appears, will be handicapped seriously without an affidavit from the missing Major De Ronde.

So Assistant United States Attorney Leo C. Fennelly was sent to South America after De Ronde, who by that time had gone on to Paris as the honorary consul of Uruguay, and therefore could not be extradited. Fennelly took ship for Paris, to get Mr. Conboy's affidavit from De Ronde, but when he got there the cupboard again was bare. De Ronde was in the Foreign Legion.

By this time Hitler's forces were coming through the low countries and his bombers were dropping their eggs on Paris. Fennelly cabled to the court for permission to return home. The message arrived during a conference of lawyers. Judge Samuel Mandelbaum, whose liberal record as an assemblyman led President Roosevelt to make him a district judge, read it to the gathering, grunted a little, and added his facetious comment:

"T'ere he is, wit' a t'irty foot Krupp gun at his rear, an' he's eskin' the court what to do!"

Chapter Eleven

I AM CALLED A MUCKRAKER

I Am Called a Muckraker

I HAVE been called a muckraker, sometimes in encomium and sometimes in disparagement. If the expression means what I think it does—if by it I am marked as a 1940 disciple of Lincoln Steffens, Ida Tarbell and Ray Stannard Baker—I accept the appellation proudly and proclaim it from the housetops.

Paul Bunyan's muckraker worked all day turning over filth, so engrossed that he had neither time nor inclination to look up and see the beauties with which God had surrounded him. That is the picture that political and civic crooks seek to invoke when they speak sneeringly of muckrakers.

But Theodore Roosevelt, who has always been something of an idol to me, had another definition. His muckraker worked in the muck of corruption so that civic health might be restored. In that sense, the one in which Steffens and Baker and Tarbell exposed graft and venality so that the people might enforce reforms, I am a muckraker.

I did not become one by deliberate choice. I hate foul odors and repulsive sights and discordant sounds as much as you do. It is not pleasant to have strangers assume, whenever I approach them professionally, that because I have done so much muckraking elsewhere I have eyes for nothing else. There is no pleasure in the company of cheap knaves who have fallen out with their fellow thieves and are ready to tell all.

Yet somebody has to do unpleasant tasks, and he who achieves a certain success with them is liable to be saddled with more than his share. Moreover, I have to confess that there is a pleasing thrill at the end to making a garden bloom where once was quicksand covered with fetid decay.

After eight years of investigating and campaigning I am proudest of two things—one, that never in that time has a suit for libel been filed because of anything I have written, though I have hit hard and often and with little reserve; the other, that of all the public reforms I have set out to achieve, only one is not within easy reach of complete accomplishment.

Once, to my knowledge, I did commit a libel. Reviewing news reports of the Seabury investigation, which took place while I was temporarily out of newspaper work and absent from New York, I misinterpreted the part played by a corporation. Fortunately the error was so obviously unintentional and without malice that the offended victim accepted a correction without unpleasantness. That episode impressed upon me the necessity of going back to source documents in controversial matters, and of checking carefully upon what for my purposes might be only secondary material.

I have been threatened with suits, often enough. One lawyer benefactor and beneficiary of Judge Manton's told his friends that if I dared mention his name he would sue. I have mentioned his name in print, frequently. I expect to mention it again when United States Attorney Cahill proceeds with the next step of the almost endless aftermath of Manton's downfall.

State Senator Julius Berg threatened, on the floor of the legislature's upper house, to sue for a story in which I told how he had helped his brother organize a pseudomedical group over which the committee headed by Senator Berg had jurisdiction. He never did, and never will. Later he killed himself while Tom Dewey waited to question him about his association with the late Dutch Schultz, and with former Motor Vehicles Commissioner Charles A. Harnett, whose indictment for taking $67,000 in bribes has not been pressed because Harnett is hopelessly insane.

Even Manton, himself, the day of my first story, hinted

vaguely and with a noticeable lack of heat that he might sue.

Such threats are the everyday annoyance of the muck-raker, like mosquitoes in a cedar grove, but they mean nothing if the investigation has been well done and its results accurately reported.

A source of greater annoyance are those who, realizing fully that they have no grounds for suit and knowing well that, with our paper at least, a phoney suit will get them nowhere at all, insist upon bringing delegations to argue about facts that speak for themselves.

Such was the Metropolitan Life Insurance Company, when I stirred the whole insurance industry with a description of the evils of weekly payment industrial life insurance three years ago. The Metropolitan sells nearly half of the almost three billion dollars worth of such insurance that is written yearly, and the furore and reforms that grew out of my articles cut heavily into that profitable business.

Such was the National City Bank, when I printed from court records allegations of how that bank permitted the estate entrusted to it by a former director to depreciate, while it protected itself during the early days of the depression.

Such was Albert W. Greenfield, the Philadelphia banker, who brought a lawyer-associate when he came to protest that, although he could disprove no item of my article about his relations with Circuit Judge J. Warren Davis, we should not print the facts because our articles were being picked up and distorted by Greenfield's mortal enemy, Moe Annenberg.

Infrequently I have been confronted with that irritating refuge of him who has talked too freely, through carelessness or in irritation, and has realized his error only when he sees in print what he said, stripped of the intervening inconsequentials with which a skillful reporter disarms his subject and disguises his goal.

In connection with my first major investigation, a lawyer who is now a judge interpreted for me a situation in which he was not concerned, by pointing out that the Appellate Division, second highest of our state courts, is not above noting political considerations. I was interviewing him for publication, and I quoted him. I have no means of knowing what happened when the article appeared, but in a similar situation later I know that another lawyer was put under intense judicial pressure to retract. In any event, my friend called up to say that he had been misunderstood, and I, realizing that probably he had to get out of a hole in a hurry, collaborated in concocting a "correction" which saved him without leaving me in the false position of having misquoted.

The then Tammany Comptroller, General Charles W. Berry, went to Europe at a time when the city was on the verge of bankruptcy. While he was in Europe we learned that the public was paying for his vacation, and printed the fact. He returned on the liner Berengaria, which docked the morning of my last day before vacation. With reporters from other papers, I went down the Bay on the seven o'clock customs cutter, boarded the Berengaria at Quarantine, and we made a bee line to ask Berry about the suite the taxpayers had bought him across the corridor from J. P. Morgan's. As the only reporter present who specialized on city affairs, I took the lead in pressing the city's $35,000-a-year fiscal chief on the matter.

"Our editors will want us to remind you that the public is interested in that two or three thousand dollars—whatever it was—for which you drew a voucher for expenses?" I told him.

There had been two vouchers, the first for $2,500 and the second for $600.

"The answer to that is brief," said the comptroller tartly. "It is none of their damned business."

"Perhaps what the public wants to know is whether such a voucher does not require some specific appropriation," I suggested, with an attempt at tact by which I hoped Berry's ire might be cooled enough so that we might get some explicit answers.

"The answer to that is the same," said the comptroller, yet more irritably. No further attempts, either by tact or by direct pressure, could get him to talk on the topic.

No politician intentionally would say for quotation, in

so many words, "the public be damned." But when I went over my notes, preparatory to telephoning from the pier to a rewrite man, I found that was what Comptroller Berry really had said. Since we were in the midst of an open and bitter campaign to upset Tammany, whose second highest elected official was Berry, I had a nugget. We wrote:

> Mr. Berry was positive in his belief that it was some Republican who started the rumor that books in the Municipal Reference Library contained all the facts he could be seeking in Europe. Likewise he gave to newspaper men who reported that the public was interested in the check he drew for expense money the brief and unequivocal reply:
> "It's none of their damned business."

That night I went to Vermont. There I received word that Berry had announced that he would not seek re-election as Comptroller, had admitted the vouchers, had explained that the $3,100 was requisitioned through a secretary's error and that he had repaid it after his return—and after the ship interview—and had denied flatly that he had repudiated the public's interest in the matter. It was, he said, only newspaper editors he had invited to be damned.

He had been "grossly misquoted." Reporters who, without consultation together over what he had said, interpreted their notes to direct Berry's remarks at the public, included those for the Times and the Herald-Tribune, who had all day to consider their meaning and were not working in the rush of afternoon reporters.

The only other person I remember who has challenged the accuracy of my quotation was the late Governor Charles M. Smith of Vermont. He did not raise the question with me or my paper, but with Vermont newspapers which questioned him after reading my articles.

While I was vacationing on my Vermont farm and visiting friends about the state, I had heard ugly rumors about defalcations in the Rutland bank of which Governor Smith was president. When I returned to New York, there was a short interval before the fall campaign, and I was sent back to check into these reports, which the local newspaper had handled only as isolated incidents when a public record was made.

I found that Governor Smith had discharged a bookkeeper from his bank who was caught after nine years of peculation, during which he had embezzled $251,000 of bank funds with which to speculate in stocks.

The governor had then held his silence while his home city employed this embezzler as its assistant treasurer. He had not notified any of those who were taking a thief into their hire to handle the public's money in Vermont's second largest city.

After gathering all of the facts I went to Montpelier, to see Governor Smith in his offices at the state capitol.

When I arrived he had a visitor. I sat in his secretary's office and watched through the open door as they talked in the gubernatorial chamber. His secretary went out to lunch, leaving me alone.

"When that man goes, walk in and talk with the governor," she told me before she left. I did.

The governor was informal, affable, frank, and gave no indication that he recognized the implications of what he said so freely.

"No, I did not inform City Treasurer Will Davis that he was employing an embezzler. Neither did I inform the National Surety Corp., which bonded him for the city job. I thought he was just a sort of glorified bookkeeper. I didn't know he was bonded."

As lieutenant-governor, Smith had been one of five committeemen representing Vermont banks in negotiations with the Federal Deposit Insurance Corporation, which insured the deposits in Smith's bank after it had written off $191,000 of the bookkeeper's embezzlements out of surplus. He did not tell the FDIC about the large theft, he said, or how it had been cared for. Neither did any of his bank associates, when four examiners came to the bank.

Though he confessed that he did not know how it had been possible for a mere bookkeeper to get away with $251,000, over a period of nine years, before he was caught, he said he had not asked the Commissioner of

Banking, his appointee and his responsibility, to look over the state's auditing system for loopholes.

"I am glad to talk with a newspaperman about this case," he said. But when I put together the isolated facts into their damning whole, and Vermont newspapers saw their implications and asked him about them, Governor Smith was quoted in denial that he had ever seen me or talked with me!

I know of nothing I have done which better illustrates the difference between two wholly different schools of newspaper reporting, in both of which I have worked.

One method is to report exactly what happened, through the eyes of others, without interpretation and with a minimum of background. It makes a record which, in theory, is completely unbiased and non-controversial. A reader of sufficient pertinacity and thoroughness, with an excellent memory and unusual powers of analysis and synthesis, can take the facts over a period of time and read into them all their significance.

The other is to present news on the theory that only professional news-gatherers have the time and the facilities to put together a whole sequence of apparently unrelated events so that each helps to interpret the others, and so that all form an intelligently intelligible but innately unbiased story.

At least some Vermont newspapers had printed most of the relevant facts of the Rutland bank scandal, but none had troubled to put them together and then to ask Governor Smith a few simple, enlightening questions. I was told, before I went to Montpelier, that the governor would not talk. To me he talked freely and without reserve. I do not flatter myself that it was my approach—which usually works better upon acquaintance than at first meeting—which led Governor Smith to talk to me. I believe that he would have answered the same pertinent questions with equal readiness for any reporter who called at his office and asked them.

It was just an illustration of the two methods of reporting. I feel that it demonstrates, to anybody who believes that voters and taxpayers are entitled to an accounting from public servants, the superior merits of the interpretive method.

But the interpretation of facts, by their assembling into orderly pattern, is muckraking, when those facts add up to prove that a public servant has proven faithless to his trust. So I am a muckraker.

It would be less than frank to claim that every time I investigate and expose some misdeed I am trying to correct a general evil. Newspapers are involved day by day and hour by hour in an intensive competition to get most of the best news first. Their work is so systematized that there is rarely opportunity for a genuine news scoop of the sort glamorized in fiction and drama. Most exclusive news is the result of digging conscientiously into a background, putting together apparently unrelated facts, and getting the story. I do my share of that. Such disclosures I do not consider as campaigns, nor do I consider that their failure to result in correction indicates the failure of a campaign.

More of my work has lain in the field of finding an evil, exploring it, publicizing it, and then keeping up pressure, publicly and privately, upon the responsible agencies until reform has been accomplished.

One day, for example, an unprominent Brooklyn lawyer and real estate man came to our office with a story about how the city had been defrauded enormously with the connivance of Jimmy Walker, when he was mayor. This informant had been there before and had been turned down. I was interested in his story, which was well documented, but it looked dangerous and I was busy, so I laid it aside.

Later, when I had spare time, I went over the records he had cited and verified his story completely.

A Long Island banker named Warren Leslie, brother-in-law of former United States Senator James A. O'Gorman and nightclub playmate of Jimmy Walker, had bought up some land at Bergen Beach, where more than forty years ago Percy G. Williams, founder of what became the Keith-Albee circuit, tried unsuccessfully to create a rival to Coney Island. Part of it was ordinary waterfront upland, and part was covered the year around by the greatest open sewer in the world, from which rose such noxious gases that the eyes of children forced by poverty to live in the neighborhood were made sore by the fumes.

When Leslie bought the property, the City had been talking for four years about taking it for an amusement park. Four months after Leslie bought it, the administration headed by his friend Walker voted formally to take the land. Leslie's title to the land under water was so questionable that a title insurance company refused to sell him a policy protecting his ownership. After the Board of Estimate rescinded a previous authorization for such action, his friend Mayor Walker signed what in effect was a deed giving Leslie the city's title to this land.

Then the city bought from Leslie the land which Mayor Walker had just quit-claimed to him from the city. The part taken by the city had cost Leslie $325,000. A Supreme Court justice awarded him $2,569,909 for it, four months after he bought it. By the time I got into the picture Leslie's claim, with interest, had climbed to $3,-700,000. More important, by that time the city's right to appeal the exorbitant price to a higher court had been permitted to lapse, because of the city's failure to act. Under the law, nothing more could be done unless the new Fusion administration was able to prove that there was fraud in connection with the transaction.

I wrote three articles on the affair. If I had been raking muck in the Paul Bunyan manner, that would have been the end. We had our sensation—a good one—and our interest would have been exhausted. But that is not my conception of public service.

Before the last article had been printed I went over to see the city's chief law officer, Corporation Counsel Paul Windels. He was out, so I talked with his chief assistant, who asked a bureau head to look into my story. Within a few days the report came back. There was nothing to it. There had been no fraud, and the time for appeal on any other ground was gone.

Then I learned through the local Community Councils, which had been interested in the situation, that the bureau head who threw down my story had been employed for six years as attorney for a title company which accepted the mayor's deed to his friend at its face value and sold insurance on its basis. I printed this, and talked with Windels, who promised to look into it.

Six months later the city of New York moved formally to vacate the exorbitant award on the ground of fraud. Windels had assigned Phillip W. Haberman, Jr., one of the most diligent, intelligent probers I have known, to the transaction, and he not only had verified my claim of fraud but had found much that could not have been ascertained without the powers of subpoena and of examination under oath which the Commissioner of Accounts, New York's official investigating agency, brought into the inquiry.

A year after my first disclosure a Supreme Court justice set aside the award, on the ground that the transaction had been tainted with fraud. Leslie hired John W. Davis, one-time solicitor general, ambassador to the Court of St. James's and Democratic presidential candidate, an attorney of eminent respectability in the community, to argue his appeal before the Appellate Division.

Almost two years after I started work on the inquiry, the Appellate Division upheld the city and threw out the award, in a decision the like of which veteran attorneys had never seen. Under the law there was only one ground on which the award could be upset—and that was fraud. The Appellate Division said there was no fraud. But it upset the award, nevertheless, and did not trouble to explain how such a thing could be!

Eventually this strange decision itself was upheld by the state's highest court, in Albany, and after a new trial Leslie was given an award of only $585,000, a saving of $3,250,000 including interest.

It took about two years and a half of work, at times intensive and sometimes intermittent, to complete this single investigation. I spent more than a year on the Fire Department's practice of rigging specifications so as to bar the products of the world's greatest manufacturer of fire-fighting equipment, and permit only favored firms to bid. It took months to insure prosecution of a ring of politicians and printers who had defrauded the state and city of hundreds of thousands of dollars. All have been barred from further sales, and some are under indictment.

One of the most troublesome bits of digging I ever did lasted for nearly two months, required the equivalent of more than a full work-week, was completely successful, and resulted in a single story on an inside page which attracted no great attention.

I had learned that Mayor O'Brien owned a number of properties which had not paid their taxes and water rents to the city, though the mayor had a good income for years and was urging other property owners to pay up. The properties were held in the name of a corporation, which had dummy incorporators and whose offices denied that O'Brien had any connection with it.

For weeks, after initial failure to prove the connection, I spent spare moments digging here and there. At last I was rewarded. As a matter of routine but with no hope of success, I checked the mayor's statements to the Board of Elections when he registered as a voter. There I found that he had said in one year that he owned the home in which he lived—which was one of the fourteen held in the name of the mysterious Hecman Realty Co., Inc. From then on all was clear sailing, and I was able to show that the mayor owed the city $48,000.

I have devoted considerable time and study to Aaron J. Levy, one of our Supreme Court justices now in his second fourteen-year term, whose handling of patronage was touched upon in a previous chaper.

In 1937 I participated in an unsuccessful attempt to prevent his re-election. Through a lawyers' committee which I persuaded Adolph Berle to head, I made available to the city's press much additional information about Justice Levy's activities. In this we were aided by another committee formed by the late Samuel Untermyer, great Jewish leader and ardent Tammanyite, who enlisted in the drive because he said that Levy's presence on the bench brought disgrace upon Jewry as a whole. The Association of the Bar of the City of New York, breaking precedent of long standing, took an active part in that drive against Levy, although lawyers ordinarily refrain from any active opposition to judges from fear of reprisal when they have to appear before those judges in court.

Owney Madden, one of New York's most notorious racketeers and beer barons, on the lam, timed his surrender for the day before Judge Levy was to sit in Special Term, Part II, where habeas corpus proceedings were returnable. His application came before Levy, and was granted on evidence which the Appellate Division and the Court of Appeals ruled afterward had no value as proof.

Justice Levy left his bench and traveled to Massachusetts, and there appealed in court, with whatever of weight his position as a jurist might lend, for his friend

Frank Cohen, who was denounced from the bench by a federal judge as prime mover in a fraud, and described by Insurance Commissioner Francis J. De Celles of Massachusetts as the wrecker of a dozen insurance companies operating in 28 states.

Justice Levy appointed his brother-in-law, the dentist Max Herbst, as receiver of the Oliver Cromwell Hotel, from which Herbst got $57,197.80 in commissions while the hotel in three years was losing under his management $126,313.69 plus interest and depreciation, though its rooms were from two-thirds to nine-tenths filled.

While Levy owed the Bank of United States $141,500, he sat in two cases in which the bank was interested. When we disclosed this fact, the judge claimed that he had not known he still was indebted to the bank when he heard those cases. We produced photographic copies of dividend checks he had received and banked, during the period, on the collateral he said that he thought had been sold to pay his debt. When eventually the banking department did sell this collateral, after the bank had been closed with great loss to the public, it failed by $85,300 to cover Levy's indebtedness.

I have given more than passing attention also to County Judge George W. Martin, a member of the highest criminal court in Brooklyn. I became interested in Judge Martin's attitude toward criminal justice five years ago, when Commissioner of Accounts Paul Blanshard and

Mayor LaGuardia were trying to clean up the bail bond situation. Judge Martin was scornful and bitter about what he described as "the hysteria for bail bond convictions," when he reproved a grand jury for indicting 43 persons for illegal bail bond activity.

Commissioner Blanshard permitted me to go over the records of his inquiry, and from them I learned that at one time 28 properties in Brooklyn were pledged for bail totalling $477,580, though the entire equity behind the bonds totalled only $144,900.

"Neither in Brooklyn nor New York has anybody been discovered at the head of a bail bond or policy racket," Judge Martin told the grand jury, but I disclosed the sworn admission of a bondsman that he was the regular agent of three policy bankers, who maintained a group of property owners for the purpose of bailing out any policy collector working for one of these bankers. One building, in which this bondsman had invested only $700, earned him $2,850 in six months.

With this as background, in the course of the Manton investigation I came across records of Judge Martin's financial involvements, and turned them over to Murray Davis, our reporter assigned to the Amen inquiry. He in turn gave them to John Harlan Amen, who had been appointed to investigate allegations of official misconduct in Brooklyn. Amplified and elaborated almost beyond recognition, this material went before the court and the state senate, but Martin was acquitted by both.

In New York's fire department, headed by a career commissioner appointed and maintained by Mayor La-Guardia, I found unsavory conditions of which most have been corrected. For a long time I studied them, and wrote stories about them. Much of the material was highly technical, and had to be reduced to simple facts which the lay public could understand. I had to work with informants who I had every reason to believe were professional bribers, with informants who were vitally interested in the outcome of my studies, with informants who were frightened half out of their wits lest Commissioner John J. McElligott learn that they had talked with me.

One of my good sources of information later was accused publicly, before the Board of Aldermen, of trying to influence public officials. One was indicted later for bribery in another matter, connected with city sales, but never prosecuted. One ranking fire department official, wrongly suspected of having given me certain information, was moved from the best fire station in the city to the worst.

Nevertheless, by sticking to provable facts, I was able to move through this maze without once getting tripped, and through a civil suit filed against the city, in which the situation was explored thoroughly on a sworn record, I was able to prove the correctness of my reports and to obtain reforms.

The situation was anomalous in that a reform mayor's department head was punishing a manufacturer for telling the truth, under oath, against Tammany's Mayor Walker.

The American-La France-Foamite Corporation has been for years the recognized leader among manufacturers of fire-fighting apparatus. Its president, Charles B. Rose, testified in the Seabury inquiry that an omnibus company in which also he was an officer had contributed to Mayor Walker's campaign chest, and had hired Walker's friend, State Senator John A. Hastings, as a "contact man" for $1,000 a week, which, he supposed, "went to a society called Tammany." This was part of the famous Equitable bus scandal, which led to Walker's resignation and departure for Europe.

Though the American-La France Company had been supplying more than its share of New York City equipment theretofore, after its president's testimony against Walker it was written off the books. Up to the time I began investigation, the company had been unable to sell the city a single piece of apparatus, though Tammany had been out of power for more than a year.

I found that the specifications were so rigged that while competitors could bid on essentially standard equipment, American-La France would have had to build to order, at exorbitant cost, to supply what the city de-

manded. I found that in buying hydrant-thawing devices, the department had pasted the specifications for one
favored make onto the requisition form, so that nobody
else could compete except with an expensive custom-made
product. I found that while old fire hose was bursting
in use, endangering firemen and impeding their work,
62,500 feet of new hose made by a leading manufacturer,
and acceptable to the Purchase Department, the National
Board of Fire Underwriters and the United States Bureau
of Standards, lay unused in a warehouse—rejected by
Commissioner McElligott. I found that the little suburban village of Great Neck, L. I., with no building higher
than five or six stories, had a better pumper than New
York, with its mighty skyscrapers, because Commissioner
McElligott declined even to look at the superior American-La France product.

As a result of this campaign, the city's specifications
were revised to provide for the best. It proved that the
best was something that no company was manufacturing,
so that all could compete on the same basis of specially-
built equipment.

Leading directly from this, I explored a proposed revision of the city's fire code which would have given to a
subsidiary of E. I. DuPont De Nemours a complete
monopoly on refrigerants used in air conditioning and
major refrigerating installations in the city, based upon a

Board of Fire Underwriters' study which the DuPont company had financed.

One successful campaign in which I took pleasure was initiated by Westbrook Pegler, who fought it out in his nationally-syndicated column for months, while I did a factual news-column survey to reinforce his sledge-hammer blows. This was the fight to extend federal and state income taxes to all public officials.

Until we won this battle, it was the established rule that under Supreme Court decisions extending back to the earliest days, no state could tax a salary derived from the federal government, nor could the federal government tax salaries paid by the states. This had been modified only to the extent that the courts, one by one, declared that a few specific agencies were proprietary, rather than governmental, and so did not come under the rule.

The whole idea was a highly legalistic application of the unchallengeable truism that "the power to tax is the power to destroy." By some mental quirk judges, who by this decision were spared income taxes, ruled that if the federal government's income tax were to apply to salaries of state officials, the federal government would be in position to tax the state out of existence, and vice versa. If there had been enacted a tax which fell heavier upon government salaries than upon other income, the courts' rulings would have been quite correct. But an income tax levied equally upon salaries from whatever source could not destroy a coördinate government without destroying all industry and all commerce.

Early in 1937 Pegler began attacking the patent absurdity and the manifest unfairness of such a system. His articles struck the popular fancy. It became evident that the tax-wearied public was in a mood to express itself effectively, if it were given the material. Pegler was utilizing striking and effective examples, but he had to produce a column a day, on various subjects so as not to weary his audience, and had no time for the necessary digging. I was assigned to get facts.

It did not take long to discover that at least 300,000 persons employed by federal and state governments, at annual salaries aggregating not less than $700,000,000, were escaping income taxes while their less fortunate fellows, earning less in private employment and without that security of tenure and those pension rights which accrue to governmental employees, were having to pay the bills.

In New York state alone I found the government employees were escaping at least $2,500,000 of income taxes. I found 531 state and local employees, more than half with salaries ranging from $6,000 upward to $28,500, who did not have to pay even one income tax, because they were "constitutional officers" and the courts had ruled that to make them pay the same taxes as other persons would be equivalent to decreasing the salaries fixed for them by the constitution.

I was able to show that the chief justice of the Supreme Court himself, while he was governor of New York at the time the income tax amendment was adopted, did not believe that government employees were exempt from the taxes levied upon others.   I found that the state was exempting federal employees, though there was no court decision requiring it and though attorneys-general had not agreed whether they should be exempt or not.

The New York legislature acted first, at the next session after Pegler's articles and my studies.   Then Congress acted.   Now government workers have to pay taxes, like any other citizens who enjoy the things that governments provide with the proceeds of taxes.

One of the unfinished businesses which has gone far enough to guarantee that it will not be a failure, whether or not it is carried to complete success, was in connection with a printing scandal of which I had inklings for some time before it broke into the open.   This exemplifies another phase of newspaper campaigning—the opening up of malefaction uncovered by other agencies and threatening to die without prosecution.

Early in 1938 an anonymous letter to District Attorney Thomas E. Dewey told about a private investigator who had discovered by accident that at least one public employee had been bribed by the company which controlled city and state printing, and that after his retirement from government service he was being carried on the printer's payroll.

Two detectives attached to Dewey's office were sent to the plant of the Burland Printing Co., where they asked questions for about two hours, and then reported back that there was no evidence of anything wrong.

About two weeks later a similar anonymous letter went to Commissioner of Investigations William B. Herlands, a former Dewey assistant, who assigned it to Louis Yavner, one of his most trusted examiners. Yavner went into the records, and there obtained enough leads to break down key witnesses and get an astounding story of widespread corruption, involving the state's supposedly impeccable assistant comptroller, a Tammany district leader very close to President Roosevelt, the recently deceased boss of Albany county, whose misdeeds Dewey heaped upon Governor Lehman's shoulders in the next fall's campaign, and many lesser figures. But this scandal Dewey did not use, because his usually efficient office had muffed it.

The state's relief organization, purchasing printing in large quantities with city money, had as its buyer of printing a former inmate of a state asylum, who had been moved from one city agency because of frequent drunkenness—the same habit which had caused his commitment to the asylum.

In the summer of 1936 his wife retained a private

investigator to obtain evidence for a divorce. She told the investigator that while cleaning out a closet, she found in an old hat $6,000. Her husband's salary was not more at any time than $40. The investigator's work was effective, and Mrs. Dolan got her divorce. Her erstwhile husband was so impressed that he asked the investigator to do some work for him.

He told the investigator that he was being paid weekly by the Burland Printing Company, because he had helped it get a monopoly on relief printing before he was fired by the state for drunkenness, unauthorized absences, and disturbances created by a woman who visited him at the office. He asked the investigator to persuade the Burland Company to give him a lump sum settlement, so he could leave the country.

The investigator thought Dolan was intoxicatedly talking through his hat, and told a lawyer friend as a matter of idle gossip. The lawyer friend, by sheer coincidence, shared offices with counsel for the Burland Company, to whom he passed the story on. This lawyer paid the investigator $1,000 and expenses to get Dolan in a hotel room, where a dictaphone had been installed, and draw out his story, which was that he had received $18,000 from the printing company in bribes. This turned out to be a considerable underestimate.

Part of this was the story written anonymously to Dewey, and later to Herlands. When the lead was followed through to the end, with Dewey's assistant, Murray Gurfein, taking over in later stages, evidence was obtained that hundreds of thousands of dollars had been spent by this company to bribe politicians and office-holders so as to obtain control over millions of dollars a year of public printing.

An anonymous tipster brought part of the story to our office, and I was sent to check it. I found that nobody knew all the facts, and those who knew them best were reluctant to talk. I was able to establish, however, that the Burland Company had admitted defrauding the city of large sums, which were estimated by the city at $500,-000, and had agreed to compromise them at $225,000.

I was told by well-informed sources that in return for this settlement the city was going to drop the matter without publicity or punishment. This I forestalled by printing enough of the story to place public officials under public scrutiny.

Months later, I was able to prepare a memorandum pointing out that the heads of the Burland Printing Company confessed to having paid to William Solomon, one of the Tammany leaders closest to the President, almost $100,000 for his services in fixing the awarding of public printing by city and state; to Deputy Comptroller Charles H. Mullens, a Republican of highest repute, almost as much for helping with the state awards; to Dolan some $30,000 for his part as buyer of relief printing; to the late Edward O'Connell, Democratic boss of Albany, a large sum for his help in controlling state printing; and to a number of lesser public employees substantial if less impressive sums.

Eventually Dewey indicted Mullens and Solomon. But his jurisdiction was limited to crimes committed within New York county, and many of these were not of official concern to him.

One day after lunching with Lieutenant-Governor Poletti, I told him something about the situation. Soon a state inquiry was launched, under the recently retired head of the state's highest appeals court, with a close personal friend of Poletti's as counsel. At public hearings officials of the Burland Company and its principal rival for state business told the sordid story under oath.

The conspirators were barred from future state business. When the next year's contracts were awarded, it was at a saving of more than $200,000.

Chapter Twelve

A FREE PRESS

⋆ 12 ⋆

A Free Press

GEORGE MORRIS, veteran political reporter, likes to tell about a dinner which he attended in Brooklyn some years ago, at a time when one of New York's sporadic drives against judicial corruption was under way.

While Morris was visiting with a group of politicians and office-holders, a judge who did not know him by sight sauntered up and joined in the conversation, which he soon turned into a monologue invective against newspapers for their criticism of the judiciary. When other expedients failed to divert the judge, an embarrassed listener took the bull by the horns.

"Judge Blank, I wonder if you are acquainted with George Morris of the World-Telegram?" he inquired.

"I wasn't," said the judge, a bit flustered. "Of course, you know my remarks were general, and don't apply to anybody here."

"Don't worry, Judge," retorted Morris, who has a trenchant tongue. "I've heard almost every crook in New York say what you were saying."

More than ever before, newspapers today are under a crossfire of criticism, some of which they deserve and much of which they do not.

Courageous, alert, independent, intelligent newspapers can be—and where they exist they are—the most impregnable bulwarks of a workable democracy. The United States is blessed with a large if not ample supply of such newspapers. Along with them, it has well-meaning but incompetent or unaggressive journals, and a small though too large group of cowardly, perverted and even corrupt hangers-on who bring disgrace upon the whole profession of journalism.

It is proper that the public should distrust newspapers which do not report the news fairly, impartially, truthfully—whether the distortion arises from ignorance, from slovenliness, from bias or from venality. It is inevitable that those who have had experience with the unreliable fringe of newspaperdom should retain a lurking suspicion of the entire profession.

But it is entirely unfair, and very harmful to our democratic processes, for shallow cynics or self-serving demagogues to promulgate the idea much too often voiced:

"You can't believe anything you read in the newspapers."

Speaking from the inside, after quarter of a century of working experience on newspapers ranging from a country weekly with 300 paid circulation and 240 column inches of advertising, up to a foremost metropolitan daily with more than 400,000 circulation and the greatest paid advertising volume in New York, I am prepared to assert flatly that you can believe almost everything that you read in most newspapers.

Except for certain well-recognized journalistic vehicles of distortion, most newspaper departures from fact are unintentional and are regretted as much by publishers and editors and reporters as by readers.

Newspapers are made by men and women, who except for their specialized training differ in no wise from their brothers and sisters who earn livings as lawyers, doctors, merchants, manufacturers, financiers, clerks, farmers and laborers. When you can point to one of these employments or any other in which no mistakes are made, it will be time to condemn newspapers because, now and again, they go off the deep end with statements that prove erroneous.

We who work on reputable newspapers do make mistakes, and the newspaper world has its disreputable fringe in which deliberate frauds are perpetrated. But we are not like potatoes. We are like eggs. One rotten potato will spoil the whole barrel. One rotten egg may nauseate the eater, but it has no effect upon good eggs in the carton.

Newspapers as an institution are under crossfire today in large part because of their very virtues—because they have accepted a responsibility which may well not be theirs, and have turned the spotlight upon corruption that is deliberate and upon negligence and incompetence that are unintentional.

Those who do wrong, whether by inadvertence, in passion, through incompetence or with malice, shun the limelight and hate that newspaper which tells the world about their faults. No man sees his own fault as others see it, and no man who recognizes his own fault likes to have it told to others. When the evidence of what has come about gradually is gathered together, and presented in damning epitome, the perpetrator is left to explain weakly:

"It wasn't like that at all. It was all a mistake. The newspaper has lied."

Every man has his friends who believe him.

When those in high places make serious errors, and do irreparable injury to the city, the state or the nation to which they are responsible, they know that their own fames and fortunes must suffer from newspaper exposure and criticism, and they likewise protest vehemently that "the newspaper has lied."

The political parties, which under our system of government assume responsibility for their protégés, and too often their churches and their lodges come to the aid of discredited corruptionists, and they too join in the outcry: "The newspaper has lied."

President Roosevelt and his entourage have gone further, on the sound military axiom that "the best defense is a vigorous offense," and have engaged for years in a deliberate campaign to create general public distrust of newspapers.

I, too, have heard almost every crook I have ever known criticize the newspapers for telling of his crookedness, and every incompetent for exposing his incompetence, and evangelists of many causes for not swallowing whole their quack nostrums. With all due respect for the sincerity of some of these, I am prepared to stand firmly upon the Scripps-Howard slogan, which I believe is the best statement yet coined of a newspaper's duty and privilege:

"Give light, and the people will find their own way."

Newspapers make many mistakes. Afternoon newspapers make more than morning newspapers. That is inevitable in the hustle and bustle of news gathering. I have never been in a city room that would satisfy the requirements of stage and screen. I have never seen a news staff running and yelling, any more than I have ever seen a besotted reporter prop himself in a telephone booth while he sent in a world-shaking scoop and simultaneously cursed his superiors all ways from Sunday and got away with it. But newspapers work under high pressure, against almost split-second deadlines. Afternoon papers may have as many as six editions in eight hours, for each of which an important story must be brought up to date. There is no time for mulling over words, rewriting whole stories, checking every possible source for every angle on every news story.

Reputable newspapers print nothing which has not been obtained or verified from the best possible sources. When such newspapers print erroneous news they do it because lawyers, doctors, public officials, merchants, manufacturers, housewives, and all of those classifications who read and often criticize the papers have themselves given false or incorrect information to reporters.

Reporters stand on the fringe of the world's activity, watching it, weighing it, checking it, telling about it. Obviously, no newspaper can maintain enough observers to be at every spot at which something might happen. Therefore reporters are maintained at strategic points, from which they can learn most quickly what is happening and either go there or check with those who were there.

Newspapers occupy no preferred position by virtue of which they can place witnesses under oath, command production of their records, and force their way onto the scene of action. All that they do is on sufferance. Reporters carry police cards or wear press badges, in most cities large enough so that they are not known personally by all public servants. Such cards admit them, at their own risk from bandits' guns, fire-wracked walls, exploding bombs or angry mobs, to the scene of action, so long as the policeman or the fireman on the spot does not choose to say:

"Reporter, eh? That don't mean nuthin' to me."

Such credentials identify reporters to public officials and private news sources, but that is all. They do not say: "This reporter is entitled to your full confidence, and you must tell him what he wants to know." Rather, they say: "This man is a reporter. If you want his newspaper to know what he asks, you can tell him. Otherwise, hold your tongue, for whatever you say may be used against you."

Reporters obtain much of their news at second hand, from those who by chance were present when the event occurred.

Some years ago a Boston dramatist wrote a playlet which required ninety seconds—a minute and a half—to produce. He invited seventeen prominent Boston business and professional men, a much higher grade of audience than the reporter must depend upon, to witness the first and only presentation of that sketch.

After watching what required ninety seconds to present, these seventeen intelligent men—who had watched the playlet with full knowledge that they were on their mettle to observe accurately, and not in the casual, lackadaisical manner of chance spectators—retired to separate rooms without consultation, and each wrote a description of what he had seen.

Of the seventeen, not one reported the same as any other, and not one reported what actually had taken place.

Most events important enough to require newspaper coverage last longer than ninety seconds. Most are witnessed at first hand by casual observers, who have no idea that they will be asked for an accurate report and make no attempt to note everything and remember it. Then a reporter comes along, and talks with as many as still are on hand and willing to talk, and tries from their incomplete, inaccurate and uninterested recollections to reconstruct a complete, accurate, vivid story of what occurred.

It is a great wonder, and a tribute to reportorial energy, assiduity and expertness, that newspaper accounts are as lucidly accurate as they are.

Not long after I went onto the staff of the old New York Telegram, I was the object of a biting criticism written by Roy Howard, which remained on the bulletin board for several days.

At that time I was on rewrite—one of the men who take information by telephone from reporters on the scene and from the coöperative news agencies, gather it together and rewrite the facts into news form for publication.

A very austere and aristocratic Park Avenue jewelry store—of the type which has no show windows and few show cases, where frock-coated gentlemen meet custom-

ers at the door, escort them ceremoniously within, inquire their wishes, and reverently produce masterpieces
of the jewelers' art from remote sanctuaries—had been
held up and robbed.

We had two reporters at the scene and several others
at vital points where the police investigation was center-
ing. The coöperative news agency had perhaps twice as
many, from whom they were forwarding reports rapidly.
I had to take information from all of these, weigh it,
analyze it, sift out errors, judge which of frequently con-
tradictory facts to accept, and write a composite story very
fast.

As almost invariably happens in the early stages of such
stories, there was a wide disparity among various estimates
of the loss. Some sources said $10,000, some said $250,000,
and others gave figures in between. The higher figure was
given early by a captain of detectives to one of our more
reliable reporters. The smaller figure was given much
later by Police Commissioner Grover Whalen.

For an early edition only the $250,000 figure was avail-
able. Its source was excellent, and I used it. Afterward
it developed that most of the store's stock had been sent
to the Palm Beach winter branch before the robbery, so
that the loss was slight.

In one edition, at least, I was a very inaccurate reporter,
apparently puffing an interesting but not large robbery into
a sensation for the sake of the story. Mr. Howard's criti-

cism expressed the intent of the management, with which I did and do agree fully, to avoid the acceptance of sensational reports without thorough qualification until they have been verified completely. This is the accepted practice of all reliable editors and reporters. But with the best will in the world, we do slip now and again, and the critics sneer:

"You can't believe anything you read in a newspaper."

The best newspaperman is the one with the most friends who trust his accuracy and rely upon his discretion.

Even in a small community the reporter can not observe personally all that happens. In a metropolitan center he can not always even reach, in time for news purposes, those who did happen to be present. He has to depend upon friends—policemen, firemen, doctors, hospital authorities, press agents, clerks, commissioners, mayors, governors and presidents. From any or all of these, he may obtain original news or be able to check the accuracy of information gathered from other sources.

Each of these has his own torch to have carried. Each has his own interests and his friends to protect or to advance. Each has his own bias of pride in achievement, jealousy of rivals, fear of reprisal. Seldom is a news source so fearless and forthright and impartial that information from it can be accepted without corroboration.

When a man of prominence speaks for quotation, unless he utters slander which when printed would be libel, or is unduly unfair or obscene, newspapers feel obliged to report what he has said without accepting responsibility for it. But a considerable proportion of the best news coming from such persons is not in the form of statements for quotation, but of information which we can use on our own responsibility at our own peril, for which the giver will not stand sponsor publicly, and often which he says frankly has come to him as rumor subject to verification. Such material must be checked with the greatest of care, and the reporter with the best friends is most likely to obtain corroboration or disproof most quickly and accurately.

I have been fortunate in my friends. Over a period of eight years they have enabled me to get more than my share of exclusive news stories; to complete successfully a considerable number of investigations and campaigns in many fields spoking outward from the hub of public affairs; to obtain fuller, more accurate and often quicker reports on events of which every newspaper learned simultaneously; and to check rapidly on news stories on which we were beaten temporarily.

Only a genius could be expert on so many subjects as I have covered with a semblance of authority, delving into legal, scientific, actuarial, economic and professional intricacies and writing of them for the scrutiny of persons who have devoted their lives to their study. On second thought, I question if even a genius could be such an expert. And I am far from a genius.

The answer, of course, is friends. Friends who are among the nation's foremost lawyers, who instruct and correct me on my way. Friends who are masters of theoretical and practical economics, of mathematics applied in many differing fields, of engineering and finance and government and industry and commerce. Friends who are actors in almost every branch of the great metropolitan drama. Sometimes they are willing to be given credit for their assistance. More often they prefer to remain in the background, permitting me to pick their minds and exploit my borrowed wisdom for my own prestige.

A friend employed in a public office telephoned one morning to tell me about a conversation the previous evening over the highballs, with an expert in the egg market. He thought it would make an interesting news story and possibly might be of public service.

It seems that while hens were laying their heads off, and farmers were losing money on every egg they could sell, the big grocery chains were holding their profits to an abnormal level which had precipitated an undeclared, unrecognized buyers' strike. Farmers were losing, eggs were rotting, housewives were buying too few eggs and paying too much for them. All this had resulted from an unseasonable January thaw, which fooled the hens into laying unduly. It was bad of itself and it was worse in prospect, because poultrymen had become disgusted with working at a loss, and had begun decapitating their hens, so that when normal winter temperatures returned there would be an actual shortage of egg production.

A couple of days spent in checking enabled me to write two stories on the situation. In the first, I remarked that "there is no known method of forcing the chains to reduce their retail price in accordance with the wholesale cost, so that consumers can use and farmers sell more eggs."

The day after the second story, the retail price of eggs collapsed, with the best eating grade declining six cents a dozen.

No quick campaign that I ever have done has brought so much comment in the trade concerned, or so much favorable reaction from readers. It all resulted from a casual friend's thought of me when he heard something of interest.

After Municipal Court Justice Harold L. Kunstler had resigned during removal proceedings based upon my investigation, Tom Dewey filed disbarment charges against him. These were prosecuted in secret before a referee. I was intensely interested in their outcome, but Dewey is not one of those friends who tells such things in secret, nor would the referee discuss it with me.

While I wondered how I could ascertain the referee's

decision before the Appellate Division's action was given out to all newspapers, a friend telephoned that Kunstler's disbarment had been recommended, and gave me a quite full and completely accurate digest of the reasons cited by the referee.

I wrote the story. Word came that the Appellate Division was greatly perturbed at the leak, and was questioning everybody who was known to have seen the report. My friend was frightened. He heard that I was to be called before the court, and given a choice of disclosing the source of my information or going to jail for contempt. I assured him that I would do the latter, if I had to make the choice, though I much preferred to go on an approaching vacation. It all blew over without trouble.

A report of major importance, worth an eight-column headline in almost every New York newspaper, was ready for publication. It had to be given first to the high official chiefly concerned, who would release it simultaneously to all papers at a time when it would be difficult for afternoon reporters to complete an adequate story for that day. One of the authors lent me a complete copy of the voluminous document two days before completion, so that I could sit in comfort and study it at leisure. When the report was made public, and other reporters rushed to the booths to begin telephoning hasty notes, our story was all in type subject to two easy corrections necessitated by last minute changes in the draft. Ours was the only afternoon newspaper whose readers got the complete story that day.

Other friends collaborated to see that I had the full story of a printing scandal. Because so much of it was potentially libelous until I knew exactly how much Dewey's office was prepared to prove, I could not use it in advance. But when Deputy Comptroller Mullens and District Leader Solomon were indicted, I was able to fill in the gaps out of a ready folder whose contents went far beyond anything yet made public.

It is friends like this that make a reporter look good.

Hardly a day passes that does not bring a letter, a telephone call or a visit from some friend, acquaintance or reader who has information that he believes may interest me. Out of them all, a small percentage offer something we can use. Some of the suggestions have been used or discarded long before. Some are self-serving and of no general interest. Some are rumors which could be explored only at a cost, in time and money, which their importance would not warrant even if there were not at least an even chance that they would prove to be untrue. Some are obviously or demonstrably true, but unprintable because they are not provable under the rules of evidence and therefore unsafe.

Out of them all, we try to select the most interesting and the most likely, in which there is the greatest possibility of combining news interest with public service. Even with this care, much time and effort is wasted on inquiries which prove unproductive.

Campaigning newspapers and their investigating reporters are accused frequently and bitterly of timidity, partisanship, hard-heartedness, and favoritism because of the stories which they decline to investigate or which they turn down after inquiry. Such accusations in general are untrue. Our judgment may be often at fault. Our willingness to go after what looks promising, wherever the chips may fall, should not be questioned.

It seems almost impossible to impress upon anybody except a lawyer that no sane newspaper will accuse its most despised foe of a crime or any moral obliquity on hearsay evidence. We believe many stories, interesting enough to print, which we never do print because they are not supported by obtainable evidence which a court of law would accept in a libel suit. We pride ourselves upon being rather good at digging out carefully hidden facts, but we are not detectives; we are not adept at false-whisker and putty-nose trailing; we are ethically opposed to acquiring documents by unethical means, or to using documents which come to us properly from persons who themselves have obtained them improperly; we can not use those methods of physical and moral persuasion utilized by the police, or those methods of search and seizure available to public prosecutors; many semi-public documents are not open to us. Moreover, we are not endowed for public service, but a commercial institution which has to pay its own way, and we can not turn unlimited man-power into an investigation, backed by large expense accounts.

We are forced, therefore, to reject suggestions which we would enjoy accepting and carrying to a successful conclusion.

I have wasted more time on official and judicial injustices, since I have become an investigating reporter, than upon any other single type of complaint. I could not even guess how many days I have spent in the aggregate, during the past eight years, listening to the harrowing stories of victims of such oppression, and going back and forth with them over their complaints trying to find some crevice in which I could get a finger hold to accomplish something. Usually I fail.

I have in my desk an extensive file on a man who has spent much of his time for several years in the alimony jail, because he can not satisfy the court's inordinate requirements and because his wife will not let him stay out of jail long enough to hold a position. It is a very sad case. I have tried to find some way to help him.

I can not criticize the court unduly, for whatever may have been the judges' wisdom, their acts have been quite proper technically. I can not place all the blame upon the wife, for I believe the husband has been partially at fault. I can not well urge that the husband's faults have been entirely in reaction against the wife's, for unfortunately he has created an atmosphere in which it would be easy for his wife or the court to raise a question whether he is not really the victim of a persecution complex.

A woman came to me, not long since, with an impressive story about how her stepson, an attorney active in politics, had defrauded his ailing father, and eventually had killed him by taking him out in a rowboat in a rainstorm when his father was already on the verge of pneumonia. She gave me perhaps half a dozen specific accusations of fraud against her son. Among other things she told me the assumed name he uses in Communist party activity.

It took some time to convince her that no court in the world would hold her stepson guilty of killing his father, on the facts that she gave, even though they should be well substantiated. As for the other things, I sympathized—but what could I do? Is it of general interest in New York that a son defrauds his father? It is being done every day in every block, more's the pity. How important is it that Joe Doakes is one of the few thousand Communist borers among New York's several million residents? She cared, for he had abused her if her story was true. But I was in no position to devote perhaps a month to putting the finger on one out of a great city's thousands of petty crooks and chiselers, if such he was.

Time after time I have been brought cases which had been fought through the courts to adverse decisions, and asked naïvely to devote a few spare minutes to correcting the injustices of those decisions.

President Roosevelt has gone out of his way time after time to lend the sounding board of his high position to that hoary accusation that newspapers are run from their counting rooms. The most recent occasion was when a group of economic royalists who happen to be pro-Roosevelt established a new afternoon publication which for the present, at least, carries no advertising.

I would not answer for all newspapers if I could. There have been some which were subject to the control of advertisers. There are some which I have reason to believe still omit news which important advertisers would dislike. In my opinion these are very few, seldom large, and so well-recognized in their debasement, that they carry little weight with readers.

I happen to know, of personal experience over a long period, just about how much influence the advertising sales department has over the editorial offices on one newspaper.

Some years ago I was called to the desk of the executive editor, to talk with him and a high business official who was intensely suspicious of the new unemployment insurance law and suggested that we make a study of it. Nobody had to tell me explicitly that this business office man considered the act a calamity and would like to have it repealed. He had not studied it himself, but had gotten his information from business office men of other papers, who felt similarly.

I spent several weeks studying the law, making trips to Washington, to Albany, and to Hartford, the nation's insurance capital. I consulted with social workers, insurance actuaries, Social Security officials, state labor department heads, industrialists, economists, and not a few others.

When I was done, it appeared that the fears voiced by our business office executive were groundless, that unemployment insurance was sound in principle and that in general our state had adopted a sound version. There were a lot of incidental faults in the new set-up, but nothing fundamentally wrong with it.

This I told to the editor and, because of the inquiry's origin, as a matter of personal courtesy to our business office executive. Neither questioned my facts or my conclusions. I wrote a series of eighteen analytical articles. In not one, from beginning to end, was a viewpoint suggested, a conclusion dictated, a fact changed or any slightest attempt made to conform my findings to the wholly different preconceptions of our executive.

Two years later, when benefits became payable under the law, a complete breakdown resulted from a combination of administrative inefficiency and faulty framework. At least some of the trouble arose out of weaknesses I had pointed out in the beginning.

Again I was turned loose with no instructions except

to find out what was wrong. Again I spent some weeks, and traveled to Albany and Washington and Hartford, and consulted with experts in every field, and again I wrote a series of articles. This time there were twelve, and every one expressed exactly what I had found, without suggestion or dictation from anybody.

In conclusion, I made a series of recommendations for statutory and administrative reforms, which I said if adopted would make the unemployment insurance system work. It was scoffed at by the administrators. It has been adopted since that time, with the exception of a single item, and today unemployment insurance in New York is working as smoothly and effectively as any government venture I know.

A cotton broker named Sidney Wolff came in one day to tell me about the evils of weekly payment industrial life insurance. A close friend of the family of Supreme Court Justice Louis D. Brandeis, he had undertaken to put across in New York state a counterpart of that savings bank life insurance which Brandeis fathered in Massachusetts in 1907, before he went on the bench. He wanted our support. His excoriation of industrial life insurance was offered in proof of the need for savings bank insurance.

The things that he said seemed incredible, and I told him so. He gave me literature alleging even more than he had charged. It included an official publication of the federal Labor Department and a book by a reputable Boston social worker. Quick check verified enough key statements in these to suggest that here might be a major evil.

The Metropolitan Life Insurance Company, a substantial advertiser, writes about half of the weekly payment industrial life insurance that is sold. I suggested to the editor that we look into the situation, and outlined the main facts briefly. He approved without hesitation.

I worked on that study for a long time, and eventually wrote eighteen articles. While they were appearing our circulation increased by some six or seven thousand copies daily. In less than a month after the last article, all back numbers containing them had been sold out. So great was the continuing demand that I arranged for a reprint, which went into a second edition and was distributed from coast to coast. The articles created an uproar in the insurance press. The courageous Insurance Examiner of Chicago supported me while most of the others dressed me out in no uncertain language, one southern publication sinking to the level of obscene personal abuse.

The articles appeared in February, after the New York legislature had been in session for nearly two months. There were before the lawmakers a bill authorizing savings bank life insurance and a resolution to investigate weekly payment life insurance, both of which had died unnoticed year after year theretofore. Before March was over both had been adopted, and temporary specific corrective measures had been adopted.

There has been a state legislative investigation, as a result of which most of the statutory changes I recommended now are law. There has been a federal inquiry by the Temporary National Economic Committee, which recently published a study confirming my findings in detail. In several states organized movements for savings bank life insurance have sprung up. The companies' weekly payment industrial business has been hit hard.

In an attempt to regain popular favor, the companies have embarked on a coöperative newspaper advertising campaign. Originally it was intended not to place these advertisements with our paper, which had started all the fuss. But they did. Courageous newspapers seldom suffer for their courage.

Three years ago I wrote from court records a long story very embarrassing to the National City Bank, one of New York's largest financial institutions, which had just arranged to run with us a series of thirteen substantial advertisements.

The original tip on this story came to me through the editor, and the story was approved by him before it ran. After it appeared, a delegation from the bank arrived to expostulate. As is his custom in such matters, the editor laid before them a copy of the story and asked them to point out, paragraph by paragraph, the errors they alleged. They could show none.

One of their number announced that in view of our uncoöperative attitude, it would be necessary for the bank to cancel its plans to advertise with us.

"Will you wait until I call Heath over?" asked the editor. "I'd like him to talk with you, so that he can write a story about the withdrawal of your advertising."

The visitors reconsidered hastily. The advertising was run according to schedule.

To these few examples of the way in which one newspaper defends its freedom to print the news as it sees it, however substantial may be advertisers who are affected, there should be added one other which in itself would prove my thesis.

Among the advertising agencies of the United States, whose patronage is the life blood of any newspaper, I know of none more important than Lord & Thomas. Nor are many individual accounts, if any, more sizable than the American Tobacco Company's advertising for Lucky Strike cigarettes, of which as a matter of court record Lord & Thomas placed as much as $2,800,000 in one depression year. Any newspaper which fears to offend advertisers would hesitate doubly before publicly branding this great advertising agency and this profitable advertiser as principals in a vicious criminal conspiracy.

The information which led to the investigation into

Judge Manton's venality appeared, until after our first article had been published and Manton had resigned, to prove that the head of the Lord & Thomas agency, at the request and as the agent of the American Tobacco Company, had bribed one of our highest judges to sell his decision and his influence in a $10,000,000 lawsuit in which the tobacco company and its officers were defendants.

That is the tentative interpretation with which I went to the editor and asked whether I should investigate. I made the facts and the inferences very clear, because in spite of all previous experiences I realized that here was a very deadly grizzly bear that I proposed to grasp by the tail.

He did not question or hesitate. My assignment was made as simply and as casually as though he were telling me to get a leg art theatrical feature offered by a press agent and blessed by a producer.

When I was ready to write the Manton articles, there was a question in our minds whether Albert Lasker knew who was the beneficiary when he lent $250,000 from which Manton profited. We have learned since that he did not. But the question whether we were about to ruin one or two of our most profitable sources of advertising never was raised by anybody, at any time.

Enormous care was exercised to avoid the most innocent error. We went to the length of weighing whether we could prove before a court even those sidelights which we included so as to be more than fair to Manton and his associates. But never did we consider who was going to be hurt by our revelations.

Just as newspapers are accused of suppressing news which would offend advertisers, so are they accused of searching unduly assiduously for news that will injure persons and institutions which they oppose. There is more to this charge, though much less than professional critics would indicate.

Without denying that sometimes reporters are sent to "get the dirt" on those whom their editors consider undesirable, I should like to cite one illustration of how misconceptions arise in this respect.

Our paper has known for a long time, as has any informed observer, that without the blessing of some administrators but with at least tacit acceptance from others, the Works Progress Administration has been permeated with Communist cells and some of its projects have been predominantly Communistic in operation and fellow travellerish in personnel.

For the second time, not long since, a W. P. A. artist was discharged from the rolls after working into his composition figures which Col. Brehon B. Somervell, the fair but realistic administrator in New York, recognized as Communistic in their significance and at least questionable in their intent. The artist had plausible though not too convincing explanations, and denied flatly that he was a Communist.

We became curious about a supervisory system which permitted the completion of such projects as huge murals, before obnoxious features were discovered, so that the taxpayers' money was gone beyond reclamation before the work was destroyed. For some days we pressed on this point. At the time I was acting as an assistant city editor. Feeling from my own pleasant experiences with Colonel Somervell that the reporter who could not see him must have been too easily put off, I sent another, who had no difficulty in talking with the administrator.

The man who was to write the story, in our office, was new both to our staff and to the city. To bring himself up to date on the controversy's background, he sent to the morgue for clippings of past stories. Going through them, he found that a man obviously the same as the discharged muralist had been imprisoned once for burning an American flag publicly and ceremonially, and had been arrested again for distributing Communist literature.

Naturally we rushed a man to the muralist's home, and obtained his concession that he was the flag-burner and the literature-distributor. Then we printed the story, which other newspapers picked up as soon as they could verify it, the next day.

We were accused by the leftist union to which this muralist belonged of having gone to much trouble to find something with which to smear their fellow traveller. Since we have been very frankly anti-Communist, perhaps some believed this. In fact, our only fault was that every New York newspaper had done slovenly work in the past, so that nobody had checked the files and discovered what should have been included in the first story that mentioned this man's name.

In the ordinary course of events, reputable newspapers take the news as it comes. Their editors decide whether to use each item, and how much space to give it, and how prominently to display it, according to their judgment of its importance and its public interest.

No newspaper can even approach the goal set for and claimed by the New York Times, of printing "all the news that's fit to print." The most voluminous daily papers can give only a cross-section of that relatively small portion of all the news which gets into the editorial rooms.

Every news story has to run the gauntlet of a series of less or more responsible editors, each of whom asks himself automatically a series of questions. Is it true? Is it interesting? Is it important? Is it fit to print? Can it be made fit to print? Is it worth the trouble of making fit to print? How does it compare with the hundreds of other stories competing for limited space?

In the end, a relatively small number of stories passes all the tests and appears in the news columns. Of these, each is graded according to its relative appeal to the public, as judged by the editors. Some uninteresting stories are important, and must be used. Some unimportant stories are intriguing, and will amuse the readers. A few brief items were requested by good advertisers—and here is the only business office influence I know. They are about physical improvements in the stores, or employees' parties, or changes in executive personnel, or innocent if unimportant promotion stunts.

Most of this news is common to all newspapers, and the profession of newsgathering and news-writing is so well organized that no newspaper can appeal for circulation on the basis of its news handling, though some try. Editors try daily to have at least a few stories which are exclusive, and which will appeal to sizable groups of readers.

Throughout this process the human equation is at work. Editors can estimate popular reaction only through their own reactions. They assume that what interests them will be of interest to the newspaper-buying public. The news which they send reporters to seek, aside from the humdrum of regular coverage, reflects the interests of the human beings who do the planning.

If an editor likes girlie pictures and intimate glimpses behind the footlights, he will specialize in such features. If he is ardently socially-minded, he will have his reporters seeking the inner significance of life's ebb and flow. Occasionally, there is an editor whose tastes and interests are universal, and who is alert enough not to become blasé. Then the world recognizes a genius, and under his delicate touch a sensationally successful newspaper is created, to last until time removes him from the scene and replaces him with an earnest grubber.

It seems to be a common misapprehension that a reporter's life is one of high romance, and that the poor chap, particularly if he works on investigations and crusading, must devote himself continuously to spurning bribes and defying threats. I am sufficiently proud of my record in this field to reject the idea that nothing I ever did was worthy of bribe or threat. Yet never have I been forced to throw out my manly chest and declaim my superiority to either or both.

I have a friend who used to work on a Jersey City newspaper, by which one day he was sent to cover a funeral. The undertaker kept reminding my friend to mention his name in the story, and always was told not to worry. My friend didn't consider it necessary to tell him that it was his paper's policy always to mention the undertaker. At the end, the reporter was offered a bill by the undertaker, to insure mention of his name. He refused it and when he turned in his story asked permission to keep the name out to punish the undertaker.

"Hell," said his editor, "why didn't you take it? It's part of a reporter's salary here. That's why we gave you the assignment."

I have had gifts from two bribers. One, who the next summer was indicted, brought me a full quart of medium grade Scotch at Christmas time, after our collaboration on a legitimate news story was long past and our relations had terminated.

The other embarrassed me greatly, so that I had to ask him to stop giving me haberdashery that made my ready-made suits look like over-used grain bags.

This man came to the office one day and wanted us to print a story about how a jury had accepted his claim that he had bribed a judge. It was dangerous to use, but of considerable news interest. He volunteered to pay for a copy of the stenographic transcript, to protect us, if we would print his story. I talked with the city editor, and we agreed. The record cost him just under $50. The story was less than one column in length. Soon afterward, he sent me three ties from a most exclusive haberdashery, which must have cost almost as much as one of my business suits.

I told the city editor, and forgot the matter until some months later the chap returned, and asked us to report that the appeals court had agreed with the jury that he was a judge-briber. Again I told him the story had news merit, but not enough to warrant our going after it. Soon he brought us a copy of the official record. I did not hear how much this cost. We ran the story. There came by mail, from the same haberdasher, six pairs of

fine French lisle sox, too small for my undainty feet. The
editor said to keep them and forget it. I took them to
the store to exchange for size, and found that the six
pairs had cost approximately twenty-five dollars.

Those are my narrowest escapes from being bribed.

Nobody ever has threatened me with anything worse
than a libel suit. Such threats are so common, so insincere
and innocuous when the work has been well done, that
they hardly count.

I have never been quite certain how close I was to
something unpleasant in one inquiry which touched closely
a number of political figures in a lower East Side district
where only good Tammany men dared go to the polls.

Aubrey Graves and I were investigating Municipal
Court Justice Kunstler. I was checking into his financial
affairs and his relationships with a courtroom hanger-on
named Charles Leef and known as "Kunstler's Fixer."
Graves was checking in court records the amazing success
of certain lawyers and their clients before Kunstler. In-
cidentally, through a tipster, he was close on the trail of a
$20,000 check which was alleged to have figured in
Kunstler's rise to the bench. My research took me to
quite respectable quarters, but Graves' brought him under
the continual attention of court employees friendly to
Kunstler.

One day we heard that by the next night the telephone
in a large office we shared would be tapped, and that all

our future phone conversations would be overheard. The next afternoon, while I was telephoning, there was a click on the line. I motioned to Graves, who ascertained that our operators had not cut in. We called telephone company workmen, who could find no tap and said none was possible. Nevertheless, we talked with discretion on the telephone thereafter.

About that same time a stranger came to the office and asked for Graves, who was signing the stories. The stranger claimed to be a private detective, hired to point out Graves to a young lady representing friends of Kunstler. He had been unable to locate Graves outside the office, he said, and asked for coöperation. If Graves would go into the neighboring restaurant, so that he could point him out to the young woman, he would have earned his fee, and would not worry that Graves would then have opportunity to identify the young woman for future reference.

This was done. Several times thereafter Graves reported seeing the blonde on his train to Westchester. She made no advances, and nothing happened. It was all quite mysterious.

We never did get our hands on that $20,000 check or prove its existence. Our tipster, who had been asked by friends of the judge if he would like to have a vacation in Florida without expense, changed his home to avoid attention. When he was finished for us, he had been

promised temporary employment with another department
of the paper at a fairly good wage. He needed and wanted
it badly.

Nevertheless, the day after final arrangements were
made for him to take us to the man who supposedly had
the check, our tipster failed to come in. Since that day,
we have heard nothing from him. He may have gone to
Florida.

Chapter Thirteen

WHAT NEXT?

⋆ 13 ⋆

What Next?

IT is of no use to delude myself that I shall ever go back to the Vermont of my childhood memories. The Vermont to which I return each summer, and where some day I hope to spend my last years, is not the countryside of my nostalgia. That has gone forever, if it ever really existed.

Radio, talking pictures, newspapers, books, magazines, automobiles and airplanes have conspired to substitute the fuller life for the simpler one. Just as they have integrated north and east and south and west, and even the ocean-divided continents, so have they standardized farmer and villager and urban cave-dweller, and made them almost as readily interchangeable as the parts for a production-line automobile.

The long, dusty hill up which young feet used to trudge from market isn't even a motor warm-up for the modern car. The morning mail brings an inquiry whether we will please mail back the deed to a right of way through our field, so that the federal coöperative can begin building an electric light system. A Boston-to-Montreal passenger plane drones briefly over South Hill; I could drive eleven miles and board it.

I try to find a man, in these days of widespread unemployment, to dig up a few dozen yards of fifty-year old water pipe from the pasture spring, and fill in the trench when the pipe has been replaced. Everybody is too busy. The neighborhood handyman speculates whether the colonel has drag enough to get him back into the C. C. C. before his proper turn comes around again. ——

This is not the Vermont of my adolescence, when a trip to town was a day's adventure; when fresh meat was a weekly treat; when residence on the Town Farm was a disgraceful confession of incompetence or slovenliness; when every self-respecting person walked from dark to dark and disaster to disaster, and horny hands were so universal that they weren't even a badge of merit.

Twenty years ago a young farmer and his wife bought a $6,000 farm on a hill in our town for nothing down and a little a month. Day after day and week after week they rose together before even the sun was up, and after they had done the morning chores they went together into the fields. Side by side they tilled the soil, planted the crops and cultivated them, hayed the fields and harvested the crops. As dusk grew thick, they drove home the cows and did their evening chores by lantern light, and tumbled into bed. In course of time the mortgage was paid off. Then fire razed their buildings down to the stone walls of the dirt cellar. The nation was depression drunk. The "world-owes-me-a-living" creed was rampant. They borrowed and rebuilt, and started paying off another mortgage.

Vermont has changed since those days. Or has it? Can it be that memory plays tricks: that just as I remember easily the fun I had in the rest areas of France and find it difficult to reconstruct the hardships of the trenches, so I remember the hard-earned pleasures of back-hill childhood and the providence and industry of the select, and forget the muscle and heart aches, and the shiftless and the shifty?

It may be that Vermont has changed less than I have —that when I am ready to go back I shall find substantially what I left. Physical changes are superficial. Social changes are for the best. Vermont is, perhaps, a state of mind.

The fields of Vermont are as green as they ever were. The woods are as inviting. Speckled trout still range the streams alert for worms, and boys and girls still trudge to and from one-room schoolhouses. Cozy farms still snuggle in the green hills. The storekeeper and the filling station owner keep tabs on our comings and our goings, since an automatic switchboard replaced the omniscient village telephone operator.

Vermont really is as unchanging as the granite that underlies its soil. You can dig and blast the granite from the hill, and tool and shape and polish its surface, but underneath it always remains granite—a composite of minerals, strong, tough, honest stone. You can build hard-surface roads through Vermont, put tourist signs on its farmhouses and filling stations in their yards; you can place radios in its homes and fly transport planes through its air; but the state of mind that has always been Vermont does not change.

It is to that state of mind, really, that I want to return.

Not immediately. There is no hurry. The world is seething. Tremendous forces are at work. I want to be where I can keep a curious eye on them. Occasionally I feel the urge to interfere, and see what I can do to divert them. It isn't really the instinct to reform, but rather the pleasure of participation and the pride of accomplishment. I would like to stick around at least until the current social revolution has stopped whirling and settled down into some recognizable pattern.

Then I want to buy that plot looking down on Lake Champlain, and build a home with a little plant in the basement where I can do some printing as it should be done, rather than as the paying customers dictate. I might take some pictures, and play some golf, and do the traveling for which there has been no time thus far. It would be nice to find out whether a newspaper operated as I would like to run one really would bankrupt itself and its owner.

There will be plenty to do, when I get ready to settle down in Vermont. There will be no excuse for loneliness or boredom.

Perhaps there will be time then for me to return to New York as an excursionist, take in some ball games, visit the Rainbow Room and the Statue of Liberty. I've always meant to, but somehow, as a New Yorker I haven't had time.

★

★ ★

TYPOGRAPHY AND COVER DESIGNED BY FRANK R. SLOAN, JR.

JACKET DESIGNED BY JOHN SHAYN

SET IN TWELVE POINT LINOTYPE JANSON

BOUND IN BANCROFT NATURAL FINISH CLOTH

COMPOSED, PRINTED AND BOUND BY

BRAUNWORTH & COMPANY AT BRIDGEPORT, CONNECTICUT

★ ★

★